CREATING VERBATIM THEATRE FROM ORAL HISTORIES

Offering a roadmap for practicing verbatim theatre (plays created from oral histories), this book outlines theatre processes through the lens of oral history and draws upon oral history scholarship to bring best practices from that discipline to theatre practitioners.

This book opens with an overview of oral history and verbatim theatre, considering the ways in which existing oral history debates can inform verbatim theatre processes and highlights necessary ethical considerations within each field, which are especially prevalent when working with narrators from marginalised communities. It provides a step-by-step guide to creating plays from interviews and contains practical guidance for determining the scope of a theatre project: identifying narrators and conducting interviews, developing a script from excerpts of interview transcripts and outlining a variety of ways to create verbatim theatre productions. By bringing together this explicit discussion of oral history in relationship to theatre based on personal testimonies, the reader gains insight into each field and the close relationship between the two.

Supported by international case studies that cover a wide range of working methods and productions, including *The Laramie Project* and *Parramatta Girls*, this is the perfect guide for oral historians producing dramatic representations of the material they have sourced through interviews, and for writers creating professional theatre productions, community projects or student plays.

Clare Summerskill is an independent academic researcher who has recently completed her PhD at Royal Holloway University of London in the Drama department. She is chair and co-founder of the UK's Oral History Society LGBTQ Special Interest Group. She is also a playwright, stand-up and singer-songwriter.

Practicing Oral History

Series editor, Nancy MacKay

Museums, historical societies, libraries, classrooms, cultural centers, refugee organizations, elder care centers, and neighborhood groups are among the organizations that use oral history both to document their own communities and to foster social change. The *Practicing Oral History* series addresses the needs of these professionals with concise, instructive books about applying oral history best practices within the context of their professional goals.

Titles fall into one of three areas of applied oral history. The first format addresses a specific stage or skill within the oral history process. The second addresses the needs of professional communities who use oral history in their field. The third approach addresses the way oral history can be used to make an impact. Each title provides practical tools, ethical guidelines and best practices for conducting, preserving, and using oral histories within the framework of acknowledged standards and best practices.

Readers across a wide array of disciplines will find the books useful, including education, public history, local history, family history, communication and media, cultural studies, gerontology, documentary studies, museum & heritage studies, and migration studies.

Recent titles in the series

Transcribing Oral History
Teresa Bergen

Practicing Oral History to Improve Outcomes for Refugees and Host Communities
Marella Hoffman

Creating Verbatim Theatre from Oral Histories
Clare Summerskill

For more information, or to place orders visit Routledge, Practicing Oral History, https://www.routledge.com/Practicing-Oral-History/book-series/POHLCP

CREATING VERBATIM THEATRE FROM ORAL HISTORIES

Clare Summerskill

Routledge
Taylor & Francis Group

NEW YORK AND LONDON

First published 2021
by Routledge
52 Vanderbilt Avenue, New York, NY 10017

and by Routledge
2 Park Square, Milton Park, Abingdon, Oxon, OX14 4RN

Routledge is an imprint of the Taylor & Francis Group, an informa business

© 2021 Taylor & Francis

Library of Congress Cataloging-in-Publication Data
A catalog record for this title has been requested

ISBN: 978-0-367-18147-5 (hbk)
ISBN: 978-0-367-18150-5 (pbk)
ISBN: 978-0-429-05977-3 (ebk)

Typeset in Bembo
by codeMantra

CONTENTS

SERIES EDITOR FOREWORD

I first met Clare on a blustery winter afternoon at the New York Public Library in December 2017. We had exchanged emails about her book idea – Clare from London and myself from San Francisco – and by lucky chance holiday plans brought us each to New York City. Over a cup of hot chocolate, Clare introduced me to verbatim theatre, a form of documentary theatre that has a strong, but under-recognised, connection to oral history. I immediately saw possibilities for a book on exploring this connection and introducing oral historians and verbatim theatre professionals to each other's fields, then providing a roadmap of best practices for using oral history in verbatim theatre. The book would fill a gap in existing literature and open up opportunities for both oral historians and theatre professionals to learn and interact with each other. The result is the book you hold in your hands.

Verbatim theatre, along with tribunal theatre, theatre of testimony, ethnodrama and related forms, is an approach to theatre that falls under the umbrella of documentary theatre. These works are created through the use of pre-existing documentary materials, such as diaries, letters, newspapers and interviews. Clare cautions readers not to take categorisation too seriously; playwrights borrow widely among genres, continually shifting the boundaries to meet their artistic goals and the ethos of the times. See **Chapter 1** for Clare's more thorough description of verbatim theatre. Documentary theatre forms, by nature of their primary source material, tend to favour topics of contemporary interest and often with an eye to bringing awareness to social injustice. Verbatim theatre, in particular, leans toward topics of social or political interest within a particular community, be that a geographical community or a community of interest.

Verbatim theatre scripts are usually created from the exact words excerpted from recorded interviews. The playwright or other members of the team conduct and transcribe the interviews, then the playwright creates characters and a plot thread based on the interviews, and selects excerpts from the transcripts to create scripts that best achieve her artistic goals. Works are performed in theatres and other public performance places to public audiences.

Verbatim theatre and oral history have much in common, particularly through the interviewing stages. Both practices place the narrator's testimony at the centre of the project, honouring the integrity of the spoken word at the spoken moment. Both value a community base and often address topics of social injustice. Above all, both honour the uniqueness of the individual's story. After the interview the two practices diverge. Oral historians are concerned with context – placing an interview within a framework of time, place and culture, that is, a microcosm in a much bigger story within a chronological timeline. Verbatim theatre artists, however, are mostly interested in creating an artistic work, a theatre piece to be viewed, enjoyed, thought about and discussed, here and now.

Another purpose of verbatim theatre, dear to Clare's heart, is the acknowledgement of the community or the individual narrator who has been made a character in the play. She writes,

> I relish the moment when a narrator attends a playreading or show and finally understands how their interview excerpts have been employed in the script of a play. They see an actor playing 'them' and speaking their own words and they feel the presence of an attentive audience around them, showing an interest in what they have been through and in what they have to say. Personal narratives presented with dramatic expertise are, for me, a winning combination, producing some of the finest works of theatre I have ever attended.

After our conversation over that cup of hot chocolate on a winter day, I knew that Clare and I would enjoy working together. Though she is best known in the theatre world, Clare has been straddling the line between verbatim theatre and oral history for some time now. She is well known in the UK for her work as a playwright, actor, comedian, musician and founder/artistic director of Artemis Theatre Company. She also has crossed over into academia (she was finishing up her PhD while writing this book) and, as an oral historian, brings the best practices of oral history into the theatre field.

This book is organised according to a format used in all *Practicing Oral History* titles, beginning with an overview of both oral history and theatre, with a strong section on ethics, followed in the second half by a practical step-by-step section on how to conduct a verbatim theatre project, beginning with oral history interviews. A highlight of the book are the examples, sprinkled throughout the text, and more extended case studies that appear in **Part IV.** Clare cites examples from her own work and the work of theatre professionals around the world to illustrate specific points, and, more importantly, how artists adapt verbatim theatre and oral history to meet their own artistic goals. Here is her example from the University of North Carolina (US) Professor Della Pollock's theatre piece *Like a Family*:

> *Like a Family* shows how the stories theatre practitioners gather in the form of interviews can be redistributed back to the members of a community, whose numbers make up an audience. Narrators in *Like a Family* were seen by Pollock as providing expert witnesses, adding their testimony and experience to the wider canon of historical knowledge and understanding, with the interviewer as the recipient of this generously shared expertise. Through Pollock placing the narrators and their fellow community members as the experts, and the student-actors as those who were eager to learn from them, the project reflected certain tenets of oral history, as later described by Frisch's notion of shared authority, whereby oral history is understood as being a joint process of learning and exchange.

As this project winds up, I'm left thinking of the universal power of the personal testimony. This testimony, realised in the form of a recorded interview in oral history and verbatim theatre, is the bedrock of human culture. Though it may be called story, testimony, narration, interview and a number of other things, I believe it all boils down to honest telling and deep listening. This quote from American writer Barry Lopez says it best:

> The stories people tell have a way of taking care of them. If stories come to you, care for them. And learn to give them away where they are needed. Sometimes a person needs a story more than food to stay alive. That is why we put these stories in each other's memories. This is how people care for themselves.

Nancy MacKay
Berkeley, California
February 2020

AUTHOR'S NOTE

I have a passion for hearing other people's stories. As an oral historian and a verbatim theatre practitioner, I know before each interview that the experiences a narrator will share with me will almost always prove to be fascinating, educational, moving and often humorous to boot! Personal narratives provide ways in which people can share their life stories and, at the same time, feel that the things they have gone through are validated by the fact that someone is eager to hear them and disperse them to a wider public.

I have always enjoyed taking the role of the listener – more so than thinking of myself as an 'interviewer' – and I have learnt so much from those who have entrusted me with their tales. I feel that the interview is almost a sacred exchange. From the minute the recorder is turned on, both narrator and listener understand that they are engaged in something important. That process might not necessarily alter the outside world, but it has a potential to change how the speaker sees their place in the world and gives them the opportunity to talk, on the record, about their own experiences relating to matters of personal, political or social importance. For narrators from marginalised communities whose stories have, historically, been under-documented, speaking publicly about their experiences takes on even greater significance.

As an actress, playwright and producer who has worked for many years in verbatim theatre where the script is based entirely on interviews, I relish the moment when a narrator attends a playreading or show and finally understands how their words have been used in the script of a play. They see an actor playing 'them' on stage and speaking their own words, and they feel themselves in the presence of an attentive audience, showing an interest in what they have been through and in what they have to say. Personal narratives presented with dramatic expertise are, for me, a winning combination, producing some of the finest works of theatre I have ever attended.

Verbatim theatre is an ideal means to address important issues which may have been overlooked or misrepresented in mainstream media, or previously undocumented in the public record. In addition to educating and entertaining an audience, verbatim theatre can stimulate further discussion among those who watch it and the communities from which the stories being told originate. Occasionally it can inspire action by those working against discrimination, prejudice or injustice who may only have learnt about a particular struggle from attending the show. Whether the theatre makers' aims are ideological, pedagogical, social or political, they will inevitably endeavour to create artistically powerful and original productions from interview material generously shared by the narrators.

I hope that as you read this book you will be inspired by the myriad of possibilities verbatim theatre offers and that it will provide you with a passion for the work as well as a practical and theoretical understanding which will inform and enhance your own project.

Clare Summerskill
London, June 2020

ACKNOWLEDGEMENTS

With thanks to the following for their permissions.

Christine Bacon, Jessica Beck, Myrtle Emmanuel, Helena Enright, John Bucher/LA Screenwriter, Maggie Inchley, Pedzisai Maedza, Roslyn Oades, Della Pollock, Gina Shmukler; Debbie, 'Eileen', 'Izzuddin' and 'Miremba'.

Currency Press:

- Extract from *Bowerbird* by Alana Valentine, copyright Alana Valentine. First Published by Currency Press in 2018. Reproduced by permission from Currency Press Pty Ltd, Sydney, Australia.
- Caroline Wake, "Towards a Working Definition of Verbatim Theatre." In *Verbatim: Staging Memory and Community*, edited by Paul Brown (Currency Press, 2010). Reproduced with the permission of Currency Press Pty Ltd, Sydney, Australia.

Johns Hopkins University Press – Journals; permissions conveyed through Copyright Clearance Centre, Inc.:

- Dorinne Kondo, "(Re)Visions of Race: Contemporary Race Theory and the Cultural Politics of Racial Crossover in Documentary Theatre," *Theatre Journal* 52:1 (2000)
- Julie Salverson, "Performing Emergency: Witnessing Popular Theatre, and the Lie of the Literal" *Theatre Topics* 6:2 (1996)

Nick Hern Books, London:

- Robin Belfield, *Telling the Truth: How to Make Verbatim Theatre* (Nick Hern Books, 2018)

Oberon Books:

- *Theatre as Witness: Three Testimonial Plays from South Africa* © Yaël Farber, 2008, by kind permission of Oberon Books.
- *Verbatim, Verbatim: Contemporary Documentary Theatre*, edited by Will Hammond and Dan Steward, 2008, by kind permission of Oberon Books.

Oxford Publishing Limited:

- Sue Armitage, "The Stages of Women's Oral History," in *The Oxford Handbook of Oral History*, ed. Donald A. Ritchie, Oxford Publishing Limited, Oxford, UK, Copyright © 2010
- Paul Thompson, *The Voice of the Past*, Oxford Publishing Limited, Oxford, UK, Copyright © 1978
- Paul Thompson with Joanna Bornat, *The Voice of the Past: Oral History*, Oxford Publishing Limited, Oxford, UK, Copyright © 2017

Oxford University Press – Journal; permissions conveyed through Copyright Clearance Centre Inc.:

- Linda Shopes, "Oral History and the Study of Communities: Problems, Paradoxes, and Possibilities," in *The Oral History Reader*, Second Edition, ed. Robert Perks and Alistair Thomson (Abingdon: Routledge, 2006)

Penguin Random House:

- Moisés Kaufman, *The Laramie Project and The Laramie Project: Ten Years Later* (New York: Vintage), Copyright © 2014 Penguin Random House LLC (US)

State University of New York Press:

- Michael Frisch, *A Shared Authority: Essays on the Craft and Meaning of Oral and Public History*, State University of New York © 1990

Taylor & Francis Group LLC – Books; permissions conveyed through Copyright Clearance Centre Inc.:

- Marella Hoffman, *Practicing Oral History to Improve Public Policies and Programs* (Abingdon: Routledge), Copyright © 2018 Taylor & Francis
- Nancy Mackay, *Curating Oral Histories: From Interview to Archive*, Second Edition (Walnut Creek, CA: Left Coast Press), Copyright © 2016 Taylor & Francis

Taylor & Francis Ltd, http://www.tandfonline.com:

- Michael Frisch, "Review: Oral History and 'Hard Times' a Review Essay," *The Oral History Review* 7 (1979)
- Michael Frisch, "Sharing Authority: Oral History and the Collaborative Process," *The Oral History Review* 30:1 (2003)
- Laurie R. Serikaku, "Oral History in Ethnic Communities: Widening the Focus," *The Oral History Review* 17:1 (1989)
- Caridad Svich, "Moisés Kaufman: 'Reconstructing History Through Theatre' – An Interview," *Contemporary Theatre Review* 13:3 (2003)
- Valerie Yow, "Ethics and Interpersonal Relationships in Oral History Research," *Oral History Review* 22:1 (1995)

Theatre Communications Group:

- *Testimonies: Four Plays* by Emily Mann. Copyright © 1997 Published by Theatre Communications Group. Used by permission of Theatre Communications Group.

University of Wisconsin Press:

- Portelli, Alessandro, *The Battle of Valle Giulia: Oral History and the Art of Dialogue* © 1997 By the Board of Regents of the University of Wisconsin System. Reprinted by permission of The University of Wisconsin Press.

PART I
Overview

INTRODUCTION

Increasingly, playwrights employ oral histories to create verbatim plays. Theatre created from interviews uses first-person narratives to tell a big story through a finely focussed lens, and oral history uses personal testimonies to balance the historical record by documenting the experiences and opinions of everyday people. Together these approaches offer exciting possibilities for addressing social justice issues, community engagement and personal growth.

Paul Thompson, who founded the journal *Oral History* in 1969 and played a key role in the formation of the British Oral History Society in 1971, was one of the first to identify connections between the two practices, observing that:

> Oral history and theatre make natural partners. Interviews are a form of performance in themselves. [...] So it is not surprising that oral history projects have often turned to drama to present the stories they have recorded, or that theatre has taken to oral history to reach out to groups and communities who may not often cross the foyer threshold.[1]

Verbatim literally means 'in exactly the same words as were used originally', and verbatim theatre refers to theatre processes in which narrators' stories, linked by universal themes, are gathered in the form of interviews, excerpts of which are then included in a script. Production and scripting methods by theatre practitioners vary enormously, but the process of creating verbatim plays, as outlined in this publication, involves interviewing individuals, usually from a particular group or community and often about a matter of political or social interest, and then creating a script from interview excerpts. The script is performed by actors who play the parts of the 'real' individuals whose words are related in the production.

Both oral history and verbatim theatre rely upon the spoken word, and both practices frequently seek testimonies from members of marginalised, vulnerable or previously silenced populations which are then documented, either in the form of oral recordings and interview transcripts, or by the inclusion of interview excerpts within a script. Where oral history and verbatim theatre projects diverge is in their intended goals. Traditional oral history methodology dictates that oral history interviews, collected to supplement or challenge the existing historical record, be archived and made available for public access and research. Information gathered by playwrights through interviews is developed into scripts and then performances. In both areas of work, either in public archives or through theatrical productions, personal testimonies are made accessible to wider audiences.

For the past twenty-five years, I have worked as a playwright, a theatre director and an oral historian. Much of my work has involved using interviews as source material to create theatre productions that have engaged audiences. Over the last two decades, in particular, the public's distrust of mainstream media has appeared to increase and people have also become wary of government spin. During this period, attention has turned to seeking alternate versions of events and information provided in the form of personal narratives. This has resulted in a growing enthusiasm for the use of verbatim theatre to address social and political concerns in a format that is not only entertaining but also makes an impact by educating, creating visibility and encouraging activism.

I have observed first-hand the connection between oral history and verbatim theatre, since both practices are centred in similar methodologies, subjects and ethical concerns, utilising the recorded interview as a common foundation to achieve their respective goals. These related practices have rarely been discussed together in any depth; this book reflects upon their close relationship, and I draw upon my own experience and that of my colleagues in both oral history and theatre to create a roadmap for practising oral history-based verbatim theatre from interviews.

The aim of this book is to address this topic from both practical and scholarly perspectives. It offers oral historians and theatre practitioners, both novices and professionals, a step-by-step guide for creating plays from interviews. It also considers existing debates within oral history scholarship, examining ways in which those discussions can inform the creation of verbatim theatre scripts and productions.

Part I introduces verbatim theatre history and explores related practices in the field. This is followed by a discussion on the close connections between verbatim theatre and oral history, and an examination of existing debates within oral history which have relevance to verbatim theatre processes. Although the disciplines of oral history and verbatim theatre have differing final objectives – one to create a broader historiography and the other, a theatrical production – both place a critical emphasis upon the practical techniques and ethical implications of the interview situation. Oral history methodology, particularly relating to the interview process, has been debated rigorously on an international level for several decades, and these discussions have led to the kind of detailed guidelines developed by organisations around the world, most notably, the American Oral History Association (OHA).[2]

In contrast to the extensive advice offered on oral history methods through publications, websites and training provided by oral history organisations, verbatim theatre practitioners have notably less scholarship and practical advice upon which to draw when seeking guidance for their own productions. The reasons for the disparity in the availability of prescriptive guidelines between oral history and verbatim theatre will be examined in **Chapter 2.** But, in short, the lack of practical advice undoubtedly stems from the fact that the role of the playwright is to gather personal testimonies for a work of art, often created with the aim of raising social or political awareness, while the purpose of oral history is to seek interviews and to preserve them intact, as a direct representation of the narrators' words, for the historical record. The playwright as an artist therefore has more license to interpret than the historian whose work must be evidence-based.

Part II discusses ethical considerations that arise in verbatim theatre work. Creating plays from interviews with 'real' people involves gathering information from interviews that playwrights develop into scripts. Although the narrator should ideally always be given the opportunity to approve their contribution to the script, the playwright has final editing control. This fact, in itself, raises ethical concerns relating to the agency and the representation of the narrator. Furthermore, working with narratives from members of marginalised or vulnerable communities – as much verbatim theatre work tends to do – means that playwrights can be susceptible to accusations of appropriation. Appropriation is generally understood as either the act of taking something that belongs to someone else, sometimes without permission, or taking an idea, custom or style from a group or culture that you are not a member of and using it yourself. In both senses, there are negative connotations attached to such action. In verbatim theatre work, personal stories are indeed 'taken', or at least 'borrowed' from narrators, excerpts of which are employed in a script by theatre practitioners who, admittedly, use the interview content for their own purposes. Such work could consequently be viewed as appropriative. But when informed consent has been secured from narrators who understand the aims of the theatre makers, and an explanation has been provided about how interview excerpts might be employed in the play then, arguably, this becomes less of an appropriative process, and more of a collaborative one. However, a thin line exists between this slightly more benign understanding of the term 'appropriation' and one which leans towards 'exploitation', where playwrights might be accused of using narrators unfairly for their own advantage. Theatre practitioners must consequently tread carefully in this work.

Part III provides step-by-step guidelines for creating a play based on interviews. If you are a theatre professional – a playwright or a director or an actor – and you wish to create a play based on interviews, then turn to **Chapters 1–5** for basic information about oral history practice and theory. Your own theatre work will benefit from that understanding. If you are an oral historian, educator or leader of a community group interested in making a play based on interviews then, once you have settled upon the subject of your research and gathered the interview content, you and your colleagues can work *AS IF* you are theatre company members, allocating roles such as playwright, director and actor to participants in your project.

Topics addressed in this 'How To' section include determining the subject of your theatre project, finding narrators and interviewing them, transcribing the interviews, editing and scripting your play and settling upon one of a variety of final production options. If you are an oral historian who has collected a number of interviews which you believe would make an engaging piece of theatre, then there will be a point in your work where you will become a 'theatre maker'. At this stage, you will need to determine who will script the piece, who will direct it, who will act in it, who it will be performed to and where it will be staged. Forms of verbatim theatre are constantly evolving, and there are numerous ways of producing dramatic projects based on interviews. **Chapters 6–12** provide a detailed outline of one way in which a verbatim play can be created which involves working with oral histories employing word-for-word content from interviews in a theatrical script with actors then speaking those exact lines. Throughout the book, however, you will find descriptions of the work of playwrights and theatre companies around the world which can serve as a springboard for your own verbatim theatre project.

Some of the plays to which I refer are ones that I have seen myself, some are ones that I have read about in theatre scholarship, some are ones which I have read in script form, some I have written for theatre companies and others are my own productions. These, I have mentioned several times, simply because I can speak with personal knowledge and a degree of authority about them, rather than because they are exemplary pieces of work! Detailed documentation of verbatim playwrights' working methods is limited and information about their relationship with their narrators is sparse. In drawing upon my own plays, I am in a position of being able to share my experiences of working with narrators, interview material and production options.

The subjects that my own plays have addressed (namely, experiences of working-class older people, older LGBT people, disabled LGBT people, people with mental health problems and asylum seekers and refugees) demonstrates only a handful of topics and issues which verbatim theatre is perfectly suited to cover since many members of these populations are from the margins of society, rather than the mainstream. But, as you will see throughout the book, the variety of matters about which narrators can be interviewed probably reflects the amount of events and experiences any number of people go through in their lifetimes, and there are really no limits to the topics which either verbatim theatre or oral history can investigate.

Part IV offers detailed examples of verbatim theatre, documentary theatre and oral history performance projects and practitioners, drawing on work from the US, Australia, South Africa and the UK. These productions, which have been performed variously by professional actors, students and community groups, demonstrate a range of working methods employed by theatre practitioners in the creation of plays from interviews addressing social, political and historical topics, i.e. verbatim theatre. Whilst some have been written using the verbatim theatre process that I outline in **Part III**, others have not, but I include them anyway to illustrate interesting and important points of comparison. Some of the plays discussed are community-based projects performed by students, and others have been produced and acted by members of professional theatre companies. It may be helpful for the reader to refer back and forth to these examples while reading the main content of the book, in order to gain insight into the working processes of a variety of verbatim theatre practitioners.

The Appendices include a template of a permission form which can be adapted for your own project, examples of how to approach your narrators, suggestions on how to prepare your narrator for the interview and a scripting exercise. Suggestions for further reading in verbatim theatre and oral history are also provided.

★

The premise behind this book lies in my understanding that, since oral history and verbatim theatre are such closely related disciplines, they have much to teach each other. Verbatim theatre makers can enhance their own practices by turning to existing debates within oral history – particularly around the interview and feedback processes – and oral historians are invited to look to verbatim theatre as a means of dispersing interview content beyond the archive. Whether you are an oral historian, a theatre practitioner, a writer, a student, a social or political activist or something else entirely, this publication will provide you with practical tools to create your own magnificent verbatim theatre piece.

I wish you a wonderful journey!

Notes

1 Paul Thompson with Joanna Bornat, *The Voice of the Past: Oral History,* Fourth Edition (New York: Oxford University Press, 2017), 302.
2 "Resources," *Oral History Association,* February 28, 2020, https://www.oralhistory. org/resources/.

1

WHAT IS VERBATIM THEATRE?

One single-sentence definition of *verbatim theatre* is 'a dramatic production based on spoken experiences shared by people who have been interviewed about a particular subject or theme'. But, like any dynamic concept in the arts, verbatim theatre processes vary – depending on the artists, practice and the context of the production. Verbatim theatre is a relatively recent dramatic form, supported by the technological development of the tape recorder – the term being first used in England in the late 1960s and early 1970s.[1] In the UK, verbatim theatre generally refers to plays that convey spoken testimony in dramatic form but a looser definition of verbatim problematises the assumption of using the exact words of the narrator. A related term for productions created from interview material is 'documentary theatre' – which is frequently now understood to be an umbrella term for plays based on interview content and other forms of documentation. Confusingly, perhaps – in the US, the preferred term for verbatim theatre is documentary theatre!

Some experts have tried to agree on specific terminology but, given the constantly evolving nature of verbatim theatre processes in many countries around the world, assigning exact names for their varying forms is not always productive. The fact is – there is no fixed set of rules for creating verbatim theatre, since every individual playwright or theatre practitioner decides on their own method of how to source interview material and then present it dramatically. While some plays cover subject matter which may prove of interest to a wider general audience, it is also the case that much verbatim theatre work has a goal that is closer to the community in which it takes place. In such pieces, interviews are conducted and dramatic productions created for the benefit of the community, perhaps for the purpose of collective healing, a call to action or simply to celebrate.

This section outlines the origins and aims of verbatim theatre, discussing well-known productions by verbatim theatre playwrights and theatre companies. Some other related dramatic forms that can be generated from interview content are also explored, which will inform your own work in creating verbatim theatre from oral history interviews.

Verbatim Theatre in Context

New and evolving fields have, by definition, a new and evolving vocabulary or terminology. Terms and their meanings may vary, but it is helpful to famil-iarise yourself with some of the terminology applied to theatre created from documentation – including interviews.

Documentary Theatre

Documentary theatre is an umbrella term referring to the creation of non-fiction plays based on documents. Such documentation involves a variety of primary sources, including film excerpts, photos, newspaper articles, letters, di-aries, statistics and interview material. Verbatim theatre is sometimes regarded as a subset of documentary theatre, since it employs documents in the form of transcribed interviews. But in this book, the term verbatim theatre, as I use it, does not refer to theatre based on other forms of documentation such as diaries, newspaper content or trial transcripts.

The term documentary theatre originated in Germany with the work of Erwin Piscator. In 1925, he produced *Trotz alledem!* (*In Spite of Everything!*), a play about the history of the Communist Party, which employed interviews, recorded speeches, newsreel footage, filmed sequences and montages. In the 1960s in Germany, documentary theatre was sometimes called Theatre of Fact, a term which was also applied to Eric Bentley's 1972 production in the US of *Are You Now or Have You Ever Been?* – which dramatised testimony presented to the United States House Un-American Activities Committee. A later example of documentary theatre (sometimes referred to as verbatim theatre in the UK) is *Guantanamo: Honour Bound to Defend Freedom*, which focusses on the issue of human rights for those imprisoned at the US Naval base prison in Cuba. It was scripted by Victoria Brittain and Gillian Slovo, and was first staged in 2004 at the Tricycle Theatre in London. The piece was based on written correspon-dence combined with personal testimony collected from released detainees, their family members, lawyers and human rights workers, as well as informa-tion from publications relating to the holding of prisoners at Guantanamo Bay.

Tribunal Theatre

Tribunal theatre refers to productions based on verbatim reconstructions of public inquiries or trial scripts. In the UK, the Tricycle Theatre presented sev-eral plays using this format under the artistic directorship of Nicolas Kent. One of the most famous of these was *The Colour of Justice: Based on the Transcripts of*

The Stephen Lawrence Inquiry (1999), edited by Richard Norton-Taylor. This piece was a dramatised reconstruction of the key events of the Macpherson Inquiry into the murder of a black teenager, Stephen Lawrence. The plays Kent produces are sometimes referred to as verbatim plays, since they are based on real-life stories. Frequently, the content of these scripts is not created from personal interviews, but from what was said, and – significantly – recorded in document form, in a trial or inquiry. In the US, one of the best-known examples of tribunal theatre is Moisés Kaufman's *Gross Indecency: The Three Trials of Oscar Wilde* (1997). A noticeable difference between tribunal theatre and verbatim theatre is that tribunal playwrights rarely conduct interviews.

Theatre of Testimony

It is understood that the term 'theatre of testimony' was first used in 1983, by the South African theatre director Barney Simon, after he directed American playwright Emily Mann's *Still Life*: a piece based on interviews with a Vietnam veteran, his wife and his mistress. While 'testimony' originally referred to personal recollection delivered from a witness box in a courtroom, in a more general context, the word is now understood to mean the telling of an individual's experience of an event or time. Theatre of testimony is frequently used to refer to plays based on interviews with people who have suffered traumatic experiences and members of marginalised or persecuted communities who are *bearing witness* to adverse events they have endured. This kind of theatre is, therefore, very closely related to verbatim theatre and, in many cases, might be indistinguishable. Some theatre scholars suggest that when harrowing testimony is related on stage, there is a responsibility on the part of the audience not only to listen, but in some way to acknowledge that they have heard and borne witness to the narrative. The South African playwright Yaël Farber states, 'The essential component of this genre lies in its capacity for healing through speaking, hearing and being heard'.[2]

Applied Theatre

Applied theatre, also known as applied drama, is an umbrella term often used in academia to describe theatre work that takes place in non-theatrical settings. These locations can include prisons, health and therapy settings, community arts centres, museums and art galleries, support service venues, housing and industrial sites. Frequently, applied theatre is constructed as a response to social and political challenges and is seen as a process which can bring about change. Other terms for applied theatre include 'socially engaged' or 'participatory' theatre and such work reflects many types of creative practices, in which verbatim interview material or other kinds of narration of life experience could be included. The guidelines suggested in this book for creating verbatim theatre from oral histories do not extend to applied theatre projects but, rather, focus on plays that are scripted from interviews and then performed by actors, professional or otherwise. However, the use of personal testimony in applied theatre projects which employ verbatim practice offers an exciting and creative way to engage with the subject matter under discussion.[3]

Autobiographical Performance

In this dramatic form, individuals, employing the first-person pronoun, perform a piece they have written themselves (or in collaboration with others) about their own lives. This can be presented in the form of a professional solo show or as part of an applied theatre project. The term also encompasses oral history performance, verbatim theatre, testimonial performance or even performance art (an art form that combines visual art with dramatic performance). The performer will usually talk directly out to the audience members, thereby breaking down the traditional 'fourth wall' that insulates the actor from the audience. Depending on the form of performance being used, the lines delivered can either be improvised or carefully scripted and repeated exactly at each performance.

Autobiographical performance is often used as a vehicle for actors from marginalised communities to tell stories about their individual and collective pasts. The political potential of autobiographical performance was initially explored in the early 1970s, overlapping with an increase in verbatim theatre in the UK, with personal stories of 'real' people gaining the interest of theatre makers and audiences alike. Verbatim theatre based on narrators' lives can be viewed as autobiographical in some ways, but it is not necessarily performed by the person whose story it tells, and the content of the script is taken from an interview. Autobiographical theatre and verbatim theatre are related forms – based on personal experiences and frequently addressing matters of political or social concern.

Oral History Performance

A range of dramatic processes fall within the definition of oral history performance. Participants in an oral history performance project might share their stories with a theatre practitioner; then enact them in some way – with the purpose of reflecting upon their experiences through this dramatic process. The focus of such work is often to create possibilities for new understandings of participants' lives and the opportunity for discussion of those revelations. Oral history performance often involves actors and facilitators seeking personal connections to their own history, then bringing these stories to life for a wider audience – who could be encouraged to join in a post-performance discussion.

Della Pollock is the author of *Remembering: Oral History Performance* (2005), a series of essays advocating oral history and oral history-based performance as the means to challenge and expand upon traditional ways of transmitting historical knowledge. In my opinion, one of the most carefully and ethically executed oral history plays is Pollock's *Like a Family*. This 1988 project, created by Pollock and her students at the University of North Carolina at Chapel Hill, resulted in a series of performances based on interviews with more than 300 members of a local working-class mill region. *Like a Family* is discussed in **Chapter 14**.

Forms of oral history performance vary considerably. There is no single understanding of the dramatic work the term describes, but it is usually based on personal experience and/or interviews. Extremely close connections can therefore be detected between this work and verbatim theatre processes.

Ethnodrama

Ethnodrama (sometimes called ethnotheatre) is used in many research fields, both within and beyond the arts world. Ethnography is the systematic study of people and cultures, and ethnodrama refers to the transformation and adaptation of ethnographic data – such as interview transcripts, field notes, statistics and journals – into a playscript later staged as a live public theatrical performance. The personal stories on which the play is based often focus on social issues and traumatic or significant events.

As with verbatim theatre processes, some ethnodrama theatre practitioners employ exact verbatim in their work and others opt for adapted versions of their interview transcripts. The creators of the piece might perform their own (autoethnographic) work and those participating in the research might perform in ethnodrama scripts about them. Both ethnodrama and verbatim theatre (in common with many applied theatre projects) can provide a space for performers and audiences alike to engage in meaningful discourse on matters of social and political concern. Unlike most verbatim theatre processes, in ethnodrama, interview scripts are often drafted and the qualitative data collected during the research period is coded during the creation of a play script.

A particularly interesting example of ethnodrama is *Her Opponent* by Joe Salvatore, a play that restages excerpts of the US presidential debates in 2016 with gender-reversed casting, in an attempt to understand how the reception of the two major candidates was influenced by gender.

Verbatim Theatre

Verbatim theatre is created from real-life stories, which are then dramatised. This work often involves a playwright creating a script from interviews with narrators sharing their experiences of a particular subject, theme or event.

The term verbatim theatre is also applied to theatre created by playwrights working with what is called 'headphone theatre' in Australia and more commonly known as Recorded Delivery in the UK when it refers to the work of Alecky Blythe and her theatre company of that name. In these productions, recorded interview material is played to the actors through earpieces, which they then narrate to the audience.

In the contemporary theatre scene, dramatic works combining dance and music with interview excerpts produce innovative and exciting interpretations of previous verbatim processes. DV8 is a London-based physical theatre company, and its productions incorporate elements of theatre, dance, film and, increasingly, text. Verbatim pieces by DV8 include Lloyd Newson's *Can We Talk About This?* (2011–12), which deals with freedom of speech, censorship and Islam.

An Overview of Verbatim Theatre

In the period following the Second World War, some playwrights questioned how far fictional theatre could adequately address the atrocities that had occurred under the Nazi regime. One writer who turned to interview transcripts to provide dramatic content was Peter Weiss, a German, who created the 1965 play, *The Investigation*, produced simultaneously in seventeen theatres in East and West Germany. The script was based on the Frankfurt Auschwitz Trials of 1963–65. Weiss turned to these court transcripts because he saw them as presenting a closer depiction of events than fiction. Although he termed his work documentary theatre, Weiss's understanding – that enacted recordings of real people's experiences could both educate and entertain an audience – remains one of the main premises of verbatim theatre.

The United Kingdom

In the UK in the late 1960s and early 1970s, Peter Cheeseman, the director of the Victoria Theatre, and later, the New Vic in Stoke-on-Trent, produced a series of plays known as the Stoke Documentaries. These productions, based on interviews with people from the local community, are regarded as the first examples of verbatim theatre. Cheeseman sent his company members out into the community to gather interviews with mainly working-class narrators, who spoke about their experiences of particular events or issues. *Fight for Shelton Bar* (staged in 1974) was one of the first plays created in this way, performed to many of the ex-steelworkers who had lost their jobs and had been interviewed. Cheeseman's work was heavily influenced by the English playwright Joan Littlewood. In 1963, with her theatre company, Theatre Workshop, Littlewood produced the documentary musical, *Oh What a Lovely War*, a satire on the First World War.

Cheeseman's work inspired a generation of theatre practitioners in the UK, intent on gathering and staging largely unheard stories from members of their local communities and presenting them back to audiences which included the narrators. Companies such as 7:84, Age Exchange Reminiscence Theatre, Banner Theatre and Eastern Angles toured their shows to non-theatrical venues such as village halls, community centres, schools, sheltered housing and residential homes. Many of their shows were based entirely on interviews and addressed matters of local interest to the narrators. In the 1990s, companies such as Joint Stock and, later, Out of Joint developed verbatim theatre processes initially explored by Cheeseman. Actors would interview narrators, then return to the rehearsal room and work with the director on how to theatrically represent their 'characters' and the narratives they had been told. This work was not 'pure' or 'exact' verbatim theatre in the sense in which I employ the term in this book – namely, creating a script from the exact words of someone interviewed – but it is still known as verbatim theatre.

There is no single way to create plays from interviews; but one shared aim of most of the theatre companies and playwrights I have mentioned was to produce theatre that gave a platform for voices in populations and communities whose stories had not been previously heard nor dramatically portrayed. In this way, it is perhaps their common desired outcome, rather than a particular methodology, that connects these forms of theatre.

After the '9/11' terrorist attacks in the US, audiences' interest in the global impact of many countries' political actions and decisions was heightened. Plays based on interviews grew exponentially, and their remit expanded from covering local and national narratives to addressing global crises. During this period, some members of the public realised that the media did not always convey the full scope of political information and social arguments on the matters discussed. Verbatim theatre became a means to address this information gap and to reflect a more authentic form of personal experience to theatre audiences. Whether or not the plays created in this way offer more accurate information than is conveyed through media outlets is, of course, debatable. Memory is undeniably fallible, and the playwright is ultimately in the position of selecting which content appears in the script.

In the UK, David Hare has written several verbatim pieces over the last two decades, although not all of these works can be defined as 'pure' verbatim plays. *Stuff Happens* (2004), written in response to the second Gulf War, is only partially based on interview material and is partly fictional. Other plays by Hare based on interviews include *Via Dolorosa* (1973), which deals with the Israeli-Palestinian conflict, and *The Permanent Way* (2003), which addresses the privatisation of Britain's railways. Since the beginning of the twenty-first century, forms of theatre created from interviews have been evolving at a fast and furious rate, addressing subjects ranging from culturally specific events and community and personal concerns, to international politics.

In the UK, playwrights such as David Hare, Robin Soans, Richard Norton-Taylor, Gillian Slovo and the director of the Tricycle Theatre, Nicolas Kent, have all contributed to verbatim theatre's movement from the theatrical fringes to the more commercially mainstream. Kent worked with Norton-Taylor on a series of tribunal plays based on trial transcripts. Their productions included *Justifying War*, a reconstruction of the Hutton Hearings (a 2003 judicial inquiry chaired by Lord Hutton, appointed by the Labour government to investigate the circumstances surrounding the death of David Kelly, a biological warfare expert and former UN weapons inspector in Iraq) and *The Colour of Justice* (previously mentioned under 'tribunal theatre'). Since the surge in popularity in recent years of plays based on testimony and interviews, verbatim productions which often tackle issues of political and social concern continue to be created by well-known dramatists and lesser-known theatre companies alike.

Another British theatre practitioner who has gained notable attention is Alecky Blythe – for her Recorded Delivery performances, in which actors receive a feed of original interviews through headphones and relate the lines they hear to the audience. Blythe's musical *London Road,* co-created with Adam Cork, was performed in 2011 at the National Theatre and was adapted into a film in 2015. The text was taken from real-life accounts and follows the impact felt by the Ipswich community after a string of murders of prostitutes in 2006. *The Girlfriend Experience* (2008), another verbatim play created by Blythe, is about a seaside brothel that specialises in services to an older clientele.

The United States

In the late 1970s and early 1980s, the playwright Emily Mann reinvigorated the production of theatre created from interviews – termed 'theatre of testimony' in the US – when she wrote and produced a number of plays in this way. One of these was *Still Life,* which explores how the Vietnam War affected three lives: a Marine veteran, his estranged wife and his mistress. In some of her later works, such as *Execution of Justice* and *Greensboro (A Requiem),* in addition to interview material, Mann added excerpts of letters, recordings, films, court records and newspaper extracts to her scripts. This arguably makes them examples of documentary theatre, rather than theatre of testimony. However, categorising the various kinds of plays created from documents is often a tricky endeavour and is not always particularly useful!

In 1979, the actor and playwright Anna Deavere Smith set out to 'find American character in the ways that people speak' and began interviewing people (more than 2,000 to date) across the country.[4] In 1983, she produced her first play based on her interviews and research: *On the Road: A Search for American Character.* With minimal set and costumes, she combined the journalistic technique of interviewing her subjects with the art of interpreting their words through performance. For her 1992 play, *Fires in the Mirror: Crown Heights, Brooklyn and Other Identities* (directed by Emily Mann), Smith interviewed and acted the parts of community members who had witnessed the Crown Heights riots in Brooklyn, New York. Both this play and her one-woman show,

Twilight: Los Angeles (1994) – in common with the earlier Stoke Documentaries in England – were performed to the communities from which the staged stories originated. Smith's work will be further addressed in **Chapter 14**.

Also of note is Jessica Blank and Erik Jensen's play, *The Exonerated* (2002), which is based on six interviews with individuals released from death row. The script employs written extracts from court records and letters, and the actors were involved in editing the material. And one of the best-known plays created from stories provided by a community is *The Laramie Project,* scripted in 2000 by Moisés Kaufman and members of his Tectonic Theater Project. The play addresses the shocking homophobia-motivated murder of a young man, Matthew Shepard, in Laramie, Wyoming. Kaufman and his colleagues interviewed 200 Laramie residents about this event. This play is also addressed in **Chapter 14**.

Australia

Since the 1990s, verbatim theatre has become prolific in Australia, due in part to playwright Alana Valentine, who wrote *Run Rabbit Run* (2004) about a community's love and support for their local rugby team. Paul Brown is another prominent Australian verbatim playwright who wrote *Aftershocks*, first performed in 1991, based on interviews with staff and members of the Newcastle Workers Club about their experiences and memories of the Newcastle earthquake. The playwright and director, Ros Horin, wrote *Through the Wire* (2005), which tells stories of asylum seekers in Australia, including that of Shahin Shafaei, who played himself in the 2004 production. Much verbatim theatre in Australia is intent on representing the lives and stories of community members who provide previously untold narratives and who, in turn, are valued by theatre practitioners for their part in the play's creation. In recent years, there has been a notable increase in the production of plays in Australia that employ testimonies provided by asylum seekers and refugees.

Australian playwright Roslyn Oades, like Alecky Blythe in the UK, also produces plays in which the actors wear headphones and speak along to edited audio interview content. Oades terms her work 'headphone-verbatim', after the form was introduced by British director Mark Wing-Davey in his 2001 workshop, Drama Without Paper, at the London Actors Centre. In such productions, actors attempt to reproduce every inflection, stumble, repetition and cough of the narrator. Oades' understanding is that 'there is as much information embedded in the *way* someone speaks as *what* they are saying',[5] a view closely aligned with similar understandings in oral history scholarship. Stuart Young and Hilary Halba have also developed a series of plays using headphone verbatim at the University of Otago, which include *Be/Longing: A Verbatim Play* (2012), based on interviews with groups of immigrants in Australia, and *Hush: A Verbatim Play about Family Violence* (2009).

South Africa

Many playwrights in South Africa have employed verbatim processes to address matters of social and political concern in their country. *The Story I Am About to Tell* (1997) was produced by the Khulumani Support Group formed through the Truth and Reconciliation Commission (TRC) and was performed by three people who testified at the TRC. It is partially fictionalised – with the intention of preventing re-traumatisation of the narrators – while still allowing a dramatic presentation of the events they endured. *The Line* (2012), by Gina Shmukler, is a piece about the xenophobic attacks that occurred in 2008 in Soweto, and this production is discussed in **Chapter 14**. *The Crossing* (2008) is an autobiographical work written and performed by an asylum seeker, Jonathan Nkala, and *Asylum: Section 22,* which presents accounts by asylum seekers in South Africa, was written by the verbatim playwright and scholar Pedzisai Maedza.

Options for Your Own Verbatim Production

Part III of this book provides a step-by-step guide for creating your own verbatim theatre piece and includes suggestions for performance possibilities but here is an introduction to get you thinking about planning a play based on interviews.

A Rehearsed Reading of the Script

A rehearsed playreading (sometimes known as a script-in-hand performance) is a relatively easy way to present a verbatim play since actors do not have to learn lines or plan for lengthy rehearsals, which a full production would involve. The actors often just read out the script while sitting on chairs or stools. An alternative is for the script to be delivered by actors after a short rehearsal period, during which the director and/or writer work with the actors who read from their scripts as they move around the stage, partially dramatising the scenes.

Theatrical Scenes Created from Interview Material

Rather than creating a full-length script, another performance option is to present separate scenes which relate to one over-arching theme. This form of theatrical presentation provides the opportunity for a facilitated discussion between theatre makers and audience members following each scene. This means that the responses by the audience to the content of the performance are more immediate than they would be if discussed at the end of a full-length show. The piece can either be performed in a traditional theatre venue or, if the production does not have a large set – or any set at all – then it can be easily presented by actors and the facilitator in a community hall or college, or at a conference or a similar event.

Verbatim Plays Performed by Students or Members of Community Groups

Another alternative is to create a verbatim theatre piece among students or community members in which they will be the performers. Since many verbatim theatre projects are based on events or issues which impact a community of interest or locality, those involved in the production will inevitably have a particular attachment to the matter being addressed. Furthermore, students, who may have been previously unaware about a subject or issue, can bring valuable fresh eyes and new understandings to the subject matter addressed by the play.

Verbatim Theatre Performed by Narrators Themselves

This form of work produces a kind of autobiographical theatre which can be extremely moving for an audience. It might consist of cast members learning and performing edited sections of their own interviews which could be presented in separate scenes or as part of a full-length play. Verbatim theatre always creates a powerful means for an audience to hear personal stories, but when they are spoken by the very people who have experienced them, extra meaning emerges both in the telling and in the reception.

If you choose to work on this kind of production, be aware that when the narrators are inexperienced as actors, they may have some difficulty learning lines and working with a director. Furthermore, where the content of the interview material is of a traumatic nature, narrators might be at risk of encountering a re-triggering of trauma when sharing those experiences on stage. If this might be a possibility, then the playwright and director have a responsibility to be ethically vigilant when asking narrators to act their own experiences. These considerations are just some of the reasons why verbatim pieces are frequently not performed by those whose were interviewed but, instead, by members of a theatre company or other performers who were not the original narrators.

Some companies, however, work creatively in ways whereby people who have a shared experience can present personal stories in a way that distances themselves very slightly from the original narrators, and additionally overcome any line-learning challenges. 'The Verbatim Formula' is a project where teenagers relate personal narratives about their experience of being in the 'care' system in the UK. In order not to be personally identified with the content or to be troubled when speaking about it, the actors narrate stories from interviews with their friends, rather than their own testimony, a device which provides them with a degree of distance from the material. The problem of learning lines is overcome by having the performers receiving the words that they deliver from an earpiece which has a recording of the original interview which they repeat out loud.[6] (This project will be discussed further in **Chapter 6**.)

A Professional Production with Full Cast and Crew and Stage Set

This would probably be presented in a traditional theatre space, perhaps on a raised stage with seating for the audience or alternatively on the flat (at ground level) with raised seating for the audience. The play could be a full-length piece (up to two hours with an interval, I would suggest, but certainly no longer) or a shorter play, which might be about one hour long with no interval. Professional theatre makers are usually employed for such a production and might include – depending on the budget – actors, a director, set and costume designers, a lighting designer and stage managers. The show could be taken on tour, presented at a number of theatres around the country, or it might be performed at just one theatre for a run of several shows which may be over one or many weeks.

Considerations in Working in Verbatim Theatre

Verbatim Theatre as a Form of Alternative Journalism

The commercial success and general popularity of plays based on interviews has come about not only as a result of an ongoing interest by the public in the 'real-life' stories of individuals, but also because verbatim theatre has been seen as filling the gap of reporting in the mainstream media. These two matters are, of course, related, since personal narratives often reveal previously under-documented version of events. Over the last two decades, particularly in the UK, there has been a rising level of distrust from the general public towards media outlets, including television and the press, which were previously regarded as reliable sources of information. This change has been due, in part, to what has been viewed by some as an ethical crisis in journalism, where, as Michael Anderson and Linden Wilkinson observe, 'commercialism, shareholder interest and economies of scale dictate an increasingly homogenised media content'.[7] Verbatim theatre has stepped into this gap in varying manifestations. Tribunal theatre provides one way in which political and legal concerns can be addressed and presented theatrically, but other forms of plays based on interview content can also dramatically investigate under-reported matters of political or social concern. These productions allow audiences to hear detailed accounts from people whose lives have been impacted by the matters addressed.

'A Ring of Truth'

When attending plays based on interviews, I have noticed that often the lines I hear the actors speak have what I would call a 'ring of truth' about them and my sense is the phrases and descriptions spoken sound extremely natural in tone and content. My observations, however, are based on a gut feeling and, as audience members, we rely on the programme notes or promotional literature to provide us with additional information about how many people were interviewed for the show and whether the script has been created using 'pure' or 'exact' (word-for-word) verbatim or 'massaged' verbatim (meaning that the original interview content has been altered in some way for dramatic purposes). But it is undoubtedly this 'ring of truth' in verbatim productions that contributes to their potential to reach and move an audience in a way, at times, unrivalled by more fictional forms of theatre writing.

The appreciation of verbatim productions from an audience member's point of view therefore comes from two levels of reception – an intellectual under-standing, *whereby I know that the play has been created from interviews with 'real' people,* and a feeling or emotional understanding that *what I am hearing and seeing sounds and appears to be somehow more 'truthful' than when I attend a play that has been scripted purely from a writer's imagination.* But the notion of truthfulness is inevitably an unruly one which, in the context of interview narrative included in a verbatim script, must be scrutinised. Although word-for-word excerpts from an interview may have been employed in a verbatim play, there are certain factors which problematise any claim to 'truthfulness' a playwright working in this genre might make, one of which is that the original account from the nar-rator will have been totally subjective, told from their own personal perspective. There will always be questions about the reliability of memory, especially when some time has passed since events which narrators may be asked about originally occurred; additionally, narrators will have had their own agenda when agreeing to be interviewed and as they recollect and narrate their experiences.

Another way in which an audience's understanding of the apparent 'truth-fulness' of the content of a verbatim play is disrupted is because the story that the playwright wishes to tell will influence what parts of the interview support that narrative goal. Theatre makers employ creative license in order to fully realise what they see as the dramatic potential of the material. But, crucially, the license employed by the playwright and theatre company members has the potential to devalue the currency of the apparent 'truth' that the audience is buying into (both figuratively and literally) when they attend a verbatim production. An example of this occurs in David Hare's *Stuff Happens* (2004), a play which presents arguments for and against the US-led attack on Iraq, mixing verbatim re-creations of real speeches, meetings and press conferences. Within the script, however, there are speculative versions of private meetings between members of the Bush and Blair administrations which could, argu-ably, confuse the audience who have come to the play believing that they are watching non-fiction scenes dramatised from interviews or other documentary materials. Without sufficient explanation that the play was part fictional, audi-ences may assume that the script of *Stuff Happens* is 'pure' verbatim and, subse-quently, may feel disappointed or even, in some way, duped on learning that a totally fictitious scene has been introduced. Others, of course, may view this as an innovative dramatic device whereby real events and personal narrative are intermingled.

The Playwright's Agenda

Verbatim plays can present the narrated experiences of 'real' people or accounts of events which may vary in their interpretation from officially documented versions, but the theatre makers who create this work, however much they might aspire to 'set the record straight', cannot, I would argue, lay any claim to objectivity. Because of the political or social nature of many verbatim productions, the playwright or producer who initiates these projects inevitably has their own agenda in the creation of the piece. The interview excerpts included may present conflict and/or revelation during the production which the playwright hopes will engage the audience on an emotional and intellectual level, but there is a risk that quotations will be taken out of context and may convey slightly different meanings than those intended by the original narrators. This is one of the most striking differences between verbatim theatre and oral history, where the interviewers will also have an agenda but where, critically, the interview content cannot be altered by them. This subject will be examined more closely in **Chapter 2**.

As a dramatic form, verbatim theatre has, at times, been criticised for the lack of contextual information provided, both about the interviewing process and how the interview content has been edited.[8] This is a perfectly valid observation since playwrights have full control over how the interview excerpts they select appear in the final piece and frequently, such information is not made available to audiences. Many verbatim theatre scripts include words spoken by narrators during an interview but leave out the interviewer's questions, resulting in what appears to be a monologue delivered by the 'character' (originally the narrator) in the dramatised scenes. However, when the interviewer's voice is absent from the final script, the audience cannot know the details relating to the set-up of the interview. They will not know where it was conducted, under what circumstances the interview occurred, who did the interviewing, why the narrator agreed to the interview, what questions were asked of the narrator – the context in which they were framed or tone in which they were asked. A playwright might feel that there is no need for this kind of information to be revealed in the text of the play or may hold the view that imposing her own voice or character within the dramatic content might not only be unnecessary, but could also interrupt the dramatic flow of action in the piece.

Some playwrights have attempted to address this apparent lack of transparency by including characters in the script who announce to the audience that they were the original interviewers, and who then speak the 'lines' of the interviewer asking the questions, thereby reconstructing the *feel* of the original interview. But even in plays in which theatre practitioners are included in the script as characters, criticism has still been levelled by theatre scholars at the playwright, suggesting that this device is only an attempt to increase the appeal to 'veracity', rather than provide any full contextual information.[8]

A verbatim play is produced by theatre practitioners for their own purposes, based on their personal or ideological viewpoints, but this does not detract from the dramatic and political strength of plays created from interviews. Issues raised by these concerns merit investigation, and **Chapters 4** and **5** address ethical considerations relating to the editing power of the playwright and the degree of personal and political agency that narrators hold in production processes.

★

Verbatim theatre processes vary enormously in style and content, as addressed throughout this chapter, and some theatre work which employs interview material involves the narrators themselves participating in the theatre work. The focus of this book, however, is mainly on verbatim theatre created when professional actors or students or community group members script and dramatise excerpts from transcribed interviews. But the following chapters will, at times, present examples of working methods that vary from this format, in order to provide the reader with a range of possibilities to inform them in their own work when creating verbatim theatre from spoken testimony.

Notes

1 Derek Paget states: 'I first heard the term "Verbatim Theatre" in 1985, in conversation with *NTQ's* [*New Theatre Quarterly*], distinguished co-editor, the late Clive Barker'. Derek Paget, "New Documentarism on Stage: Documentary Theatre in New Times," *Zeitschrift für Anglistik und Amerikanistik* 56:2 (2008): 132.

2 Yaël Farber, *Theatre as Witness: Three Testimonial Plays from South Africa in Collaboration with and Based on the Lives of the Original Performers* (London: Oberon Books, 2008), 19.

3 If you wish to explore some applied theatre work, you may be interested in the work of Geese Theatre Company in England, which comprises a team of theatre practitioners who present interactive theatre and facilitate drama-based groupwork, staff training and consultation for the probation service, prisons, young offender institutions, youth offending teams, secure hospitals and related agencies throughout the UK and abroad: Geese Theatre Company, http://www.geese.co.uk/.

4 Anna Deavere Smith, *Fires in the Mirror: Crown Heights, Brooklyn and Other Identities* (New York: Anchor Books/Doubleday, 1993), xxiii.

5 "About," *Roslyn Oades*, February 28, 2020, http://www.roslynoades.com/about.

6 For more information about The Verbatim Formula, see "The Verbatim Formula," *People's Palace Projects*, February 28, 2020, http://www.theverbatimformula.org.uk/.

7 Michael Anderson and Linden Wilkinson, "A Resurgence of Verbatim Theatre: Authenticity, Empathy and Transformation," *Australasian Drama Studies* 50 (2007): 153.

8 Deidre Heddon, *Autobiography and Performance* (Basingstoke: Palgrave Macmillan, 2008), 131. In this excellent publication, Deidre Heddon places verbatim theatre processes under well-needed critical scrutiny and examines ethical concerns relating to this field of work.

2

ORAL HISTORY AND VERBATIM THEATRE

Similar but Different

Since this book is for oral historians who intend to create verbatim theatre and theatre makers who wish to turn to oral history to inform their practice, readers from each discipline will benefit from understanding the fundamentals of the other. The principal difference between oral history and verbatim theatre lies in their goals. The oral historian's goal is to balance the historical record by including the voices of everyday people. The verbatim theatre playwright's goal is to create an artistic work. This chapter examines connections between oral history and verbatim theatre – both historical and contemporary – and highlights some of the main differences.

Oral history methodology follows a prescriptive process, previously developed but still open to revision, as a means to operate ethically and yield the most productive results when gathering data and historical research material in the form of interviews. Traditionally, oral history seeks to preserve the interview fairly intact, as a direct representation of the narrator's words, for the historical record in an archive. The role of the verbatim theatre playwright, however, is to gather personal testimonies for a work of art, often with a goal of raising social or political awareness. In this process, the playwright may or may not use the narrators' words verbatim or in the original context. Material gathered can contribute towards historical understanding, but will generally be employed only as dramatic content in a play, and not be archived, as oral histories are. One of the most striking points of connection between oral history and verbatim theatre is the shared attention both disciplines give to seeking verbal testimonies from members of communities who may not otherwise have had their stories sought and dispersed.

The narratives in both forms of work are mainly secured by recorded interviews, and consequently both have been entirely dependent on the technological development of recording devices. The early 1890s saw the invention of wax cylinders or discs (hard wax surfaces into which sound grooves were cut), and ethnographers employed these devices to record stories or, in some cases, songs. The steel wire recorder was invented in 1898, and in 1928, a coated magnetic tape was invented in Germany. But it was not until the 1970s that portable tape recorders became available to members of the general public, and oral history and verbatim theatre projects grew in popularity during this period. Both areas have developed apace since that time with no signs of the popularity of either practice abating in a world which appears to hold a continuing fascination with recording personal narratives and hearing about the experiences of 'real' people. Furthermore, verbatim theatre and oral history are also forms of story-telling which can inform and educate. It is somewhat inevitable then that these practices will have many overlapping features. But, at their core, they still have different aims and objectives.

Purposes of Oral History Projects

- Throwing light on the lives of marginalised people and communities, and neglected social issues.
- Adding to the historical canon and creating a broader historiography.
- Documenting aspects of historical material which tend to be missing from other sources relating to lived experience.
- Empowering individuals or social groups through the process of remembering and reinterpreting the past, with an emphasis on the value of process as much as historical product.

Aims of Verbatim Theatre Productions

- Producing playscripts from personal real-life testimony and experience which are then shared with audiences.
- Disseminating personal, social and political information, thereby creating a form of educational entertainment.
- Staging stories narrated by members of marginalised groups, making their lives and concerns visible, and celebrating communities.
- Revealing political or social injustices that have not been adequately covered in the mainstream media (or presenting an alternative version).
- Creating performed historiography, whereby stories are enacted about those whose lives have not previously been documented, allowing for a reassessment of those histories.
- Interviewing members of a community about a difficult event, then feeding their stories back to that community, providing narrators with reflective, as well as healing opportunities.

History from Below

In 1948 Allan Nevins initiated an oral history project at Columbia University in New York. He interviewed people who were deemed to be significant in American life – those from the political, economic and cultural elites. The project has since been viewed as a 'top-down' form of oral history, as opposed to the 'bottom-up' approach, whereby narrators were sought from the less powerful sectors of society. This bottom-up approach has become more prevalent in recent decades.

In Europe, some of the origins of oral history lay in the systemic folklore collecting of nineteenth-century Scandinavia, while other oral history projects in the twentieth century were more rooted in social and cultural history and allied with political movements on the Left. All of this work had the shared aim of seeking the voices of those previously excluded from national narratives. By the late 1960s and early 1970s, the bottom-up approach of oral history was emerging on both sides of the Atlantic as more popular than using recorded interviews to inquire into the lives of the rich and powerful. In the US, Studs Terkel, a veteran writer of the Works Progress Administration (WPA) – which had hired unemployed writers to chronicle the lives of ordinary citizens including former black slaves, workers and homesteaders – published a popular work entitled *Hard Times* in 1970. This book contains more than 150 testimonies from people of varying socio-economic status who lived in the US during the Great Depression. Oral historian Michael Frisch, when discussing the reviews of *Hard Times*, commented, 'The critics described the book in terms of literature, rather than history'.[1] This observation shows how interview material can lend itself to literary or even artistic forms, in addition to producing a form of alternative historical documentation.

Until the 1970s, when oral history (in the form of recording, transcribing and archiving interviews) was finally accepted as a legitimate discipline by history departments within mainstream academia, academics had assumed that records of historical events existed only in the form of political legislation, published memoirs of public figures and legal documents. The desire to seek out the stories of ordinary people, largely invisible in the public record, issued a challenge to historians who had previously employed a far more document-based approach to gathering historical information.

In 1966 in the UK, the social historian E.P. Thompson published an essay in *The Times Literary Supplement* entitled 'History from Below'. This work introduced the phrase to historiography and referred to the new historical interest in the lives of the poor, disenfranchised, oppressed and otherwise under-documented sectors of society. This viewing of history 'from below' links to Paul Thompson's suggestion that, by interviewing those from the working classes, oral history can enable a radical change in the way we interpret social elements of history.[2] It also ties into his reference to testimonies from the working classes as 'Evidence from the underside'.[3] In the late 1960s and early 1970s, with the increasing availability of recording devices, Paul Thompson and other oral historians argued that their practice could enable these voices to be heard for the first time not only by historians, but also by working-class people themselves. Significantly, this understanding was also shared by several verbatim theatre practitioners in the UK during the same period, as explained in the following section.

Verbatim Theatre Practitioners Seeking Working-Class Stories in the UK

The growing interest in working-class history and culture was apparent in the 1957 series of 'Radio Ballads' created by Charles Parker for the BBC. These were produced in collaboration with Ewan MacColl and Peggy Seeger, and, rather than being performed by actors, they featured the actual voices of fishermen, railwaymen and construction workers, a practice which was unheard of at the time. The narratives were interspersed with songs composed and arranged by MacColl and Seeger. During the 1960s, discussions were held among oral historians about ways in which working-class histories might be retrieved and the Radio Ballads offered one form in which the general public was able to listen to a seldom heard range of voices.

Another way in which the stories of working-class people came to be more widely dispersed in the UK at that time was through the creation of the 'Stoke Documentaries' by Peter Cheeseman, whose work was directly influenced by Parker's Radio Ballads. During the late 1960s through to the 1980s, the focus of many of the productions created by Cheeseman and then by several of his colleagues and contemporaries was on stories told by working-class narrators. These practitioners include Chris Honer (artistic director of the Gateway theatre, Chester, 1976–80), Chrys Salt (who wrote *Of Whole Heart Cometh Hope*, 1983, created from the memories of the Cooperative Women's Guild, for Age Exchange Reminiscence Theatre Company) and the playwright Rony Robinson, who worked with Cheeseman on several plays during the 1960s and 1970s. Cheeseman's productions provided inspiration and practical guidance for many other playwrights and theatre companies in the UK at the time and in later years.

In the latter part of the twentieth century, companies were touring plays based on interviews to non-theatre settings such as community centres, working men's clubs, day centres and residential homes, where they could share working-class or regional stories with audiences from similar communities. The relative simplicity of set, props and lighting allowed them to travel light with small-scale productions and reach audiences who might not otherwise attend the theatre.

Oral historians and verbatim theatre practitioners alike have seized upon opportunities to employ spoken testimony from members of marginalised communities. The result has been an ever-increasing dispersal of stories from minority groups in society in the form of archived oral histories and in the production of plays based on interviews. From an initial focus on working-class narrators, oral history and verbatim theatre have both extended their search for previously unheard and untold stories to other groups who have been silenced, shamed or even criminalised in the past. While neither practice is focused solely on marginalised communities, both are well positioned to respond to pressing contemporary issues and have, over recent decades, brought the voices of women, LGBTQ people, people from the BAME (Black, Asian and Minority Ethnic) population,[4] homeless people and immigrants into public awareness. In oral history, this is accomplished by making interviews available through historical record and in theatre, by disseminating information through productions to wider public audiences.

In recent years, the subject matter of many verbatim plays has expanded to address human rights abuses, and universal issues of crisis and/or controversy such as war, natural disaster, political debates and criminal acts. Interestingly, however, much of the commercially successful verbatim theatre in the UK – staged in well-known and well-funded London venues and sometimes adapted for film – does not always focus on the stories of marginalised communities. It often addresses contemporary political debate (as seen in works by David Hare) or stories about a marginalised community which are purposefully written from a middle-class perspective (as seen in many of Alecky Blythe's plays). Conversely, the stated aims of other theatre companies, such as Ice and Fire and my own company, Artemis, involve dramatising the stories of members of marginalised and silenced populations including refugees and asylum seekers and those who have historically been dispossessed of a voice in society or a platform from which to disperse their testimonies.

What Can Verbatim Theatre and Oral History Teach Each Other?

Although I have outlined some of the shared aims of oral history and verbatim theatre, I am certainly not suggesting that these two practices should be conflated. Rather, I am interested in examining ways in which both processes can learn from each other – especially how oral history debates and methodology might inform verbatim theatre. Below, I summarise my observations of some of the connections and differences, based on my work in both fields.

Shared Aims and Practices

- Many verbatim theatre productions and oral history projects seek stories from members of marginalised communities who have not previously been able to speak publicly about their experiences or had their stories recorded by historians or sociologists.
- In the 1960s and 1970s in the UK, many oral history projects and verbatim theatre productions focussed on recording working-class testimony.

- Both practices involve sourcing thoughtful narrators who are prepared to share their experiences about a particular subject or event.
- The material recorded in an interview is often transcribed in full by an oral historian or a verbatim theatre playwright.

Similarities between the Two Disciplines

- The recorded interview is the essential component and foundation for verbatim theatre productions and for oral history projects.
- Oral history projects and verbatim theatre productions are totally reliant upon the narrators, who take a prominent role. When the interview transcript is sent to the narrators for approval and feedback, they are afforded a greater sense of involvement in the work. The review process can also inspire narrators to reflect and make sense of their past. This reflective stage, and the effect of the interview process on the narrator, has been explored in far greater depth in oral history than in verbatim theatre scholarship. But, unlike oral history in which the narrator can only reflect upon their interview, narrators who contribute to verbatim theatre projects also have the opportunity to witness 'themselves' portrayed on stage, with their own words being spoken by actors.
- Both practices can involve a *feeding back* of the material from interviews to members of the communities who shared their stories. In oral history, this can occur in the form of exhibitions, open-archive days and other events which involve showcasing the interview content. With verbatim theatre, the main aim of the work is to disperse the interview content through dramatic means.
- Oral history projects and verbatim theatre productions often seek the *alternative* version of a current or historical event – one that was not recorded in more 'official' forms of documentation.
- Verbatim theatre productions can create a version of performed historical documentation. The narratives employed in such plays may not always be available for academic scrutiny and interpretation in the way that archived oral histories are, but as performances and published scripts they can contribute to gaps in historical and social knowledge.

Differences between Oral History and Verbatim Theatre

- Oral historians, as historians, are careful to place an individual narrative or a current social issue into a larger picture of time, place or cultural phenomenon. Context is everything for historians. Thus, record keeping is an integral part of any oral history project. All stages of the work are documented by oral historians, including identifying their own agenda, the project concept and what they hope to achieve from their research. They often document the circumstances of the interview and use the interview as a springboard for further research. The aims of verbatim theatre productions can be political, social, educational or ideological, but playwrights are primarily artists. The transcribed interview is all they need, and from that they develop a script. After it is finalised and handed over to the actors and director, there is usually no need to keep either the recorded interviews or information relating to the narrators.

- Since the ultimate aims of oral history projects and verbatim theatre differ – one usually being for research purposes and the other a dramatic production – the interview is approached differently. The questions asked and the way they are asked differ. The playwright might, for example, encourage a narrator to speak in more detail about a subject which the playwright feels may have dramatic potential. Or, when asking about a social or political matter, the playwright/interviewer might not feel obliged to conceal her own opinion, as an oral historian will generally endeavour to do. While oral historians attempt to maintain a neutral position in their questioning of narrators, the political, social or ideological agenda that theatre makers hold often provides the motivation for the productions they create.
- In oral history practice, after the interview has been completed and the content transcribed, the interview recording will be preserved intact and archived. Editing of the interview transcript or the actual recording takes place only under special circumstances. In the process of creating a play based on interviews, however, the playwright critically selects which excerpts to employ in a script and the original transcripts are rarely seen by anyone else.

As discussed in this chapter, oral history and verbatim theatre have different final aims but some striking similarities. Whether you are reading this book as an oral historian intending to create a piece of theatre from interviews or a theatre practitioner looking to oral history scholarship to enhance your work, noting both the points of intersection and of divergence provides important insights. Your interview-based plays will consequently be informed by a deeper understanding of the historical background, the working methods and the aims of both practices.

Notes

1 Michael Frisch, "Oral History and 'Hard Times', A Review Essay," *The Oral History Review* 7 (1979): 72.
2 Paul Thompson, "The Voice of the Past: Oral History," in *The Oral History Reader*, Third Edition, ed. Robert Perks and Alistair Thomson (Abingdon: Routledge, 2016), 39.
3 Thompson, "The Voice of the Past: Oral History," 37.
4 BAME is an acronym currently used in the UK to refer to Black, Asian and Minority Ethnic people.

3

DISCUSSIONS WITHIN ORAL HISTORY THAT INFORM VERBATIM THEATRE PROCESSES

By examining some of the debates in which oral historians have engaged over the last fifty or so years, my intention in this chapter is to explore how scholars and practitioners of verbatim theatre can gain valuable insight from their findings and discover much to interest them as they create their own plays scripted from interviews. Four main areas of oral history discussion which I believe have direct relevance to verbatim theatre are as follows:

- Identifying of the **positionality** of the interviewer and the narrator.
- **Possibilities of reflection** being afforded to narrators in verbatim theatre processes.
- Applying the notion of **shared authority** to theatre created from interviews.
- Decisions about **whether or not to include the interviewer's voice** in a script.

Positionality

In this section I use the term 'positionality' to refer to the relationship between the interviewer and the narrator, determining whether the playwright is from the same population as their narrators or a different population and whether or not they have shared experiences with those whom they interview. Over the last few decades, following postmodern feminist thinking and employing the tools of intersectionality, oral history discussions have addressed power dynamics within the interview situation and identified how levels of trust between a narrator and an interviewer can affect both the quality and the quantity of disclosure during an interview. Both these matters are relevant to verbatim theatre processes since playwrights rely on interview excerpts to create their plays, and richer content provides greater possibilities during the development of a script.

As discussed, verbatim theatre practice is susceptible to accusations of appropriation since narrators' stories are used to create a play which helps realise the aims of the theatre maker. Additionally, interview excerpts are frequently employed in a script without being contextualised. Such criticisms are of particular concern when the narrators might be considered to be in some way vulnerable, or if they are from communities that have suffered oppression or prejudice, since, in such situations, there is more potential for exploitation. In both verbatim theatre and oral history projects, power imbalances are inherent between the interviewer, who has usually initiated the project, and the narrators, especially those who come from sectors in society that are marginalised or have previously been silenced or dispossessed. Power imbalances are less likely to occur in interview situations where the narrators hold positions associated with a higher status, such as politicians or legal professionals.

Oral historian Sue Armitage has noted that, in the process of gathering women's interviews in the late 1970s and 1980s, 'the reality of multiple (especially racial) differences ended notions of a unitary women's culture'.[1] The feminist debate determined that a first-world woman could not and must not speak for all women, especially those who come from a different social class or race. From this debate came the realisation that every narrator is situated in a specific social location, which they are encouraged to recognise.[2] Armitage states that the consequence of this discovery was that 'we learned reflexivity by becoming aware of our own subjectivity and learned to state clearly our own partiality and "positionality"'.[3] Since the interviewing process is such an integral part of verbatim theatre work, Armitage's comments about the positionality of the interviewer in oral history projects are also relevant to playwrights who conduct interviews for their productions.

Although charges of appropriation may be inherent within verbatim theatre processes, because theatre makers do 'use' other people's experiences to create plays – work which will often benefit the theatre makers' own careers and reputations – there are ways to mitigate possibilities of narrators being *used* in this area of work. One of these is for playwrights (or others who are involved in the interviewing process) to identify their own positioning in respect to the narrators. This involves the interviewer asking questions such as:

- Do I come from the same population as the narrators?
- Am I of the same ethnic or racial background?
- Do I hold full residency of a country where a narrator does not?
- Am I from a different class than the narrator?
- Do I share the same sexual orientation or gender identity (for instance transgender identity)?
- Am I the same or a different gender?

The significance of recognising these differences or similarities is that often these identities will carry with them notable power discrepancies. A white person in a predominantly white country will hold greater power in that society. A heterosexual person will generally hold more power than a homosexual man or a lesbian. A man more than a woman. And so on. Identifying positionality in this way, using the tools of intersectionality, will enable interviewers to gain a deeper understanding of the power dynamics within the interview situation. This, in turn, will help them prepare for the interview and conduct it with greater sensitivity when asking the narrator questions, especially if they relate to matters which reflect wider power imbalances within society, such as women's experiences in particular roles or areas of work, and the same with people who are BAME (Black, Asian and Minority Ethnic), or LGBTQ people's struggles with accepting their sexual orientation or gender identity, or asylum seekers' adverse treatment in a host country.

When determining the positionality of an interviewer in relation to a narrator, the matter of power and authority is not the only criterion that merits identification. It is also helpful to examine whether the interviewer is an 'insider' (referring to someone who shares the same identity or experiences) or an 'outsider' (someone who is of a different identity and has had completely different experiences in life) in relation to the narrator. These terms are, of course, also often related to power imbalances, and they are binary definitions, which are sometimes limiting and not always applicable. But I introduce the notion of insider/outsider awareness within interviewing work for the purpose of opening this discussion, while acknowledging that the full picture is always more complex.

In the late 1970s, when discussions regarding the insider/outsider positioning of an interviewer in relation to a narrator were first addressed, Paul Thompson suggested that 'in any tight-knit community [...] the insider knows the way round, can be less easily fooled, understands the nuances, and starts with far more useful contacts and, hopefully, as an established person of good faith. All this has to be learnt and constructed by the outsider...'.[4] But Thompson also cautioned against an insider approach which might be viewed as one way to smooth out possible inequalities, stating, 'It is not necessarily true that an interviewer of the same sex, class, or race will obtain more accurate information. If the social relationship in an interview becomes, or is from the start, a social bond, the danger towards social conformity in replies is increased'.[5]

Over recent decades, oral historians have engaged in critical reflection on their insider or outsider status when writing about their projects. Perks and Thomson, in the introduction to *The Oral History Reader* (2016), point to examples which demonstrate the advantages of holding an insider position when interviewing. One case they present concerns Akemi Kikumura's interviews with her own mother, an Issei woman from Japan, who immigrated to the US in 1923. Kikumura believed that her mother would *only* have spoken openly to her because she was a family member and therefore, an insider.[6] For Perks and Thomson, although 'outsider' status may bring a sense of objectivity and distance, having an 'insider' perspective brings particular insights that the outsider lacks.[7]

My own understanding from an examination of such studies, as well as from reflecting upon my oral history and verbatim theatre work, is that when narrators come from a marginalised or vulnerable community, the importance of the interviewer sharing a similar identity – or at least some of the same experiences as the person interviewed – is far greater than when interviewing people from the more mainstream or powerful sectors of society. But I agree with oral historians who have found the binary terms 'outsider' and 'insider' somewhat limiting and who have sought to employ more fluid forms of definition in their work. Olga Lidia Saavedra Montes de Oca, for example, when interviewing Cubans about how it felt to be a transgender person or a family member of a transgender person in Cuba before and after the 1990s sexual revolution, refers to herself as an 'insider-outsider'.[8] In that project, she saw herself as an insider, in that she was a Cuban-born researcher, and an outsider, presumably (although she does not state it) because she was neither transgender nor a family member of someone who was. Performance artist and scholar, E. Patrick Johnson, in his interviews with African American queer women in the South, refers to himself as an 'outsider/within' since his interlocutors and he shared what he saw as many of the same identity markers (e.g. queerness, Southern) but not others, such as gender or class position.[9]

RIGHTS OF PASSAGE

In my own play, *Rights of Passage*, based on interviews with lesbian and gay asylum seekers in the UK, 'Miremba' (not her real name) is a lesbian originally from Uganda, whose story provides one of the three main narratives in the piece. She told me that it was precisely *because* she and I shared the same sexual orientation that she had agreed to come forward to speak to me.[10] Her comments on this matter convinced me that her disclosure about very difficult past experiences which had occurred in her country of origin was broader in scope and detail than it might have been to an interviewer who was not a lesbian. But, in identifying my positionality in relation to Miremba as an insider, I also had to acknowledge the power imbalances that existed between the two of us. I share the same sexual orientation as Miremba and the other asylum-seeker narrators I interviewed for this play but, until they gained refugee status and, after that, became full citizens, they did not hold the same state of residency in their new country as I did. Until that point, they would therefore not be in a position to enjoy the power and advantages that come with it and, aside from our nations of birth, other significant power and status imbalances existed between some of us in the form of ethnicity, class, education, and so on.

In addition to seeking historical and social knowledge in the form of interview material, oral historians examine interview practice and methodology, endeavouring to create a deeper understanding of what is revealed and also what is hidden in interviews. Forensic exploration of the dynamics of the interview situation may not be of interest to the playwright in the same way it is to oral historians, since the recordings are conducted for a different purpose. But the robust discussions relating to positionality that occur within oral history scholarship are undoubtedly of interest to theatre makers when reflecting upon their own working processes.

Possibilities of Reflection

In *The Voice of the Past*, Paul Thompson famously contends that oral history 'can be a means for transforming both the content and the purpose of history'.[11] He also suggests that 'oral history gives history back to the people in their own words. And in giving a past, it also helps them towards a future of their own making'.[12] If participating in an oral history project can, as Thompson suggests, help a narrator towards 'a future of their own making,' then arguably, a narrator for a verbatim play, through sharing their stories with the interviewer and then, at a later date, seeing them enacted on stage, will also be in a position of examining their own experiences in a way that may enhance past, current and possibly future personal understandings. I have witnessed such journeys with some narrators who have contributed to my own plays, and I am particularly interested in how oral history discussion on this matter can inform verbatim theatre processes.

The very act of being interviewed affords narrators an opportunity to reflect, both on their past experiences and on the way that they see and situate themselves in the present. Michael Frisch states that oral history also offers a tool to see 'how people make sense of their past, how they connect individual experience and its social context, how the past becomes part of the present, and how people use it to interpret their lives and the world around them'.[13] The Australian oral historian, Alistair Thomson, also examines the ways in which narrating experiences can illuminate the past and its meanings in the present lives of individuals and society. He suggests that being interviewed can allow the narrator the possibility of what he refers to as 'composure'.[14] His understanding is that, when interviewed, we compose our memories to make sense of our past and present lives.

Michael Frisch's and Alistair Thomson's observations contribute towards an ongoing debate within oral history around the impact that recalling and retelling stories and memories has upon the person who shares them. But possibilities of composure and of reflection extend to narrators who share their stores with playwrights. An interview for a play can also provide an opportunity for reflection to an individual or even to a community. In Moisés Kaufman's *The Laramie Project*, we hear from community members who share their thoughts about the murder of Matthew Shepard. In the follow-up play, *The Laramie Project – Ten Years Later,* we then hear from some of the same narrators, as well as several new ones, who reflect upon the intervening years and speak about how Shepard's killing, the interviews conducted for the play, and the play being produced around the country and internationally, impacted them and members of their community.

It seems clear that recalling an event, then rearranging memories about that incident and composing a narrative during an interview can create the possibility for further reflection on something that might have been stored deeply in one's memory. Laurie R. Serikaku suggests that this can be particularly important for oral histories gathered from people from ethnic minority communities.[15] She observes that 'an understanding of where one has been as a group offers insight into the values, sense of identity, weaknesses and strengths that characterise the individual and his or her group in the present'.[16] Furthermore, Serikaku argues that 'minority groups can use self-awareness as a powerful tool for ensuring the survival of their culture and identity'.[17] The process to which Serikaku refers can occur in verbatim theatre productions, especially in those where interviews from people from a marginalised or vulnerable community are sought and then played back to members of that community.

Examining Possibilities of Reflection for Debbie in Hearing Voices

HEARING VOICES

Another of my own productions is *Hearing Voices,* based on interviews with a group of patients who met on a secure psychiatric ward at a London hospital. One of the narrators and main 'characters' in that play is Debbie who had been admitted to hospital because she suffers from bipolar.[18] After the play was staged, Debbie posted a couple of on-line reviews about the production describing her experience of seeing herself played on stage by an actress who narrated her words. I was delighted to read her feedback in this form since it allowed me an insight into the experience of someone who shared their stories to be employed in a verbatim play.

When I was conducting academic research on this play a few years after it was performed, I arranged a follow-up interview with Debbie in which I asked her specifically about her involvement with the whole project: how she felt about being interviewed initially, then on seeing a rehearsed playreading, and later, when she attended the full production.[19] Her feedback was invaluable to me on many levels and will inform and help me with my own future working processes. But it also showed me that the possibilities of reflection for narrators interviewed by oral historians do apply in equal measure to narrators in verbatim theatre processes. There is even a possibility that they may occur to a greater extent, since narrators to a verbatim play will see a version of themselves acted on stage, speaking the very words they initially delivered in their interview.

From her involvement in the theatre project, Debbie appeared to gain a deeper understanding of her situation as someone who had severe mental health challenges. Being interviewed for the play also enabled her to re-evaluate her views about what she regarded as the poor standard of treatment she received at the hands of the psychiatric system provided by the National Health Service (NHS) in the UK. Debbie had told me how, over the many years that she had been a patient in the psychiatric system, she had been treated quite badly and occasionally with force when she was on a bipolar 'episode'. One incident she recalled also involved her family members and concerned a time when she knew she was not well. She had called the police voluntarily, explaining that she was on a lithium comedown (when coming off lithium too quickly can produce a rebound manic or psychotic episode) and had asked them to take her to hospital. A while later, when they still had not arrived at her home, she decided to make her own way to the ward. After she set off, the police came to her house, where her partner Sean was, with their four young children. The police could not gain entry and subsequently broke into the property, looking in every room for Debbie, shining torches on the faces of the children in their beds, shouting and terrifying them. This was one of the scenes that was dramatised in the play, narrated by the actress who played Debbie from the word-for-word account provided in her interview. Even though Debbie had recounted this tale for use in the script, seeing it portrayed on stage had, she explained, made a formidable impression upon her.

Watching this scene gave her the chance to reflect upon what had occurred during that incident, as well as on how she had generally been treated by the police and by nurses and consultants within the psychiatric system over the years during which she had been ill. In the follow-up interview about her experience of seeing the enactment of the police breaking into her house, she commented: 'That scene, with the police coming in and shining the torch on them, and everything that happened that day, it was a terrifying experience, and just to see that, happening in a play in front of me, it brings it all home. I felt sorry for us'. She added: 'I'm not so hard on myself and the kids because we've been through a lot that if I hadn't seen the play, I probably wouldn't have realised'.[20]

Another area where I noticed a high level of reflection occurring for Debbie was from comments she made about watching scenes in the play which showed mentally ill patients (including herself) in distress being ignored or treated harshly by the psychiatric nurses. Again, viewing these incidents portrayed dramatically allowed Debbie to reassess her views about the behaviour of the nurses towards her when she is ill. In her follow-up interview with me, she said: 'Seeing the play brings it home that, hang on a minute, that isn't normal. You shouldn't be treated like that. I shouldn't be treated like that. But when they lock you up against your will, you feel like you've done something wrong'. She commented: 'They've taken me away. They've locked me up. They've sectioned me for twenty-eight days. That's a sentence. What's my crime? Oh yeah, of course, I'm bipolar. That's my crime'. And in her on-line review, Debbie wrote:

> Clare Summerskill's play has opened my eyes, because the treatment that Clare perceived as wrong, inhuman, unjust, uncalled for I had been accepting that as the norm. Because I was a bad, naughty, bipolar person, I felt I'd deserved it, because I was hyper-manic. However, after watching the play, seeing just how it was for all of us, showed me and the rest of the audience that there is a big problem in the nut house with the NHS that could be changed, should be changed.[21]

Debbie witnessed a dramatic representation of herself on a bipolar episode, something which was somewhat disturbing, but which gave her greater insight into what others around her might have experienced during those times when she herself was unable to control her behaviour. But the play afforded her another level of comprehension about how she had always seen her illness as something for which she deserved to be punished, an observation which is, of course, a huge indictment of the way she had been treated by those working in the psychiatric system.

From the feedback provided by Debbie about her involvement in the play, as well as a handful of other similar examples from narrators to some of my other plays, I am convinced that possibilities for personal reflection on the part of the narrators, which have been examined within oral history scholarship, can also be observed in verbatim theatre processes.

Implications of Frisch's 'Shared Authority' for Verbatim Theatre Processes

The oral historian, Michael Frisch, popularised the term 'shared authority' in his 1990 publication *A Shared Authority: Essays on the Craft and Meaning of Oral and Public History*. In an examination of the interview setting, this notion refers to the process as well as the desired outcome of the process. Frisch understands the interview as a co-construction between the interviewer and the narrator, an understanding which has implications for verbatim playwrights who seek ways to increase the personal agency of narrators in their production processes.

Frisch's interest lies in determining who the actual author is within an oral history interview, asking: 'Is it the historian posing questions and editing the results, or the "subject" whose words are the heart of the consequent texts?'.[22] Several oral historians write about sharing authority in a series of articles in *The Oral History Review* (2003) but Frisch, when commenting on this collection, highlights the difference between the two terms that were beginning to be used interchangeably: 'sharing authority' and 'shared authority'. He explains: 'The latter term has a different tonality. In choosing it, I intended to suggest that in an important sense authority is shared in oral history by definition – in the dialogic nature of the interview, in the history-making offered by both interviewer and narrator, in the answer to the always appropriate question "who is the author of an oral history?".[23]

While a discussion about shared authority involves identifying who the author is in an oral history interview and who holds the authority on the subject being addressed, the use of the altered term, 'sharing authority', also creates a vibrant and ongoing debate within oral history scholarship and practice about ways in which the narrator can be seen as a co-editor of the interview. I suggest that the implications of the two slightly differing interpretations of Frisch's shared authority extend to verbatim theatre processes.

Oral historians have engaged in discussions about how they can find ways to focus less on simply eliciting and utilising interview material provided by narrators and pay more attention to the value of the information being imparted and the experience of those who are interviewed. As the American oral historian Valerie Yow explains, the wider investigation into the relationship between researched and researcher, spearheaded by Frisch and other leading oral historians in the 1970s and 1980s, led to the understanding that 'The stance that there is a researcher and there is a subject is replaced by the conviction that two people, each bringing a different kind of knowledge to the interview, share equally in a process of discovery'.[24] I wonder what the implications might be if the same thinking was applied to narrators who share their stories in verbatim theatre processes. With the inherent possibilities in this work of playwrights appropriating interview content and the risk of the narrator experiencing a diminished sense of agency within the production process, it is important for theatre practitioners to explore ways in which narrators may be able to experience beneficial outcomes from their involvement.

Narrators' Reasons for Their Involvement in Verbatim Theatre

One way to determine how narrators feel about their involvement in a verbatim theatre production is to ask them why they wish to share their stories with members of a theatre company. Christine Bacon, the artistic director of the UK theatre company Ice and Fire, presents playreadings and full productions created from interviews often conducted with asylum seekers, refugees and migrants. She told me that not only is she intent on creating such plays because 'I feel that people need to hear these stories' but also, critically, she added: 'A lot of the asylum seekers and refugees are activists themselves. A lot of them have left their country *because* they stood up to authority and because they believed in speaking out. So, they understand why it's useful to speak out and get stories heard'.[25]

Bacon recalls how she mentioned to certain narrators for *Asylum Monologues* that the piece was going to be performed as a playreading at the British Home

Office and asked if they would like to join in the post-show discussion there. They replied that they were keen to be part of that because they felt there was something very 'direct' about witnessing how their stories were received by people who had created the systems which had caused them difficulties and often suffering, namely, asylum-seeking procedures and forced detention. This example demonstrates one way in which narrators were able to use the production to some extent for their own purposes, rather than being *used* by the playwright, who would have had her own agenda when creating the script. For the narrators to Christine Bacon's play, one of the main benefits was through telling their own stories to a wider audience, and also being heard by those in positions of power who might influence policies that could affect their lives. In this way, the transaction between the theatre maker and the narrator – one which could potentially be seen as appropriative and even exploitative – is, perhaps, not quite as one-sided as it might initially appear.

RIGHTS OF PASSAGE
In the research period for this play, I had approached the leader of an LGBTI asylum-seeker group, with whom I arranged some writing workshops for the members, and she asked the members if any of them would agree to be interviewed by me about their experiences. This is how I first met Miremba. A few months after all the interviews had been conducted and the play had been scripted, I took the opportunity to re-interview Miremba, with whom I had stayed in touch, and I asked her why she had initially agreed to be interviewed for my play. This was her reply. 'Talking about my life. Maybe it was something like "Oh maybe if I talk about it might be something to make me heal." I also wanted my story to be heard because I knew I'm not the only one that have gone through such hardship, and knowing you do write plays and other people are going to see that play, and they will tell another person about that play, and probably when the play comes out another person will see that play and probably they will do something about it'.[26] These comments indicate to me that Miremba experienced a sense of personal agency in her involvement as a narrator.

Including or Omitting the Interviewer's Voice

The final part of this section takes a closer look at how the co-creation that Frisch believes occurs within oral history work can also apply to verbatim theatre productions. Oral historians have engaged in discussions about whether the interviewer's voice should be included in the transcription of an interview. In the US, Columbia University's custom of transcribing oral history interviews omitting the interviewer's questions was challenged in the early 1970s, initially by Duke University, and then by the British Oral History Society who rejected this method of working within their own practices and chose to include the interviewer's comments. Alessandro Portelli observes that the voice of the narrator becomes 'distorted' when the researcher's voice is removed. Presenting the text of a transcribed interview without the questions that prompted the narrator to respond impacts the way their responses are perceived and suggests that the narrator will always say the same thing, regardless of the circumstances. In other words, Portelli says, it gives the impression that a person speaking is 'as stable and repetitive as a written document'.[27]

Verbatim theatre playwrights frequently choose to omit the interviewer's voice in their scripts, often because it can prove to be artistically problematic to leave it in. Having an actor performing the part of the interviewer and asking questions about the experiences of the 'characters' in a play can interrupt the dramatic flow of the piece and potentially cause confusion for the audience. However, some playwrights have devised theatrical ways in which the audience is made aware of the interviewer's presence while hearing the accounts from narrators. In *The Laramie Project* by Moisés Kaufman and members of his Tectonic Theater Project, there are times where the actors play the parts of some of the interviewers whose questions and comments have been left within the content of the script. In the original production, the theatre company members who had conducted the interviews were the actors in the play, playing themselves. But as the piece then toured around the US and then to other countries, different actors were brought in to play the parts of the company members/ interviewers.

In *The Laramie Project*, as well as some of the interviewers' questions being included, we also occasionally hear explanatory comments about the interview process delivered by the company members. For example, at one point, the script reads as follows:

NARRATOR: Company member Leigh Fondakowski:

LEIGH FONDAKOWSKI: This is one of the last days on our second trip to Laramie. Greg and I have been conducting interviews nonstop and we are exhausted.

GREG PIEROTTI: We are to meet Father Roger at seven-thirty in the morning. I was wishing we could skip it all together, but we have to follow through to the end. So here we go: seven-thirty A.M., two queers and a Catholic priest.

FATHER ROGER SCHMIT: Matthew Shepard has served us well. You realise that? He has served us well. And I do not mean to condemn Matthew to perfection, but I cannot mention anyone who has done more for this community than Matthew Shepard.[28]

Although *The Laramie Project* is one of the most widely performed verbatim plays in the world, it is by no means a common practice for playwrights creating scripts from interviews to include the interviewers' voices in their productions. One of the notable benefits of Kaufman's choice in this piece is that audience members are reminded throughout the performance of the processes of representation involved in its creation and, moreover, that they are watching a play based on the words of real people: the theatre company members and narrators they interviewed.

This chapter has examined some discussions and practices in oral history which are relevant to verbatim theatre processes. In the creation of scripts from interviews, when playwrights edit the content to align with their own personal, professional or artistic aims for the piece, there is a risk that the personal narratives with which they work can be viewed merely as source material, to be employed in a dramatic piece. The power of the original voice and the reason the narrator may have agreed to be interviewed can become obfuscated, since it is the playwright who holds the editing control in this work. However, we can also see that when narrators are viewed by playwrights from a co-authorial perspective, rather than simply as people whose words provide script content, verbatim theatre processes can produce beneficial outcomes not only for playwrights and audiences but also for the narrators themselves.

Notes

1 Sue Armitage, "The Stages of Women's Oral History," in *The Oxford Handbook of Oral History*, ed. Donald A. Ritchie (Oxford: Oxford University Press, 2010), 174.
2 Armitage, "The Stages of Women's Oral History," 175.
3 Armitage, "The Stages of Women's Oral History," 175.
4 Paul Thompson with Joanna Bornat, *The Voice of the Past: Oral History*, Fourth Edition (New York: Oxford University Press, 2017), 211.
5 Paul Thompson, *The Voice of the Past* (Oxford: Oxford University Press, 1978), 116.
6 Akemi Kikumura, "Family Life Histories: A Collaborative Venture," in *The Oral History Reader*, ed. Robert Perks and Alistair Thomson (London: Routledge, 1998), 141.
7 Robert Perks and Alistair Thomson, "Interviewing," in *The Oral History Reader*, Third Edition, ed. Robert Perks and Alistair Thomson (Abingdon: Routledge, 2016), 137.
8 Olga Lidia Saavedra Montes de Oca, "Opening Other Closets: Remembering as a Transgender Person and as a Family Member," *Oral History Journal* 45:2 (2017): 83.
9 E. Patrick Johnson, "Put a Little Honey in My Sweet Tea: Oral History as Quare Performance," *Women's Studies Quarterly* 44:3/4 (2016): 57.
10 All the quotations cited 'Miremba' (not her real name) come from an interview I conducted with her in London on 8 October 2015.
11 Thompson, *The Voice of the Past* (1978), 2.
12 Thompson, *The Voice of the Past* (1978), 226.
13 Michael Frisch, *A Shared Authority: Essays on the Craft and Meaning of Oral and Public History* (Albany: State University of New York Press, 1990), 188.

14 Alistair Thomson, "Anzac Memories. Putting Popular Memory into Practice in Australia," in *The Oral History Reader*, Third Edition, ed. Robert Perks and Alistair Thomson (Abingdon: Routledge, 2016), 244.

15 Laurie Serikaku employs the term 'ethnic minority communities' in her writing, but the term BAME (Black, Asian and Minority Ethnic people) is currently in use in the UK.

16 Serikaku, "Oral History in Ethnic Communities: Widening the Focus," *The Oral History Review* 17:1 (1989): 77.

17 Serikaku, "Oral History in Ethnic Communities," 77.

18 I have not termed Debbie's mental condition as bipolar 'disorder' as some mental health campaigners take objection to the fact that the word 'disorder' is added to the end of many psychiatric terms. See Noah Rubinstein, "The Dirtiest Word in the DSM," *Good Therapy*, January 30, 2014, https://www.goodtherapy.org/blog/the-dirtiest-word-in-the-dsm-0130147.

19 The information cited by Debbie comes from an interview I conducted with her in London on 12 February 2012.

20 Debbie, interview with Clare Summerskill, London on 12 February 2012.

21 Debbie's review, "*Hearing Voices* by Clare Summerskill," posted on-line on 30 May 2009, is now no longer available. The quotes cited are taken from my personal copy of the review.

22 Frisch, *A Shared Authority*, xx.

23 Michael Frisch, "Sharing Authority: Oral History and the Collaborative Process," *The Oral History Review* 30:1 (2003): 113.

24 Valerie Yow, "Ethics and Interpersonal Relationships in Oral History Research," *Oral History Review* 22:1 (1995): 53.

25 Christine Bacon, interview with Clare Summerskill (via Skype), August 24, 2016.

26 'Miremba', interview with Clare Summerskill, London, October 8, 2015.

27 Alessandro Portelli, "What Makes Oral History Different?" in *The Oral History Reader*, Third Edition, ed. Robert Perks and Alistair Thomson (Abingdon: Oxford, 2016), 55.

28 Moisés Kaufman, *The Laramie Project and The Laramie Project: Ten Years Later* (New York: Vintage, 2014), 62.

PART II
Ethics and Verbatim Theatre

4

ETHICAL CONSIDERATIONS AND GUIDELINES FOR VERBATIM THEATRE PROCESSES

In this chapter, I discuss how playwrights working with interviews can turn to existing ethical debates and practices in oral history in order to inform and improve their own projects. I also outline the ethical issues at stake within verbatim theatre processes and provide a set of guidelines for practitioners to follow.

Ethical behaviour is the fabric which binds human society. It consists of rules, implicit or explicit, that govern the way we treat one another. Though few rules are universal, all systems of ethics have a shared aim of treating people fairly and working towards the betterment of our communities. Discussions around what constitutes ethical behaviour are often heated as this is a subjective area; yet many professions have developed codes of ethics to which their members subscribe. Furthermore, in research where information is gathered by one person interviewing another – such as anthropology, sociology, ethnography and oral history – ethical considerations are foregrounded.

The American Oral History Association (OHA) has, since 1968, published guidelines outlining a set of principles and obligations for those working within that discipline. Some of the OHA guidelines relate purely to ethical concerns, and others involve practical considerations but, at times, these matters can overlap, for example, when informed consent is sought from a narrator.[1] The 2018 OHA 'Principles and Best Practices' summarise how to work with narrators and interview material. Oral history societies and groups in other countries than the United States, such as the Oral History Society in the UK, Oral History Australia and The National Oral History Association of New Zealand have also published ethical and legal guidelines.[2]

Since the interview lies at the core of verbatim theatre, I suggest that many ethical guidelines from oral history practice can be adapted or even applied directly to verbatim theatre processes. First, we will look once again at some of the critical similarities and differences between the two disciplines, this time through an 'ethical lens'.

Can Ethical Practice Inhibit Artistic License?

There are currently no agreed guidelines for creating verbatim theatre. A handful of practitioners have documented their own working methods, including some of the ethical challenges they face. However, very few open conversations have taken place *among* verbatim theatre practitioners relating to their working practices and there may even be a reluctance to create guidelines.

Janet Gibson, in her article 'Saying it Right: Creating Ethical Verbatim Theatre', explains why there could be some value in the impulse to resist ethics in the theatre: She states:

> Given the increasing codification of ethics and ethical standards of conduct in business, government and other institutional arenas, I am concerned that these paradigms, emboldened by the weight of law, and possibly without discrete reflection on specific theatre/performance pieces, may encroach on the creative practices of theatre-makers, compromising the autonomy necessary to their political and artistic efficacy.[3]

Gibson's concerns are seemingly focussed on the playwright's artistic license which she fears might be curtailed by the introduction of any ethical directives. She also highlights the importance of the theatre makers' autonomy. In oral history work, although interviewers are encouraged to identify their own aims in running a project, the understanding is that their personal agenda should not interfere either with the interview situation or with the analysis of the content. But, for Gibson, the autonomy of playwrights is crucial to their working method: they select interview excerpts for their dramatic potential and relevance to the main subject matter of the play, which reinforce the playwrights' own artistic, political or ideological vision.

Although there are no written ethical guidelines for verbatim theatre playwrights to follow, individuals nonetheless think long and hard about such issues. The Australian playwright Alana Valentine advises that, when working with those who contribute their stories, you should, "'Be trustworthy': Keep the promises you make, act honourably, be honest about your intentions".[4] And Robin Belfield, in *Telling the Truth – How to Make Verbatim Theatre*, states: 'I do require – in fact, I demand – that my conduct and creative pursuits are led by respect, honesty and integrity'.[5] The underlying premise behind these comments appears to be that the ethical conduct of verbatim theatre practitioners is guided more by their own individual moral compasses than by any external rules or laws. The qualities of 'respect, honesty and integrity' which Belfield mentions are laudable, but are inevitably open to varying interpretations.

The principal ethical concerns relate to how the narrator is treated at various stages in the theatre production process and how their words are employed in verbatim scripts. The suggestion that adherence to fixed ethical procedures might limit artistic possibilities is a valid one and should not be dismissed lightly. However, I believe that our practice (at least up to transcription stage) is similar to oral history and we would do well to respect the ethics of that discipline. Below, I offer some guidelines for theatre makers to follow throughout the interviewing and scripting process.

Guidelines for Working Ethically in Verbatim Theatre Processes

1 Identify the agenda of the playwright and the aims of the production
2 Identify power dynamics between the theatre makers and the narrators
3 Secure informed consent from narrators
4 Endeavour to increase the narrators' level of agency during the production process
5 Make ethical decisions about the naming of the narrators in the script
6 Demonstrate sensitivity and respect for narrators in their theatrical representation – particularly those who come from marginalised or vulnerable communities.

1. Identify the agenda of the playwright and the aims of the production

Before embarking upon a verbatim theatre project, playwrights must identify their own aims and agenda in pursuing this form of work. Do they wish to educate a wider audience about a historical, political or social matter which they believe has been previously neglected by the media or unknown by the general public? Are they keen to show support for and increase understanding about a particular group of people from a community of shared interest or geographical locality? Addressing the theatre makers' aims and agenda will help them to seek ways to accomplish their primary objectives without causing harm to the people they interview and represent.

In oral history, the project organiser and any other interviewers involved will identify the project concept before their work begins, and then ask themselves whether they have an agenda that could prevent them from being neutral in regard to the material the work addresses or to the narrators they interview. Many playwrights, however, accept the fact that they are not neutral. They may be drawn to verbatim theatre precisely because they *do* hold a strong position about the subject matter. But it is still a helpful exercise to identify this agenda and the aims of the production. Working with the stories of 'real' people is a challenging endeavour, and the common areas of ethical concern within both oral history and verbatim theatre relate to the protection of, and respect for the narrators.

2. Identify power dynamics between theatre makers and narrators

Oral historians follow post modern feminist thinking in their examination of power dynamics between interviewers and narrators such as inequalities in class, ethnicity and gender (as discussed in **Chapter 3**). Verbatim theatre practitioners (the playwright/interviewer and possibly the actors too) must also identify power imbalances between themselves and those they interview and theatrically represent. An interviewer may well hold more power than their narrator, who in turn may hold information that the interviewer wishes to obtain. But identifying inherent dynamics will enhance playwrights' understanding of the interview situation, leading to them demonstrate a greater duty of care towards narrators and gain a deeper understanding of their own theatre work.

The playwright David Hare has stated that 'people like talking to theatre people, and they trust them' adding that 'they like their stories to be told'.[6] While his comments may well be true in some circumstances, they require analysis. The knowledge that the narrator's personal story will be employed in a script and acted on stage may, indeed, be a compelling reason to agree to be interviewed for a play. But even when playwrights gain narrators' trust with ease, they must also recognise the power imbalances in that exchange and accept that this work involves an increased level of ethical awareness.

In a typical interview situation, the narrator may well have less power than the interviewer. For some people, being interviewed might be reminiscent of the benefits office, the police interrogation, immigration assessment, job interview or doctor's appointment. The person behind the desk, with the notepad or recording device, has the authority to take their personal information – even the entire story of their life – and use it in ways over which they have little or no control. This is the scenario into which the oral historian or verbatim theatre playwright enters, voice recorder in hand. Class, gender, 'race' and status can all play a part in cementing inequality – or the perception of inequality. For example, a lesbian may not wish to recount her romantic history to a heterosexual woman researcher; a former miner in the UK may not rush to recount his feelings about the years Margaret Thatcher was in power to a history professor in a suit and tie. When narrators for a verbatim play hold a degree of power or status within society, concerns about exploitation are not completely absent, but they are far less evident than when members of marginalised communities are interviewed. Furthermore, ethical concerns are heightened when narrators are deemed in some way vulnerable. In such cases, an even greater degree of ethical vigilance and practical care is required.

If the interviewer has led a similar life or had similar experiences to the narrator, the dynamics may appear more equal. However, there are always other issues at play here. The playwright will take the person's story and use it to create a stage show, enhance their own professional reputation and probably receive payment. The narrator may lose control of how their own story is used. There is potential for real harm if a narrator feels their contribution has been misused or misinterpreted, if they do not like what they see onstage, if they feel misrepresented or if their input has been forgotten or undervalued. It is crucial for the theatre practitioner to bear all this in mind. A playwright might be on a low income, from a working-class or minority background or nervous about an interview, but still it is important for them to recognise their own power in this situation.

HEARING VOICES

One play that I wrote and produced, called *Hearing Voices*, was based on interviews with narrators with serious mental health issues, who I had met while we were all patients on a secure psychiatric ward. This work involved my making many important ethical decisions about how and when I interviewed my friends and closely examining the power dynamics between us. It is worth noting that, at the time I interviewed them, all of the narrators for this play appeared to me to be a lucid state of mind and they provided thoroughly intelligent and coherent accounts of their life stories. I would certainly not have employed testimony of anyone with mental health issues who I judged could not understand the purpose of my interview. In the UK, the 2005 Mental Capacity Act provides legal protection for those who have a limited mental capacity, whether temporarily or permanently, by illness, accident, disability or another disorder or trauma. In these instances, 'mental capacity' refers to the narrator's ability to understand and retain information, weigh it as part of decision making, and communicate their decisions. Marella Hoffman, writing about oral history work with public policies and programs, argues that oral history interviews should generally not be conducted with such people as they cannot give fully informed consent, except in circumstances where 'the medical and legal authorities responsible for the person's well-being have authorised that some form of oral history interaction would be beneficial for the person'.[7]

None of the narrators to *Hearing Voices* were patients in hospitals at the time I interviewed them. If they had been, in my mind, there would have been no question of my interviewing them for a play, but as people who had been hospitalised in the past, and who I knew quite well, I was keen to hear their stories and share their experiences of the psychiatric services in Britain and present their stories theatrically. But in doing this work, it was imperative to critically analyse the power dynamics between myself, as their friend and as the playwright, and them, as narrators from a vulnerable population.

Discussing ways in which oral historians might gain a greater understanding about inequalities that have previously been unnoticed and unaddressed, in 1995, Valerie Yow stated: 'We seek to become more aware of the political situation in the interpersonal relationship and of the political context within which interviews can be used. We analyse the effects of differences in gender, race, class, status, age, and culture'.[8] Nowadays, her comments would also apply to sexual orientation and gender identity. Debates about power dynamics within an interview and the positionality of the interviewer in relation to the narrator are particularly important to oral historians because their work is used for historical or social research. But when verbatim playwrights conduct interviews, power imbalances between the interviewer and the narrator can also affect how a narrator speaks about a particular event or subject. Being aware of this dynamic helps playwrights think about ways in which they can improve the interview situation for the narrator and seek ways whereby there can be a more equal footing. Gaining trust can benefit both parties as the narrator will feel safe to disclose more, and **Chapter 7** offers further suggestions on how interviewers can help narrators to feel more comfortable about sharing their stories.

3. Secure informed consent from narrators

Informed consent is a legally non-binding term that refers to an agreement among parties about what will happen and why. It usually takes place in the form of a conversation between interviewer and narrator at the beginning of the interview process, although it can also be outlined in written form: a letter, an email, or a brochure describing the project. In verbatim theatre projects, after fully understanding how their recorded words are to be used for the purpose of creating a play, narrators are then asked to sign a consent form. (See **Appendix 2** for an example of an informed consent form.)

A verbatim playwright (and other theatre company members, if they are also conducting interviews) must secure the informed consent of those they interview. This process is not as simple as producing a consent form and asking the narrator to sign. It involves explaining to narrators the intended form of the final theatre production and the ways in which their words may be employed in a script and performed by actors. Gaining 'informed consent' rather than just the 'permission' of narrators is therefore of utmost importance here.

Within oral history, the term 'informed consent' rather than 'permission' is employed, and the difference between these terms is important since it signifies that it is the duty of the interviewer not only to obtain the narrator's consent but also to ensure that the narrator fully comprehends the scope of the project. The OHA defines informed consent as 'an agreement that documents, verbally or in writing, that the narrator has been given all the information necessary to come to a decision about whether to participate in the oral history project', but most oral historians seek written permissions.[9]

In verbatim theatre projects, informed consent must be secured from narrators by firstly explaining to them the purpose of the interview and exactly how the content will be used in the future and then asking them to sign a form saying that they agree to this. I recommend that the consent form be signed at the end of the interview, when the narrator knows what they have said. Some playwrights, however, ask the narrator for their consent during the recording process so that the permission is in the form of a spoken agreement. But for the sake of transparency and to allay any ethical concerns, I would strongly advise theatre practitioners to ask for written consent. But there will always be situations where this might not be preferable.

Some cases where an oral informed consent could be secured is when the narrator connects a recent trauma or distress with signing a written document, or when the narrator is physically unable or is unaccustomed to a reading/writing culture and word of mouth is more appropriate. The use of written consent forms for narrators has been brought into question by the playwright and scholar Pedzisai Maedza who, in his own productions with asylum seekers and migrants in South Africa, has noted what he refers to as the 'scriptocentralism' of this practice. He argues that these narrators, 'whose material condition and being is largely governed through "texts and the bureaucracy of literacy", i.e. through passports, Section 22 permits, arrest warrants and deportation orders, may experience and be disoriented by papers which they may read to be inaccessible and charged with the regulatory powers of the state'.[10] Bearing these exceptions in mind, you will make your own choices about how to operate with ethical integrity in regard to securing informed consent from narrators for your theatre work.

4. Endeavour to increase the narrators' level of agency during the production process

Appropriation can occur when someone takes possession of something or makes use of it exclusively for themselves and exploitation is the action of making use of and benefiting from resources. The creation of theatre productions from personal stories provided by 'real' people could therefore be seen from some perspectives as an appropriative or even an exploitative form of work. The risk of appropriation or exploitation can be mitigated by increasing the degree of agency a narrator holds in the process. This might occur in various ways, for instance: by sending the narrators the interview excerpts that the writer intends to use, for their approval; by inviting the narrators to attend a playreading, where their feedback will be incorporated into further drafts; and by inviting them to attend the final production and participate in post-show discussions.

When I interview people, I always take time to explain to them what verbatim theatre is and I outline the working process that I employ for my own plays. I tell narrators about the subject matter of the piece and let them know that I intend to use some of their interview excerpts in the script (as recommended in the previous section). But Pedzisai Maedza raises an important matter when he acknowledges that, at the point of interviewing, playwrights do not know themselves what the final product will look like. Writing about his own play, *Asylum Section 22*, he states:

> I could do no more than tell the subjects that I am a playwright; divulge the research topic and then ask for an interview. This being the case, I am inclined to suggest that the consent granted is not complete [...] If the playwright does not have any idea in advance of what would be on the tapes or how they will subsequently use the recordings, the interviewee cannot really know to what they are consenting.[11]

One way in which to address this concern raised by Maedza is to ask narrators for their initial consent at the time of the interview and then, after the script has been written, show them their excerpts so that they can see which parts of their interview content are being employed. Such a step gives narrators a greater sense of involvement, and therefore agency in the production process. This is a practice I employ myself, but it is not one that is followed by all verbatim play-wrights. Some have concerns that their artistic vision might be compromised if they hand over a portion of editorial control to narrators in this way.

Playwrights must decide whether or not they wish narrators to have any form of say in the scripting of their stories, and if they do seek feedback from them, they must decide at what point they will take that step. Will they choose to send the narrators their excerpts to look over before the final creation of a script? Or just before the rehearsal period? Or will they invite the narrators along to a rehearsal? Or ask them for their feedback after a playreading? Or after the first performance, in the form of a post-show discussion? Playwrights' working methods differ widely in this regard.

The playwright Alecky Blythe, has stated that she would dread the thought of any real-life contributor coming into the rehearsal room, but she says, 'As a way of thanks, I invite them to come and see the show'.[12] But Christine Bacon, the artistic director of Ice and Fire, views the theatre company's relationship with the narrators in a very different way. She states, 'We encourage them to come and see something before we interview them so they get an idea of what we do'. She tells narrators: 'We will send you the edited transcript when it's finished. You can change anything you like and it will be honoured. You can withdraw permission at any stage. Even when it's already running, you can withdraw your permission'.[13] Bacon's working practice affords narrators a substantial degree of agency within the production process and responds to the need to involve narrators and to let them know how much their contribution is valued. But if they do not wish to be identified as narrators and therefore would not want to join in a feedback process or participate in post-show discussions, they can still be invited to the final performance as audience members.

One of the main differences between oral history and verbatim theatre is that an oral history is regarded as a co-creation between the narrator and the interviewer. This matter has been addressed in **Chapter 3** in relation to Frisch's notion of 'shared authority' but it is also highly relevant in a discussion of ethical considerations about the narrators' agency within verbatim theatre processes. Nancy MacKay, in *Curating Oral Histories*, comments: 'The finished oral history is considered to be a collaborative document with the narrator being the primary creator, acknowledged as the first author in cataloguing and citations'.[14] But verbatim theatre work seldom follows this convention.

Occasionally playwrights creating scripts from interview and documentary material will acknowledge verbally, perhaps during a post-show discussion, that their plays are the result of a form of co-creation with those who have been interviewed. But on the front cover of a published script, the playwright usually will be named as author. While it might not be realistic to list all the narrators there, they can be named in the programme and in the preliminary pages of the script (if published). First names, full names or character names may be used, depending on the contributors' preferences.

An additional area of ethical concern that relates partly to the narrators' agency and partly to the matter of informed consent, discussed above, is when excerpts that a narrator has agreed for inclusion in a play are used for another purpose after the production. One such scenario might be if a play is published after it was performed, then the playwright should ask the narrators *again* for their consent to having their excerpts included in the published script. Written permissions should again be sought if parts of the play are uploaded to YouTube or broadcast on television or radio. Asking for narrators' consent as a project develops into other forms is a way of including them in the working process and acknowledging that the production would not exist without their generously shared testimonies.

5. Make ethical decisions about the naming of the narrators in the script

In verbatim theatre scripts and performances, sometimes the characters who speak the words of the original narrators are called by their own names and sometimes other names are chosen by the playwright for

them. These decisions are ethical ones, since they relate to the representation of 'real' people (rather than fictional characters) who, by the nature
of the work for which they have been interviewed, often come from
marginalised communities.

My own working practice when naming characters in plays is to con-
sult the narrators who form the main characters in the script and ask them
what they would like to be called in the play. For minor characters and
for 'composite' characters that have been created by using excerpts from
interviews from two or more narrators, I do not deem this necessary, and
believe that a playwright can invent names for those parts. Surnames are
rarely employed in verbatim theatre scripts, so the names under discussion are usually first names. When I have asked narrators what name they
might prefer to be called, some have replied that they want their own
name used; others say they would definitely not like their real name employed; and some opt for a name that has some personal meaning to them,
but one which would not be recognised by the audience – their middle
name, for example. In *Rights of Passage*, one refugee narrator wanted to be
called the name by which he was known in his country of origin, rather
than the name he had called himself since he came to the UK because, as
he explained to me, the former name represented a previous life he had
now left behind.

One of the advantages of verbatim theatre productions is that they allow narrators who may wish to remain anonymous for a variety of reasons, to still
have their story told publicly. For example, some LGBT narrators might be
in the closet, some asylum seekers might fear deportation or a domestic abuse
victim may not want to be recognised. Also, as addressed in **Chapter 1**, many
verbatim plays are created from the narratives of people within a relatively
small community, either a community of interest or a geographical locality.
If the play is performed to an audience within a small or a closed community,
the possibility increases that the 'real' people who gave their stories might be
recognised from lines spoken in the script. In such a situation, those who have
shared their experiences might appreciate the fact that they have not been personally named.

In some plays, however, a narrator might be a well-known figure, such
as the UK Member of Parliament, Diane Abbott in the play *Riots* by Gillian
Slovo. This was a piece based on interviews from politicians, police, rioters and
victims involved in the London riots of 2011, produced at the Tricycle Theatre in 2011. Another example of someone being interviewed for a verbatim
play who has a reputation within a particular profession is Dr Rufus May, in
my own play *Hearing Voices*. May was a British clinical psychologist, who has
used his own experiences of being a psychiatric patient to promote alternative
recovery approaches for those experiencing psychotic symptoms. In cases such

as these, it is common practice for narrators to be fully identified, since their narratives have usually been secured to provide informed expertise to the matter under discussion in the play.

Some areas of oral history practice relating to the narrator diverge slightly from other interview-based research methods. One of these is the general assumption that narrators should not automatically remain anonymous. While other disciplines may see anonymising narrators as a means of protecting them from public exposure, oral history practitioners are aware that narrators may *want* to be identified as historical witnesses. Choices around the naming of narrators which are made jointly between the playwright and narrator, therefore, go some way towards producing Frisch's aims of 'shared authority' and the co-production of knowledge.

Decisions about using the real names of members of vulnerable communities who are interviewed can present challenges for the playwright. For example, while the initial instinct of an interviewer working with people with mental health problems may be to anonymise the names of all those involved, such a situation requires a deeper level of scrutiny since people with mental health problems have historically had their voices silenced. The stripping away of identity combined with their historical silencing means that they are possibly even less likely to have their stories told and their voices heard than those from other marginalised groups of society. The ethical implications of interviewing narrators from this population for an oral history project or a play and employing their own words in a script, but then renaming them are, therefore, particularly problematic. This was a dilemma I encountered in the scripting of my play *Hearing Voices*. For this play about people's experiences in the psychiatric system, I interviewed five former patients. One of the main 'characters', Debbie, said she wanted her own name to be used in the script. Another narrator said that he would like to be given a name that he sometimes uses, and three other narrators asked that I use a pseudonym.

6. Demonstrate sensitivity and respect for narrators in their theatrical representation – particularly those who come from marginalised or vulnerable communities

Dramatic choices made by theatre makers can impact those who have given their stories for use in the production and are therefore matters of ethical consideration. Questions relating to accurate representation of the narrators and possibilities of misrepresentation of the original content are of particular significance when people who have shared their stories come from marginalised or vulnerable communities.

Whilst conducting interviews for one of his plays, Robin Soans describes how he was once cautioned by the sub-warden of a bail hostel in Leeds, England, where ex-offenders are housed, to:

'Never forget that it's someone's life'

Soans states that: 'I have been aware ever since of the potential for titillating an audience at someone's expense'.[15] His comments provide us with a sobering reminder that not only are we representing 'real' people in our work, but narrators will frequently come to see the show to which they have contributed.

Whatever form of representation a verbatim playwright settles upon, the main rule in this work is to consciously and ethically strive to **DO NO HARM** to narrators, either during the script-writing process or when portraying them on stage.

Since the late 1960s, when verbatim and documentary theatre productions began to increase in number and popularity, theatre makers around the world have taken different approaches to how they represent narrators in their plays. Some playwrights choose to employ 'exact' or 'pure' verbatim, where there is nothing in the script that has not been said by a narrator during an interview; others use 'massaged' verbatim which employs narrators' excerpts in a more flexible way. Some theatre practitioners opt for the headphone verbatim method (also known as Recorded Delivery), where each actor wears an earpiece through which they hear – and immediately speak – the recorded words of one or more narrators. In this way, they attempt to replicate the exact words and tone of the narrator as they receive it. And in other forms of verbatim theatre, playwrights and directors have asked actors to portray the 'essence' of the narrator, rather than relate the actual interview content.

My own practice in creating verbatim theatre is to employ the exact word for word testimony of those I interview, only occasionally inserting a very light sprinkling of 'fictional' lines in the script at critical moments to enhance dramatic presentation. A few years after I produced the play *Hearing Voices*, I re-interviewed Debbie and asked what it was like to come to the production and see an actress play her on stage and speak the exact words she had delivered in her initial interview. We briefly discussed her views on the efficacy of verbatim theatre and, at one point, I mentioned that, when writing the piece, I had been faced with the option of fictionalising the people I had interviewed, rather than employing narrators' exact words. Debbie's response to this suggestion was adamant: 'But then it wouldn't have been the same! The thing about the play was that it was verbatim and that's what made all the difference. That's why it was definitely us! It wasn't your characterisation of us, it was our words'.

Out of Joint is one example of a theatre company that, rather than using the exact words of narrators, has instead employed their testimony in an improvised form of narrative.

OUT OF JOINT

Max Stafford-Clark was the founder and artistic director of Out of Joint theatre company in the UK and, among many other plays, he directed Robin Soans' *Talking to Terrorists* and *A State Affair* and also David Hare's *The Permanent Way*. In several Out of Joint productions, Hare and a group of actors interviewed narrators in pairs or groups. They then returned to the rehearsal room and assumed the role of the narrator while the rest of the group asked them questions, after which process, the actors would improvise and develop their 'characters'.

These types of productions by Out of Joint are generally regarded as verbatim plays, but did not involve using the precise words of narrators in the final script. Instead, the theatre practitioners employed the narrators' stories more as a jumping-off point for the creation of characters for their own productions. On the one hand, these examples demonstrate how exciting and creative possibilities can emerge when plays are produced from interviews with real people, but on the other hand, such working processes could raise ethical concerns about misrepresentation of the original narrators.

During the scripting process, playwrights focus on how they can best arrange the interview content to create a dramatically powerful and informative piece of theatre. In the rehearsal room, however, when actors are brought in to play the parts of the narrators, theatre makers must work with the material at hand in a way that is mindful and respectful of the original narrators and display sensitivity to how they will be dramatically portrayed on stage. If the actors have not conducted the interviews themselves, they will usually not know the narrators and will endeavour to work creatively with what they understand about their 'character' as it is written in the script, just as they do in other forms of theatre work. Occasionally, however, their acting may have to be reined in a little by the writer or director, if they experiment with exaggerated performances which do not sufficiently do justice to or are not respectful to the original narrators. The playwright may point out either to the director (if there is someone else in that role) or to the actor that the 'real' narrator did not act like that and might even be slightly offended to see themselves portrayed in such a way. The playwright or director can then suggest ways to help the actor create a more accurate and respectful representation of the person. How this direction process takes place will depend entirely on the theatre company's own way of working dramatically with the interview content.

I have found that having the writer in the rehearsal room working with the director, or the writer also being the director of the piece, can help actors when searching for their own dramatic interpretation of the 'real' character they play. The actors may find it useful to listen to the voices of the narrators on the original interview recordings; or even meet them, if the director decides to invite them into the rehearsal room. But whatever theatrical choices the director, writer, and actors finally settle upon with respect to the way characters are represented, those decisions must be taken with a sensitivity to the fact that real people are being portrayed who will often come to see the show and whom they will possibly meet.

While some practitioners may have concerns about the possibility of ethical considerations restricting the artistic license of a playwright, we must remember that no verbatim play would exist without the narrators. Playwrights, therefore, have to balance these two factors. When scripting plays, I would personally encourage you to employ, wherever possible, the exact words that were spoken by narrators, thereby mitigating concerns of misrepresentation. But, even when excerpts from narrators' interviews are used word for word, ethical concerns can arise relating to how their narratives are dramatically portrayed. It is important for playwrights working with interview content to operate with personal integrity and ethical vigilance, and to extend a duty of care towards the narrators who have made their plays possible.

Notes

1 "Principles and Best Practices: Principles for Oral History and Best Practices for Oral History," Oral History Association, 2009, https://www.oralhistory.org/about/principles-and-practices-revised-2009/.
2 See, for example: "Ethics & Practice," *National Oral History Association of New Zealand*, March 4, 2020, http://www.oralhistory.org.nz/index.php/ethics-and-practice/; "Is Your Oral History Legal and Ethical?" *Oral History Society*, March 4, 2020, https://www.ohs.org.uk/advice/ethical-and-legal/; "Guidelines of Ethical Practice 2007," *Oral History Australia*, March 4, 2020, https://www.oralhistory australia.org.au/files/oha_guidelines_for_ethical_practice__2007.pdf.
3 Janet Gibson, "Saying it Right: Creating Ethical Verbatim Theatre," *NEO: Journal for Higher Degree Research Students in the Social Sciences and Humanities* 4 (2011): 2.
4 Alana Valentine, *Bowerbird: The Art of Making Theatre Drawn from Life* (Strawberry Hills, NSW: Currency Press, 2018), 66.
5 Robin Belfield, *Telling the Truth: How to Make Verbatim Theatre* (London: Nick Hern Books, 2018), 103.
6 David Hare, "David Hare and Max Stafford-Clark," in *Verbatim, Verbatim: Contemporary Documentary Theatre*, ed. Will Hammond and Dan Steward (London: Oberon Books, 2008), 70.
7 Marella Hoffman, *Practicing Oral History to Improve Public Policies and Programs* (New York: Routledge, 2018), 67.
8 Valerie Yow, "Ethics and Interpersonal Relationships in Oral History Research," *Oral History Review* 22:1 (1995): 53.
9 "Informed Consent," *Oral History Association*, March 4, 2020, https://www.oralhistory.org/informed-consent.
10 Pedzisai Maedza, *Performing Asylum: Theatre of Testimony in South Africa*. African Studies Collection, 66 (Leiden: African Studies Centre, 2017), 123–24. A Section 22 permit is an asylum seeker permit which is valid for six months and makes it legal to stay in South Africa while waiting for the Department of Home Affairs (DHA) to decide whether it will grant refugee status or not.

11 Pedzisai Maedza, "Theatre of Testimony: An Investigation in Devising Asylum" (MA diss., University of Cape Town, 2013), 105.

12 Alecky Blythe quoted in Chris Megson, "'What I'm Aspiring to Be Is a Good Dramatist': Alecky Blythe in Conversation with Chris Megson," *Journal of Contemporary Drama in English* 6:1 (2018): 228.

13 Christine Bacon, interview with Clare Summerskill (via Skype), August 24, 2016.

14 Nancy Mackay, *Curating Oral Histories: From Interview to Archive*, Second Edition (Abingdon: Routledge, 2016), 6.

15 Robin Soans, "Robin Soans," in *Verbatim, Verbatim: Contemporary Documentary Theatre*, ed. Will Hammond and Dan Steward (London: Oberon Books, 2008), 36.

5

ETHICAL CONSIDERATIONS IN THE CREATION OF PLAYS FROM INTERVIEWS WITH MEMBERS OF MARGINALISED COMMUNITIES AND VULNERABLE NARRATORS

Verbatim productions vary significantly in respect to who is interviewed and what they are asked to speak about. The final script may consist of narrative excerpts from people who share a common identity or experiences or, in some cases, a play can tell the stories of a wide range of narrators from different sectors of a society. But many verbatim plays are created to dramatically disperse previously unheard stories from members of marginalised communities or people who are in some way deemed vulnerable; these narrators, by virtue of their background or identity, might be unaccustomed to having their experiences and views made public, let alone performed in front of audiences in a theatre. This chapter will discuss ethical considerations pertaining to shows which draw upon interviews with members of such populations.

Can Verbatim Theatre 'Give a Voice to the Voiceless'?

Because of its ability to theatrically disseminate narratives from groups of society who may not previously have had a platform to voice their views, verbatim theatre, like oral history, is often understood by playwrights and audiences as giving a voice to the voiceless. The so-called 'voiceless' are, of course, not without a voice, but their voices have often been sidelined by the mainstream sectors of a society. Verbatim theatre playwrights can feel that they are ideally placed to produce plays which will allow stories from these people to be heard – at least by theatre audiences.

Although there are some similarities between the two dramatic forms, verbatim theatre is not the same as autobiographical performance in which people enact their own experiences in plays that they have sometimes also scripted themselves. Verbatim theatre playwrights present selected excerpts in their scripts from the interviews they have attained in a way that creates a form of artistic representation as well as advancing their own political and ideological agenda. Bearing this in mind, we might consider whether verbatim theatre can indeed provide a means for people from marginalised communities to voice their experiences. The answer is both yes and no! Verbatim theatre does allow recorded stories, experiences and views of those whose voices may often go unheard in a society to gain a wider audience, but the playwright wields a heavy editorial hand when it comes to making decisions about how the interview content is theatrically presented.

If verbatim theatre were to provide a means to give a voice to the voiceless, the narrators or storytellers would be the producers and performers. Although such scenarios do occasionally occur in some forms of professional verbatim theatre work, they are the exception rather than the rule. This is usually because disempowered people do not always have the means to set up a theatre company, source professional actors – who may have had experiences relating to the subject being addressed in the play – and be in a position to secure the funding required for creating such a production. As theatre makers, we must recognise that, albeit with the best of intentions and with a sincere desire to share stories that are not gaining the level of public attention we feel they should be, the playwright will have full editing control of the material presented in the final script and is often the person who will source the funding and initiate the project. Furthermore, playwrights never hold a neutral position in this kind of work. Our agenda – whether it is ideological, political, social or artistic – as well as our power is located at the core of any play created from interviews.

The Challenge of Speaking for Others

The creator of a verbatim play has to make political as well as artistic choices in this work. In addition to determining the subject matter of the production, choices include deciding whether the piece will be about members of a community who are from a similar background as the theatre company members or whether they will gather stories from people about whom they may have previously had little personal knowledge, and with whom they have no shared experience. When narrators come from a different population than the playwright, and most especially when power imbalances exist, playwrights have to decide how to represent the narrators and, in doing so, must acknowledge the fact that they are now in a position of *speaking for others*.

In her article, 'The Problem of Speaking for Others', the philosopher and scholar of women's and gender studies, Linda Alcoff, discusses the positioning of a speaker who is speaking for others and the intentions of that speaker.[1] This matter is significant not only for verbatim theatre playwrights but also for all who work with interview content, since those who wish to speak for others often originate from a position in society that is far closer to the hegemonic classes than those whom they wish to represent. Alcoff believes that the practice of speaking for others is often rooted in an innate 'desire for mastery', whereby an individual accords herself the privilege of truly understanding the reality of another person's situation, or champions a just cause and gains kudos by doing so.[2] These concerns apply to verbatim theatre practitioners and processes but in any area – dramatic, academic or political – the possibility exists that one person who claims to speak for another might be doing more harm than good. This is because, however well-meaning their intentions, the interviewer or researcher, in claiming to represent another, can potentially take the voice away from those for whom one claims to speak.

Sue Wilkinson and Celia Kitzinger, writing from a feminist perspective about issues of representing 'the other,' suggest that one solution to the ethical dilemma of speaking for others is to refuse to be drawn into representing others at all. They suggest that, rather than speaking for others, we might think about maintaining a 'respectful silence' and instead work towards creating a social and political environment in which others will be enabled not only to speak for themselves on their own terms, but also be heard.[3] If theatre practitioners were to follow this line of thinking, one possible outcome might be a dearth of drama for and about marginalised communities rather than an increase in the creation of projects initiated by those who come from such populations. In societies where members of minority groups suffer prejudice or are oppressed, ignored or even silenced, people from those communities are often not in a position to create the platforms they need in order to be heard by those who hold the power within a society.

In examining ethical ways of approaching work with what they term 'Self and Other', Wilkinson and Kitzinger refer to the methods of feminist social psychologists who give representations back to the represented for comment, feedback and evaluation.[4] They explain that the idea behind such practice is that those who are represented are then described 'not as "subjects", or even "research participants" but as "co-researchers"'.[5] This suggestion, which reflects Frisch's notion of 'shared authority', can be implemented in verbatim theatre processes by the playwright sending narrators interview excerpts that are to be included in the script and asking again for their final consent. Feedback from narrators can also be sought after playreadings which may be performed for narrators and other interested parties before the production is presented to the public in its final form.

Another approach is to engage a professional ethnographer to gather a community narrative. This practice is occasionally employed in applied theatre projects based on interview material, as well as in anthropological research. Ethnography is the branch of anthropology that deals with the description of specific human cultures, using methods such as close observation and interviews. In a theatrical context, the ethnographer works with and between the theatre company members and the other people involved in the project.

However, the author, feminist and social activist, bell hooks contests the idea of an ethnographer working within or beside a community who comes from outside that community and speaks for its members. Writing as an African American woman, she is wary of those who say that they are going to tell the story of the others. In the following powerful statement, hooks imagines how the outsiders might regard their ethnographic work, and the subjects about whom they are speaking:

> No need to hear your voices when I can talk about you better than you can speak about yourself. No need to hear your voice. Only tell me about your pain. I want to know your story. And then I will tell it back to you in a new way. Tell it back to you in such a way that it has become mine, my own. Re-writing you, I write myself anew. I am still author, author-ity. I am still the coloniser.[6]

hooks raises a critical concern that can also be encountered in theatre work when a playwright 'mines' other people's stories, employing them for their own purposes and personal advancement.

Ethical Concerns in Creating Plays from Interviews with Asylum Seekers and Refugees

The last section of this chapter discusses ethical concerns that arise in the creation of plays based on interviews with asylum seekers and refugees. Asylum seekers or refugees who are interviewed for plays have often been persecuted and may well have suffered trauma. Even if they wish for their personal experiences and matters relating to asylum processes to be more widely understood by the general public, they are still vulnerable to exploitation by those who interview them and create theatrical productions from their stories. Although your own work might not involve working with narrators who have suffered as many asylum seekers have, presenting an overview of some inherent ethical concerns in this area of work may be helpful for your own practice.

Over the last decade, the number of verbatim plays and applied theatre projects based on stories provided by asylum seekers and refugees has increased significantly. Playwrights and theatre practitioners in countries such as Australia, Germany and the UK (which are all refugee host communities) reflect in their work the conversations being held in their countries about the rising levels of migration occurring around the world. They also use plays and drama projects to comment on the existing treatment of those claiming refuge in host countries. When theatre practitioners employ testimonies from people who have been persecuted, whose lives have been under threat and who have then had to relate those experiences in interviews for border officials in the host country, ethical concerns around practice are foregrounded.

One of the main ethical considerations when members of vulnerable populations are interviewed for verbatim plays is whether their involvement in these projects will present any risks or dangers for them. On the other hand participation in the project may afford them some personal benefit. These two outcomes are, of course, not mutually exclusive. Personally, I would like to see increased attention in verbatim theatre scholarship paid to the experience of the narrator. I have always had a deep interest in the role and experience of a narrator to verbatim theatre processes, and, it is because of this that I have chosen to re-interview some of the narrators from some of the plays I have written and produced. In these follow-up interviews, I asked narrators about their experience of sharing their stories with a playwright and then seeing themselves portrayed on stage by an actor.

RIGHTS OF PASSAGE

'Izzuddin' was originally interviewed for *Rights of Passage* and, in a follow-up interview, when I asked him why he had responded to an advert I had posted seeking lesbian and gay asylum seekers for my play, this was his reply: 'Initially it was because I just wanted to get my story out there, because I always planned to write a book about me because everyone said to me "You should write a book, 'cos your story's so interesting". But it's going to be a long time before you see the book or maybe never and, when I saw the ad, I just thought "this is my opportunity to get my story out". Because I think the aim really is to help others who are in the same boat or experiencing similar issues in this country who have not been able to find information elsewhere. So, I thought by having my story being presented in a play, it could reach the wider public and that's the reason why I offered to be interviewed'.[7]

I was fortunate to be in a position to hear detailed feedback from Izzuddin about his involvement in the play and am indebted to him for providing it, but relatively few verbatim theatre practitioners document their working practices in a way that can be shared with other playwrights or theatre scholars. It is therefore often difficult to determine the range of reasons why narrators agree to be interviewed for plays or to analyse any benefits they may gain from their involvement in production processes.

The Canadian theatre practitioner and scholar, Julie Salverson, has written about the experience of some of the narrators to her own plays based on interviews. She created a drama project entitled *Are the Birds the Same in Canada?* which presented dramatic sketches and interview clips from narrators who are refugees. She states, 'As artists and educators, we must continually ask ourselves: in what context are risky stories being told? Within what frameworks did they originate?' and she asks: 'what is the cost to the speaker?'.[8] This is a question that we, as verbatim theatre makers, must keep at the forefront of our minds when working with all narrators, but particularly with those who have suffered trauma and those who may be deemed to be vulnerable participants. We are (usually) not social workers or therapists but, as playwrights who gather interview material to be employed in our scripts, we must work intentionally – with care, consideration and respect for our narrators.

The possibility of triggering discomfort or in any way causing harm to contributors by asking them to narrate personally traumatic experiences will always exist in verbatim theatre processes. However, that risk can increase when the narrator has experienced a stringent and often harrowing interview process when applying for asylum. Theatre scholars and practitioners are rightly concerned that the interview process for the theatre project may mirror or re-trigger some of the more traumatic aspects of the asylum interviews. In order to mitigate such risks, the playwright must work with extreme sensitivity, making sure that narrators feel completely comfortable in speaking about their experiences, informing them that they can stop talking whenever they need a break and assuring them that absolutely nothing will be asked of them that they are not happy to share.

Creating verbatim theatre from vulnerable or traumatised narrators is challenging work, ethically and practically. But when the aims of the production have been clearly explained to narrators and if they give their full and informed consent to being interviewed, in the knowledge that a play will be created from their own words, the narrator can experience benefits by participating. Hopefully, the benefits will outweigh any inherent risks.

Verbatim theatre provides a perfect means for people who might not wish to be identified publicly to share and disperse their personal stories. Christine Bacon says that, in her experience, the narrators she interviewed for *Asylum Monologues* were generally delighted when they found out that a professional actor would be playing them. She states, 'Half of the attraction of this project for interviewees is "Great! My story can be out there and I don't have to repeat it a hundred times"'. She comments: 'Having an actor present their story is a very attractive thing. It's actually a sort of relief. It's like "OK. I just have to speak with you. We'll have a conversation, and then that's it. I'm done with it"'.[9] She also explains that when the narrators attend the show and see the impact of their stories on the audience: 'That is very often an eye-opening moment for them as well because they think "People do care about what I've been through"'. Bacon's observations remind playwrights that we are in a hugely privileged position to be able to disperse deeply personal experiences through theatrical means. Our plays have the potential to enlighten audiences about matters of which they were previously unaware but verbatim productions can also increase the personal agency of narrators, who might never otherwise have had the opportunity to share their important stories with the wider public.

★

Ethical concerns in verbatim theatre mainly relate to the treatment of narrators. Theatre makers' vigilance in this regard must begin at the point of choosing the subject matter of the play, then continue as they approach narrators and interview them. Playwrights must be alert to the ethically related decisions they take during the scripting process of the play, and actors and directors must think carefully about the dramatic representation of the narrators. There are also ethical implications in choosing whether or not to ask the narrators for feedback when finalising the script and deciding how or whether to involve narrators in post-show discussions. Asking them, after the production is finished, about seeing themselves and their words spoken by actors can inform playwrights about ethical choices in their future work. Shows created from interviews are produced for many reasons, and the working practices of playwrights, as well as the form their final productions take, vary enormously from theatre company to theatre company. But, ultimately, the main ethical responsibilities theatre makers have in this work are twofold: to critically reflect upon our own working practices and to treat the narrators with respect and gratitude for their contribution.

Notes

1 Linda Alcoff, "The Problem of Speaking for Others," *Cultural Critique* 20 (1991–92): 5–32.
2 Alcoff, "The Problem of Speaking for Others," 29.
3 Sue Wilkinson and Celia Kitzinger, "Representing the Other," in *The Applied Theatre Reader*, ed. Tim Prentki and Sue Preston (Abingdon: Routledge, 2009), 86.
4 Wilkinson and Kitzinger, "Representing the Other," 91.
5 Wilkinson and Kitzinger, "Representing the Other," 91.
6 bell hooks, "Marginality as a Site of Resistance," in *Out There: Marginalisation and Contemporary Cultures*, ed. Russell Ferguson, Martha Gever, Trinh T. Mind-Ha, Félix González-Torres and Cornel West (Cambridge: MIT Press, 1990), 343.
7 "Izzuddin," interview with Clare Summerskill, London, June 29, 2016.
8 Julie Salverson, "Performing Emergency: Witnessing, Popular Theatre, and the Lie of the Literal," *Theatre Topics* 6:2 (1996): 181.
9 All quotations from Christine Bacon (unless otherwise cited) are from: Christine Bacon, interview with Clare Summerskill (via Skype), August 24, 2016.

PART III

Creating a Play from Interviews

Step by Step

6

GETTING STARTED

Having reflected upon the history of verbatim theatre and some of its related dramatic forms and examined connections between oral history and verbatim theatre processes, it is now time for you to get started on your own project. This chapter outlines the initial steps you need to take, starting with how to develop a nugget of an idea you might have for a play and continuing through to making a decision about the final shape of your production. Once you have settled these matters, **Chapters 7–12** provide you with complete practical guidance on how to create your verbatim play.

In order to be able to identify what needs to be done and who else you need to help with the project, ask yourself the questions below. Your answers will guide you through the steps required in planning a project. Each step is described under a heading in this section.

Q: What is your current position in relation to your project?
- You might be a solo oral historian, educator or theatre practitioner who wishes to create a play based on interviews,
- Maybe you are already working with a group – perhaps a group of older people or students – and you would like to formulate a project around the group's interests and abilities.
- Perhaps you are a playwright or a theatre director who wishes to create a verbatim theatre play but you have limited or no previous experience of working specifically with verbatim theatre.

Q: How far along are your ideas and research?
- You may be starting-from-scratch, meaning that you would like to write some kind of dramatic representation based on interviews but you have not

yet conducted the interviews and have not even thought about the theme of the final production.

- You already have a topic in mind but have not conducted any interviews.

- You already possess a collection of interviews about a subject or theme and want concrete advice on how to go about writing a script and producing a piece of theatre.

- Or you may be a seasoned playwright who knows exactly what research area you wish to explore through interviews but you are aware that it involves a sensitive or controversial topic and want to be sure to work with your narrators in a caring and appropriate manner which demonstrates ethical awareness.

Q: What skills do you have which you can utilise in this work?

- If you are an oral historian, then you know the basics about how to find narrators, conduct an interview and transcribe the interview content. Whether you are working alone or with other oral historians, you probably need no extra help in sourcing interview material which will later be employed in the script.

- If you are an educator who has no experience with oral history but are excited to use interview material for a verbatim play, then you need to learn the basics of oral history practice. Researching the fundamentals of oral history theory will also prove immensely helpful for you (see **Appendix 6** on Suggested Reading).

- If you run, or are part of a community group, and have no experience of oral history practice or theatre work, you need to do a little extra research on both of those subjects, and this book will equip you with the means to create a play based on interviews.

- If you are a theatre maker – a playwright, director or one of a group of actors who is drawn to the idea of creating a play based on interviews, then understanding the basics of oral history practice during the interviewing and transcription stages (as outlined in this book and other publications listed in **Appendix 6**) will inform and enhance your theatre work.

Q: What practical resources do you have at your disposal?

- Technical Equipment – You will need at least two audio-recording devices.

- Physical Space – If you work in a school or college, you might be able to gain access to a theatre space when the time comes for the production and to a rehearsal room in the weeks before. If you work as part of a community group, you may be able to work in available room for the rehearsal period which is currently used by that group, but you probably will need to find a theatre venue where the play can be performed.

- Funding – Whether you are working in an amateur theatre capacity (with actors who have not been professionally trained) or with professional actors, you will probably need to secure funding for some, or all of the stages of your production (see **Appendix 4** for information on projected expenditure).

The following sections of this chapter address the steps to follow in order to begin your verbatim theatre piece:

Step 1: Define Roles and Skill Sets
Step 2: Undertake Project Research and Design
Step 3: Discern Project Motivation or Goal
Step 4: Consider the Community at the Heart of the Project
Step 5: Think about Production Options
Step 6: Consider Your Budget Requirements

If you are a theatre practitioner, then you are already aware of the roles needed to create a production and you can move on to Step 2. Alternatively, you and your colleagues and/or students or community group members must fill the different roles of theatre makers yourselves. You will therefore be acting **AS IF** you are members of a theatre company. Box 6.1 shows the main 'players' you need to move forward with your work. It is followed by a detailed description of the responsibilities of each of the roles mentioned, with additional roles suggested for those of you who intend to create a full production in a theatre or a tour of the final show.

Step 1 – Define Roles and Skill Sets

In order to create a play from interviews, you do not need to fill all of the positions suggested in Box 6.1 below. Depending on the size of your budget and whether or not you choose to work with professional theatre makers, your production might be less ambitious. For example, it could be performed in a community hall, without a set or lighting equipment, and with actors who are students or community group members. Alternatively, you might aim for a professional production with a designed set, trained actors, an experienced theatre director and as many crew and production members as your budget allows.

There are many options for this kind of work, and it is up to you and your co-creators to decide how you want your final performance to look. The following list of possible members of your team begins with the playwright, whom I define as the person with the original idea for the play.

Playwright

The playwright's role could be filled by anyone with a good idea and a passion for oral histories: anywhere from an oral historian or community activist without theatre experience to a professional playwright with a great deal of theatre experience. This person might initiate the project and manage it all the way through the production process. She may have already collected some fascinating oral histories around a theme and now wants to write a script based on them. The playwright could be the person who will transcribe the interview

BOX 6.1 THE ROLES OF PARTICIPANTS IN A VERBATIM THEATRE PROJECT

Playwright	The **Oral Historian, Educator** or **Community Group Project Leader** assumes the role of **Playwright**. Usually, the **Playwright** will conduct the interviews and script the play. The **Playwright** might also take the role of **Director** or engage a **Director** to work alongside her during the rehearsal period.
Director	This role can be taken by the **Playwright** or by someone else with directing experience.
Producer	This role may be taken by the **Oral Historian, Educator** or **Community Group Project Leader** or by someone else.
Interviewer(s)	Interviews can be conducted by the **Playwright, Oral Historian, Educator** or **Community Group Project Leader**. **Actors, Students** and **Community Group Members** can assist in this work.
Interview Transcribers	Interviews can be transcribed by the **Playwright, Oral Historian, Educator** or **Community Group Project Leader**. **Actors, Students** and **Community Group Members** might be asked to assist, or this work can be outsourced to a professional **Transcriber**.
Actors	Professional **Actors** could be employed for the production, or **Students** and **Community Group Members** might perform as **Actors** in the play. They will be auditioned by the **Director** and/or the **Playwright**.
Stage Managers	Professional **Stage Managers** can be employed for the production or **Students** and **Community Group Members** might be asked to fill these roles.
Other company members	The **Oral Historian, Playwright Educator** or **Community Group Project Leader** may ask suitable people they know to fill these positions, otherwise professionals will need to be employed.
Lighting Designer	
Graphic Designer	
Set Designer	

material and then select excerpts to be included in a script. The playwright might be a high school or college teacher with an idea of working with students on a verbatim play created from interviews about a particular subject or theme. The students could participate in decisions about the subject matter of the play and whom to interview, and they might conduct and transcribe interviews. Students might participate in the productions as actors or other members of the production team.

The playwright could manage the entire project – having come up with the idea for the play, she could conduct the interviews, write the script and then choose the actors for the play. She might also direct the piece. In verbatim theatre work, writers who have gathered and scripted interview material tend to be far more involved in the rehearsal and production processes than playwrights who produce more fiction-based scripts. It is quite common for verbatim theatre playwrights to also direct the piece since they are the ones who interviewed the narrators and often have strong views on how they want 'their' narrators to be theatrically represented and portrayed.

Producer

In the theatre world, the term producer can refer to someone who is not directly involved in the creative process but who might raise money for the play or even financially back the production themselves. A producer can oversee the booking of venues where the play will be performed as well as attend to matters relating to publicity and marketing. Having come up with a great idea for a production, the playwright might therefore seek a producer to work on the financial and practical side of funding, booking and touring the show. In some scenarios, the producer will seek a playwright to create a play that they would like to see performed.

Interviewer(s)

Some playwrights choose to conduct all the interviews for their project, and this is a common practice in verbatim theatre. Alternatively, for those who may not want to work alone or hold sole responsibility for producing the piece, a small team of people could be involved in the play's creation; in which case, several people might then conduct the interviews. One of the benefits of students or community group members conducting interviews is that they will be more engaged in the project and also this stage can be completed in a shorter period of time. Equally important is that it has an educational value for the interviewers and provides them with the opportunity to meet people and develop new skills. Take note, though, that inexperienced interviewers will need to be instructed about basic interviewing techniques, and it will be necessary to supervise their work.

In some theatre companies, actors are sent out by the director and/or playwright to interview people, as demonstrated in the work of Peter Cheeseman at the New Vic Theatre in the UK, and also in productions created by Joint Stock and Out of Joint theatre companies and, in the US, by members of Moisés Kaufman's Tectonic Theater Project. But I have always chosen to work on my own in conducting interviews and when developing the script. Playwrights – of verbatim theatre or otherwise – tend to have a very personal artistic vision of how their final work may look and sometimes the presence of too many people contributing ideas can result in differing or conflicting aims for the piece which can, in turn, undermine its efficacy.

Transcribers

Transcribing recorded interviews is a time-consuming but vital part of creating verbatim theatre. It also is a highly skilled job. Though many playwrights like to transcribe their own interviews time constraints sometimes lead them to outsource the task. If oral historians are on the project team, they will be familiar with transcribing and qualified to do it. If you are working with students, or members of a community group, they will need training and supervision. (**Chapter 8** provides detailed information about the transcription process for verbatim theatre projects.)

Actors

Whatever form your final production takes, you will need actors to play the parts of the 'real' people whose stories you are telling. The actors could be students, members of the local community or a group with whom you are working, colleagues in the oral history project that has led to the creation of a script from interviews, or they could be professional actors, employed specifically for your show. In this case, they will usually be employed through an audition process where they will be cast on their abilities to work with verbatim performance (a matter addressed in **Chapter 12**), and on how well they can play the parts of the 'real' people who the playwright has now scripted into characters within the play. Professional actors will, of course, need to be paid professional rates for their work.

Director

You need a director for the piece who will work with the actors in the rehearsal period and make the script come to life on stage. In fiction-based theatre, as opposed to verbatim theatre, the director frequently works alone with the actors in the rehearsal room, without the writer being present. But in some verbatim theatre practices, and in most of my own work, the playwright assumes the role of the director. The playwright may want full directing control over the piece during the rehearsal period, since she might be the one with the artistic vision of the project and the final product. Furthermore, since the playwright often serves as interviewer, it is likely that she will feel a closeness to those who provided their stories and will be keen to make sure that they are dramatically represented respectfully and accurately.

Alternatively, a director could be employed at the rehearsal stage to work with the playwright's script. One advantage to this scenario is that a director who is not the playwright, and has not interviewed the narrators can bring an 'outside eye' to the piece. As a playwright, I have performed the role of director in many of my own plays and I have also employed professional directors to work with the actors. Each working process is different and presents its own challenges and rewards, but successful results can be achieved in each scenario.

Other Company Members

If the play is to be performed in a traditional theatre space, on a stage and with fixed audience seating, you will need the help of several company members to create a theatrical production. Some of these roles are vital, and the play cannot go on without them. Others are optional, and your ability to fill some of them will depend on funding. I recommend that novices to theatre work keep it simple. But if your experience is substantial and if the budget allows, other important company members required to create a theatrical production might include the following:

Stage Manager(s) – to source props required for the show and to assist the director and actors during the rehearsal period. They may also be needed to operate sound and lighting cues during the final production and, if the play is touring, sometimes to drive the van.

Set Designer – to work with the director and the writer on designing and building a set.

Lighting Designer – to work with the director to create a lighting design for the play.

Costume Designer – to design and make or buy the costumes.

Sound Designer/Visual Technician – many shows nowadays include projected images, video footage streamed onto a backdrop and soundscapes, which form part of the set design.

Graphic Designer – to design the flyers and posters needed to publicise the show.

Publicist – to work on marketing and promoting the production to secure good attendance.

Step 2 – Undertake Project Research and Design

Now is the time to think deeply about the primary theme of your play. Perhaps you want to interview people about one particular event that has impacted them, or you may want to ask them about their experiences of, and opinions about, a matter of political or social concern – or something else entirely. But whatever the topic or theme being addressed by the piece, you must now firm up your ideas for your verbatim theatre production.

Deciding Upon the Subject Matter of the Piece

Like oral history, verbatim theatre is ideally suited to the telling of stories that have not been widely heard. Those stories might come from members of groups in society who have not previously had a platform from which to express themselves. You may begin with a strong idea, or even just a hunch, about the topic you want your dramatic production to address. Don't worry if you begin with a general theme; it will become more focussed as you listen deeply to your narrators' experiences. You might already have a 'story' that you believe to be important and want to explore, something unknown, underreported or poorly represented in the media. Your theatre piece based on interviews will bring this topic to a wider audience and enable it to get the attention than it deserves.

Verbatim theatre often covers social or political issues, particularly as they relate to a local community. In fact, verbatim theatre (and its related forms of documentary theatre, tribunal theatre and theatre of testimony) with its foundation in personal storytelling is a perfect medium to touch the hearts of an audience about social injustice, educate them about a matter which they may otherwise not have known about and potentially galvanise a community toward action.

Examples of Plays Relating to a Political Matter, a Local Concern and a Social Issue

A play based on political concerns:
This Much is True is a verbatim play about the fatal shooting of Jean Charles de Menezes, a young Brazilian mistakenly identified as a terrorist, by the Metropolitan Police at Stockwell tube station, London. The script is based on testimony provided by witnesses, police, lawyers, family, friends, and Justice4Jean campaigners. The piece was written by Sarah Beck and Paul Unwin, and first produced in 2009 at Theatre 503, London.

A play based on local or community matters:
Aftershocks: A Project of the Newcastle Workers' Cultural Action Committee, about the 1989 Newcastle earthquake, is based on interviews conducted

with thirty-two people who experienced the collapse of the Newcastle Workers' Club. *Aftershocks* was first performed at the Newcastle Playhouse, Australia, in November 1991. The writer in residence for this play was the Australian verbatim playwright and scholar, Paul Brown.

A play based on social concerns:
Notes from the Field was written and performed by Anna Deavere Smith and staged off Broadway in New York City in 2016. It was subsequently adapted into a feature film by HBO and released in 2018. The piece depicts the personal accounts of students, parents, teachers and administrators caught in America's school-to-prison pipeline and investigates a justice system that pushes minors from poor communities out of the classroom and into incarceration. (The work of Anna Deavere Smith is discussed in greater depth in **Chapter 14).**

When Your Focus Shifts during the Research Period

If you have already settled upon a topic for your play, then you are ready to begin your project. But even if you are at this point, be prepared to change course if necessary, or to revisit your initial ideas. Sometimes playwrights realise that the play they had originally intended to create, or even the focus of the subject matter they wanted to address, has shifted either slightly or, in some cases, significantly from their initial idea. If this is the case, don't worry. It is common for ideas to evolve over time, especially when working in the areas of current interest that are so often covered in verbatim theatre, such as migration, homelessness, gender inequality, LGBTQ concerns and so on. Embrace the change and turn it to your advantage. Taking time to reflect critically (and often) upon what you now want to say through the piece of verbatim theatre that you are creating is always worthwhile. The evolution of your thinking will enrich and inform your final theatre piece.

Step 3 – Discern Project Motivation or Goal

Many verbatim theatre productions begin with a theme or conviction close to the heart of the creator, or an act of injustice that the playwright wishes to shed light on. As you begin your project the act of identifying and articulating your motivation will help you find the heart of your project, that is the central point, around which the plot develops. Ask yourself:

- What social, political or personal issue prompted you to take up this project?
- Who influenced your decision, and in what way?
- What do you want your production to achieve?

- Do you wish to educate the audiences who see the play?
- Do you want to provide a space for stories to be heard which might otherwise be neglected, forgotten or silenced?
- Are you trying to fill in some gaps in historical documentation?

It may be that your responses are informed by the discussions addressed in **Chapter 5** about 'who is speaking for whom' in plays created from interviews.

In the following examples, playwrights explain what motivated them to create theatre projects based on interviews. The first play is based on interviews with people about a period of time in history, and the project therefore creates a form of alternative history; and the second example shows why a playwright working with narratives of migrants, asylum seekers and refugees chooses verbatim productions to disperse those stories.

Example 1

THE EXETER BLITZ PROJECT

The Exeter Blitz Project was written in 2012 by Jessica Beck and Helena Enright. Between 1940 and 1942, the city of Exeter in the UK was raided by the German Luftwaffe nineteen times. Members of Viva Voca Theatre decided to create a theatrical experience to share and celebrate the real-life stories of those who experienced the Blitz in Exeter and interviewed over twenty people who were between the ages of six and twenty-five in 1942.

Jessica Beck explains how she approached the subject matter of this play:

> 'When creating any play from scratch, it is essential that the core of the piece is clear from the beginning. In this case, we wanted to tell the story of the Exeter Blitz, through the words of those who were there. So in that way, we had an obvious structure – what Exeter was like before the war, wartime Exeter, the increasing raids, the May 4th Blitz, the aftermath, VE day, etc. With over forty hours of interviews, we could have made several different plays with this material. But by bouncing the material off the 'core' idea, you get a clear sense of what goes into the play and what doesn't.'[1]

From these comments, we can see that the writers of this play decided that the direction of the script was going to be a chronological one, which is often a fail-safe way to approach the telling of one event or an historical period of time, during which something particularly remarkable occurred.

Example 2

Another way of looking at verbatim theatre work is to see it as a relatively easy and safe way for people who are vulnerable to tell their stories without risk, since they themselves will not be on stage. I conducted an interview with Christine Bacon about her work as artistic director of the UK theatre company, Ice and Fire, whose productions, often presented as playreadings, focus on the lives and experience of migrants, asylum seekers and refugees in the UK. We discussed how accusations of appropriation or even exploitation are occasionally levelled against verbatim theatre practitioners, and Bacon responded in the following way:

> 'The reason I'm doing this is because I care and because I feel that people need to hear these stories, and the people who talk to me feel the same. And many of the asylum seekers and refugees that I've spoken to are activists themselves. A lot of them have left their country *because* they stood up to authority and because they believed in speaking out. And so a lot of them have an implicit understanding of what activism means and why it's useful, and why is it useful to speak out and get stories heard.'[2]

Step 4 – Consider the Community at the Heart of the Project

Verbatim theatre productions address a vast range of topics, and theatre makers and oral historians alike are drawn to creating theatre from interviews precisely because of the seemingly endless possibilities which arise from asking people to speak about their personal experiences and then dramatising those stories using the narrators' own words. The subject matter of the plays can focus on events shared by narrators within small communities or extend to matters relating to global politics. The themes running throughout the scripts vary from extremely personal narratives about one subject, to which relatively few other people may be able to relate (such as the play *bald heads and blue stars*, written by the Australian playwright, Sarah Peters, in 2014, and based on interviews with women with Alopecia – a condition that causes hair to fall out in small patches) to stories told from a totally subjective perspective, but which have a universal resonance (for example, productions based on experience of prejudice, war, violence, trauma).

One commonality between many plays created from interviews is that they frequently draw on narratives provided from members of a community of one kind or another. This may be because the narrators are chosen for something they have in common, such as a geographical locality where they have collectively experienced an event (as seen in *The Exeter Blitz Project*), or because of a common interest – people who have shared experiences even though they do not live near one another. Women with Alopecia, asylum seekers or people with mental health problems are examples of communities of interest. There are other subject matters which verbatim theatre can, and has addressed, but the purpose of this section is to gain an understanding of some of the implications of creating plays based on interviews with members of one particular community, since verbatim theatre, as a form, lends itself so well to such productions.

Plays Created from Interviews with Narrators from One Locality or Community

1   **Plays addressing a local matter which generally do not tour beyond the narrators' original community**
    If you are an oral historian, or someone who is new to scripting plays and you want to create a piece based on interviews, it is likely that, rather than choosing to cover topics relating to national or even global developments, you might prefer to begin your journey by looking for subject matter – and subsequent interview content – that is nearer to home. Within your own region, town or city, you can interview residents about a local topic, something they may have experienced in the recent or more distant past, such as *The Exeter Blitz Project,* or something that they are still experiencing in the present day, such as *The River,* a play by Helena Enright. *The River* is presented as a tapestry of stories from people about their experiences and memories of the River Shannon in Limerick, Ireland. It was performed by Enright on an eighty-foot Dutch Barge on the River Shannon as part of Limerick City of Culture 2014.

    Because of the specificity of the subject matter and the locality in which you are working, plays created from interviews which relate to these kinds of topics will often be performed close to home before an audience of community members and will undoubtedly hold a special interest for members of the community where the interviews and the performance take place. This kind of local affiliation invariably helps in finding narrators and attracting publicity in the form of newspaper and online articles. It also makes it easier to secure well-attended audiences for the show that might consist of family members and friends of the original narrators as well as people from the locality who have an interest in learning about local history or current concerns relating to where they live.

2   **Plays created by a professional theatre company addressing a local matter with a universal theme, which then tour beyond the original locality where the interviews were sourced.**
    One consideration when interviewing people who come from a small geographical area is that there is a strong chance that some of them could be identified by the audience members, even when the playwright changes their names in the script. Certain narrators might enjoy this recognition,

but others may feel strongly that they want their comments to remain anonymous. At the scripting stage, the playwright must, therefore, be vigilant about including something said in an interview which could be regarded as offensive to somebody else or unfair, inaccurate or even libellous. As a dramatic form, verbatim theatre is well suited to presenting different views or arguments about a particular subject provided by several narrators. But the playwright must script this content in a way that does not publicly expose anyone who might differ in their views from other narrators. By the time a script is ready for actors to begin rehearsing, any potential concerns in this regard will have been addressed and ironed out, but playwrights must work with utmost care and ethical vigilance in this respect when creating a play from interviews with members of a small community and then performing it back to that same community.

The Laramie Project includes excerpts from interviews with many people who hold noticeably contrasting views, not only about the brutal murder of Matthew Shepard and why it happened, but also about salient issues in the play relating to drug use, homosexuality and religion. At one point, an interviewee, Marge asks the interviewer 'Well, uh, where are you going with this story?' And Greg (one of the company members) replies, 'Oh well, we still haven't decided. When we're finished, we are going to try to bring it around to Laramie'. Marge then replies 'Okay then, there are parts I won't tell you'.[3] Marge's response to being asked about Shepard's death is seemingly informed by her understanding that her comments, voiced by a character in the play, might be traced back to her by local audience members.

The Laramie Project is an interesting play for many reasons, one of which is that, although it was created from interviews with narrators who all came from the town of Laramie in Wyoming, after it was first performed in Denver and then taken to Laramie, it toured internationally. The popularity of this verbatim/documentary play around the world is unrivalled, possibly on account of its universal themes and powerful dramatic narrative arc. The script begins with descriptions of a striking crime – the murder of a beautiful young man – and then, through excerpts from narratives provided by members of the town, audience members seek to determine the course of events that led to Shepard's death and try to understand the real reasons behind the murder.

The play you create may well have a successful afterlife and be performed for years to come around the world, as *The Laramie Project* was, but there is also the possibility that its content might be regarded as either locally specific or more ephemeral than a fictional script might be. This can occur if the play relates only to one geographical locality, or if it is of interest only to a very small section of society, or if it is based on a political matter that is of current, but possibly passing interest in the news (or even *not* in the news, since you wish to raise awareness about it). Although this is frequently the case with verbatim plays, in no way does it diminish the importance of their subject matter or their worth; verbatim theatre is simply a form of drama that is written by playwrights who tend to respond to what is happening around them, be that matters of local or historical interest or issues of current social and political concern.

Plays Created from Interviews with Narrators Who Come from a Community of Interest

A play created from interviews from members of a community of interest generally addresses a matter about which all of the narrators have had some experience. When such plays are performed, it is useful, and often essential for others who have shared those experiences to be in the audience. When this occurs, the power of verbatim theatre cannot be understated, particularly when the play is followed by a post-show discussion held between the theatre makers (playwright, director, actors), sometimes people working in a professional capacity related to the content of the show, and the audience about what has been staged. This form of theatre can validate other audience members who might have been through some of the same experiences that they have just seen the actors dramatise. It can also educate and inspire a wider audience about a matter of which they previously had little or no knowledge or understanding. Having audience members who come from the same community of interest as those who shared their stories in interviews can empower the narrators who are invited to attend the performance.

GATEWAY TO HEAVEN

Eileen was a narrator to my play, *Gateway to Heaven* and, in her interview, she told me about her experience of receiving a dishonourable discharge from the WRNS, (the Women's Royal Naval Service) in the UK, in the early 1970s, after admitting that she was a lesbian. Eileen attended the rehearsed playreading of the show to which narrators, their friends, and members of LGBT groups and organisations had also been invited. Several years after the production, Eileen told me, 'I did have a lot of sympathy that night... I remember that. It was there in the audience'.[4]

From her reflections during a follow-up interview I conducted with her, I understood that when she witnessed 'herself' and the scene of her dismissal acted on stage, she also saw that she and these events from her life history, rather than being in any way judged adversely, were celebrated. I suggest that this afforded her the possibility of moving from a place of silence and shame to one of validation and pride, and this occurred precisely because the audience members *were* from the same community as she. When recalling her experience of watching the play, she told me 'It was like telling my story to family'.

The Australian verbatim theatre playwright and scholar, Caroline Wake, suggests that when a play is fed back to a community through public performances, 'the wider community can listen to a story about an issue or an event that has affected them, and pause to reflect on what has happened since then: in this way the play might change the community'.[5] Whether or not your own play will prove to have such a powerful impact, there are many advantages to working with members of your own community, geographical or otherwise. Narrators will usually be easier to source and may well suggest other people to interview. When the play is performed, it is almost guaranteed that there will be interest from other members of the community with whom you are working. And members of a community – of either interest or locality – will frequently feel pleased or even honoured to be asked to participate in a project which not only allows them to share their stories, but also challenges them to reflect upon their own lives and those of others who have undergone similar experiences.

Step 5 – Think about Production Options

At some point during the early stages of your work, you must decide upon the nature of the final performance. Will it be presented in a conventional theatre space or somewhere else? Will it be acted 'in the round'? Will it be in the form of a playreading or a full-length rehearsed play? At this point, making these decisions is necessary not only for artistic purposes, but also for seeking funding, since grant application considerations are based on the exact kind of theatrical work you intend to produce, and of course, the budget needs of the project.

Chapter 1 offered examples of various forms of verbatim theatre work created over recent decades. This section provides more detail about some of those production options and outlines some additional versions of verbatim theatre. **Chapter 14** presents further examples of theatre created from interviews by theatre practitioners from around the world so, after reading through the options below, you might want to look over that chapter briefly, in order to make an informed decision about your own production.

Performance Space Options

Decisions about your performance space will depend on a number of factors which include potential audience numbers, the size of the cast, and even the philosophy behind the production.

You may want your show to be performed in a traditional theatre venue (with a proscenium arch and a raised stage and fixed seating, or raked seating leading down to a performance area on ground level). However, many professional theatre companies, particularly those who perform to members of a local or regional community, stage verbatim plays in smaller venues such as village halls, school halls, residential homes or day centres. Such choices align with a philosophy historically associated with theatre companies whose work addresses areas of social and political concern, whereby shows are 'fed back' to those who provided the stories for the script in their own community or environment, rather than in a more traditional theatre setting. Depending on the content of the script and your own ideological and artistic aims, you might want to consider this option.

For a performance with a larger cast, staging it 'in the round', perhaps in a hall, could be an option. This involves the audience sitting in a large circle with the actors performing to them from within that circle. Depending on the artistic vision of the director, it might be that the actors who are not involved in the scene being presented could sit at the edge of the space until it is their turn to perform. (This form of performance was employed by Peter Cheeseman at the New Vic Theatre for many of his Stoke Documentaries.)

Production options include
- A rehearsed playreading of a script based on interviews
- Theatrical scenes created from interview excerpts
- Verbatim plays performed by students or community group members
- Verbatim theatre performed by the original narrators
- A staged production with professional theatre company members
- Holding a post-show discussion

A Rehearsed Playreading of a Script Based on Interviews

One way of presenting verbatim theatre is in the form of a playreading, where actors read directly from a script. The company Ice and Fire, for example, whose work is based on human rights issues, presents many of their productions in this way. Ice and Fire often presents several plays at different venues in different parts of the country performed by different actors simultaneously. This is only possible because, as playreadings, they are simpler to produce than full productions (see **Chapter 14** for a description of this company's work).

One of the main advantages of this kind of presentation is that the actors do not have to memorise their lines, thereby avoiding a lengthy rehearsal period. They can hold their scripts in their hands and even sit on chairs as they read the piece. Some rehearsed playreadings are presented in a partially-staged fashion, with the actors still reading from their scripts but, after having had a few days of direction, they move around the stage performing with their fellow actors. This small amount of staging enhances the quality of the dramatic presentation. A further advantage to the scripts being performed without a long rehearsal period is that the material can be altered if necessary, reflecting any life-changing circumstances that impact the narrators. An example of this might be if an asylum seeker mentioned in a play has, in real life, recently attained a successful claim and been granted temporary residence in a country.

PIONEERS: VOICES OF THE WINDRUSH NURSES

Pioneers: Voices of the Windrush Nurses is a verbatim theatre piece written and directed by playwright Adeola Solanke. A rehearsed playreading of the script, performed by professional actors, was filmed and has since been presented in video form at conferences and other events in the UK.

Post-war immigrants from the Caribbean, named the Windrush generation, were so-called from the ship, HMS Windrush, which arrived in the UK in 1948 and brought with it the first group of more than half a million migrants. After the end of the second world war, the newly established National Health Service (NHS) recruited extensively from Jamaica and Barbados after facing a hiring crisis in the UK, and this practice later extended to other Caribbean islands.

The script dramatises stories told by the nurses about how, despite having the required qualifications, only a small minority of them were accepted onto the state registered nurse training and even fewer received promotions or opportunities to move up the ladder and pursue their own ambitions. The project was initiated by researchers from the University of Greenwich: Dr Myrtle Emmanuel, Professor Tracey Reynolds, and Dr Leroi Henry, who were keen to document the voices of some of these migrant nurses.[6]

Theatrical Scenes Created From Interviews Excerpts

Another effective way to create verbatim theatre is, rather than script a full-length play from the interview material, to write a few scenes, not necessarily linking up dramatically or chronologically to each other, but each addressing a theme discussed by narrators in their interviews. This kind of performance works well when combined with a facilitated discussion and has the advantage of increasing the participatory engagement of the audience.

JUST LIKE THE COUNTRY

In 2000, I wrote a piece in this style for the London-based reminiscence theatre company, Age Exchange, under the artistic directorship of Pam Schweitzer. The production was called *Just Like the Country*, and it was a sequel to the original play, written by Joyce Holliday for Age Exchange in 1990. The project addressed the impact that the building of the inter-war housing estates, erected on the outskirts of London, had upon residents who were selected to live there due to health issues caused by their previous accommodation in tenements in inner London. The tenants of the new Cottage Estates, as they were termed, discovered the joys of having an inside bathroom, hot running water and a garden for the very first time. But the residents often missed their relatives who they had left behind, many miles away. Their stories reflect the first time that extended working-class families in London split up to live in different areas of the country.

The show was performed for older people in residential homes, sheltered housing, and day centres who had lived in the areas mentioned in the production. Two actor-musicians in the show played the parts of the narrators and also performed songs from the period when the houses were built, which audience members recognised and joined in with. After each scene, I facilitated a discussion with the audiences about what they had just seen, asking for their own memories and stories relating to the subject matter. One of the reasons I believe that this theatrical format worked so well with older people is that, if the discussion had been held at the end of all the scenes being presented together as one piece, (which would have lasted over an hour), some of the audience members' memories and reactions may have been forgotten in that space of time, and their comments and feedback would not have been so immediate and, consequently, productive.[7]

Verbatim Plays Performed by Students or Community Group Members

This type of production could be initiated by a teacher, community group leader, theatre professionals or an oral historian who has an interesting and vibrant collection of interviews and wishes to dramatise them in some way. Whoever is running the project, whether an individual or members of an artistic team, will need to consider the logistics of exactly how many people are to be involved in the final production. It may be that the students or community group members, working in conjunction with an oral historian or project leader, collectively decide the subject or theme of their play. Under supervision from the project leader or oral historian, the students or group members can seek narrators, conduct and maybe transcribe the interviews, returning to the project team with the transcribed interview content, which can then be scripted and performed. With such work, the project leader (educator, oral historian or drama expert) should have experience in working with verbatim theatre, in order to organise the participants effectively, supervise their work and coordinate their findings in such a way that advances the original aims of the project.

Verbatim Theatre Performed by the Original Narrators

This option provides an opportunity for people who have been interviewed about their experiences to present their own stories on stage, basically acting themselves. One way of creating such a production is, first, for those who wish to tell their stories to be interviewed by the playwright who will then transcribe and edit the interview content. Excerpts from the interviews can be given back to the narrators in a scripted form for them to learn and perform, acting 'themselves'. Although it is closely related to autobiographical performance, in my view, this kind of dramatic representation cannot be described as such since it involves the playwright distilling the content of the narrator's interview and then selecting excerpts which they think work best theatrically, rather than the performers creating their own show.

I have worked in this way with a couple of projects; one entitled *Staying Out Late,* which was a piece based on drama workshops and discussions with older lesbian, gay and bisexual participants on the concerns of older LGB people about being in care or receiving care in later life, whether in a residential home or in their own homes. The other project was called *Vis à Visibility,* again, based on workshops and discussions held over a number of weeks and created in association with the disabled LGBT group, Regard. In both of these projects, some of the scenes in the final productions involved participants learning and then performing excerpts of interviews which I had conducted with them. Although both shows involved working with members of marginalised communities, many of who had suffered prejudice and trauma, I did not notice that the actors had any difficulties in dramatically narrating their own experiences in this way.

Inevitably, ethical concerns are heightened in such work and theatre makers must be vigilant when asking people from any marginalised community or vulnerable population to perform their own narratives. The project director must identify and address early on any concerns among the narrator-performers about any aspect of the project. After all, it is their life stories that are being made public. I would note that, in both theatre projects I have mentioned, the participants who played themselves on stage welcomed the opportunity to do so and found it to be a rewarding and empowering experience.

One drawback to this working process is that it can be quite demanding for narrators who are not professional actors and who may have difficulty in learning lines. In productions I have created in this way, as both the writer and director, I have, at times, had to be a little strict when the narrator-performers are tempted to improvise their own words! It is difficult to explain to them that, although the 'lines' you are asking them to narrate were originally spoken by them, they will work best dramatically if they are presented in the edited and scripted form you have written. However, when performed successfully, this form of work produces a powerful sense of authenticity for the audience.

THE VERBATIM FORMULA

The Verbatim Formula (TVF) is an exciting collaborative participatory arts project based at Queen Mary University of London, that uses verbatim theatre techniques to convey the voices of care-experienced young people, care leavers, and adults responsible for their care and education and to create a conversation and dialogue among those groups. *(See note below for an explanation of what the project leaders of TVF understand the term 'care experienced' to mean).*

The testimonies that are performed are attained by young people who have themselves been in care. They interview each other, edit the recordings, and perform them while listening through personal headphones, repeating the words they hear. The identity of the original speaker remains anonymous, which means that although, to some degree, the content of the script is auto-biographical, the performers and narrators can still maintain anonymity.

An audio clip of an interview with one of the participants in this project who provided her own stories for the script and then performed excerpts from other narrators' experiences is posted on the TVF (The Verbatim Formula) website. The participant explains: 'I was very nervous and very unsure because I felt that you've got to trust people so much giving that piece of me and such a personal story to someone else to read out. When you're in care, you have to be tough. Because when you have to grow up fast, you react a lot differently than a normal kid would. So, it's definitely hard-hitting when you have to say someone else's story. It's like putting you and the audience in the same shoes, because you're both kind of hearing it, well not for the first time obviously, but you're both reacting to it in the same way because it's not you'.[8]

Note on use of terms: The theatre practitioners who created The Verbatim Formula explained to me that they adopt the term 'care-experienced' because they work with young people as co-researchers, experts in their own experience, who are well positioned to enable adults to listen better and to change their practices.

A Staged Production with Professional Theatre Company Members

My definition of a professionally staged production is one that involves hiring and paying several theatre company members, such as actors and a director and other company members whose duties are described in Step 1 of this chapter. This is the most 'polished' level of theatre making, and should only be considered by projects with a sufficient budget and a professional director. If this is your aim, you will probably need to secure a conventional theatre space which you might have to hire, if you are not working with a box office split from the owners of the theatre (which is when the theatre agrees to pay you a percentage of the income it receives from selling tickets through the box office).

A full-length play generally lasts up to two and a half or even three hours, with an interval. But I would suggest the optimal time for an audience to pay full attention is approximately two hours with an interval, maybe with the first act around fifty minutes and the second act around forty-five minutes. But plays vary considerably in their length and construction and there are no firm rules on this matter. A full-length play, with or without an intermission, could be staged either at one theatre for a run (of a few days or one week or even several weeks), or it could tour to a number of theatres that have been booked around the country where the theatre makers live, and even performed in other countries, if the play has international appeal and funding.

Holding a Post-Show Discussion

Depending on the subject matter, you may decide to hold a post-show discussion involving the cast members, the director and audience members from the same communities (of interest or of locality) as those being portrayed in the play. You might also want to invite outside experts on the subject matter addressed by the play to participate in these discussions. For example, for a show about asylum seekers, you could approach members of asylum groups and organisations or legal professionals who work in the field, asking them to attend and participate. These outside experts will enliven and add depth to the discussion and may offer information or opportunities for audience members to further engage with the subject matter.

Step 6 – Consider Your Budget Requirements

Whether we like it or not, every creative work has some financial needs. Verbatim theatre, with its roots in the community, can sometimes be performed successfully on a very small budget, substituting passionate volunteers and donated space for money. But productions performed in theatres can become expensive, as you will probably need to pay for the theatre space, and professional actors, a director and the theatre crew must be paid professional rates. **Appendix 4** (at the end of this book) provides an outline of some of the main expense items needed for your production and tour (if applicable), but to give you an overall idea at this stage of the resources you need to create your play, here is a short list of some basic requirements:

Human resources:	Playwright
	Interviewer(s)
	Transcriber(s)
	Director (if this role is not taken by the Playwright)
	Producer
	Actors
	Production crew (stage managers, set and costume designer, etc.)
	Marketing manager
Other resources:	Technology: computers, mobile phones, camera for publicity shots (if a professional photographer is not employed)
	Space: office space, rehearsal space, performance space
	Publicity: printing of scripts, programmes, flyers, adverts
	Stage design: costumes, props, set, set-building space
	Sound and Vision: Music tracks and video projection equipment
	If touring: Travel expenses, accommodation, van hire

Applying for Funding

In order to raise the money that you will need to produce your play, you will almost certainly have to apply for funding from a grant-giving body (unless you are fortunate enough to secure financial support from an individual benefactor). You must research how to apply to art-based funding bodies but also expand your ideas to include approaching oral history or history organisations or heritage grant-giving bodies and, if applicable to the subject matter of your play, health organisations. I mention funding at this stage because it will influence the kind of final performance that you are able to create and, if the production is dependent upon funding, you will probably need to begin the grant-writing process at least one year before the final production. A general note is that anniversaries of events that you might be covering in your play are a good time to apply for grants from funding bodies, so you might want to check if the subject of your piece ties in with any approaching anniversaries.

Conclusion

When they are not interviewing, oral historians often work alone. After the interviews have been conducted, they might find themselves transcribing the material, detailing information about the narrators and the content of the interviews, working with a repository to ensure best preservation of the interviews and sometimes writing about the interview content.

Creating a play from interviews, however, is a public, social endeavour, with a core purpose to engage with other people. The playwright and actress, Anna Deavere Smith, interviews narrators herself, listens back to the content and then either improvises the words the narrators spoke or employs the interview content verbatim in a script. She then performs her own work, playing all the characters, but she still needs many other people to help her create the final performance. Even a 'one-woman' or 'one-man' show (where there is only one actor on stage) involves working with a producer, a director, possibly a script editor, a stage manager (or more than one), a set and costume designer, a lighting designer and maybe other company members as well. But a production created with several participants, whether they be students, community group members or professional actors, will always require the talents and commitment of many people, and this is the stage where you have to figure out who you will need to work with when creating your play and how to prepare them for the forthcoming project.

Notes

1 Jessica Beck and Helena Enright, *The Exeter Blitz Project* (Exeter: Short Run Press, 2013), vi.
2 Christine Bacon, interview with Clare Summerskill (via Skype), August 24, 2016.

3 Moisés Kaufman, *The Laramie Project and The Laramie Project: Ten Years Later* (New York: Vintage Books, 2014), 15.

4 Quotations cited from "Eileen" (a name chosen by the narrator for the publication of the playscript) are from: "Eileen," interview with Clare Summerskill, London, February 14, 2012.

5 Caroline Wake, "Towards a Working Definition of Verbatim Theatre," in *Verbatim: Staging Memory and Community*, ed. Paul Brown (Strawberry Hills, NSW: Currency Press, 2010), 4.

6 For more information about this project, see Sian Moore, "Intergenerational Legacy of Windrush Nurses," *CREW Blog*, University of Greenwich, November 16, 2018, https://werugreenwich.wordpress.com/2018/11/16/intergenerational-legacy-of-windrush-nurses/.

7 For more information about this show and other Age Exchange productions, see Pam Schweitzer, *Reminiscence Theatre: Making Theatre from Memories* (London: Jessica Kingsley, 2007).

8 For more information about this project, visit "The Verbatim Formula," *People's Palace Projects*, February 28, 2020, http://www.theverbatimformula.org.uk/.

7

THE INTERVIEW

If you are an experienced oral historian or verbatim theatre playwright, you will already know that *preparation* is key when it comes to the interview, and the information in this chapter provides guidelines on how to prepare for the interviewing process. If you are new to either discipline and to interviewing in general, you can read some helpful literature on interviewing (as suggested in **Appendix 6**) or you may want to consider taking an oral history training course.[1]

Oral history is, in many ways, a stricter discipline than verbatim theatre since an oral history is conducted in order to provide a form of historical record and a play is an artistic venture. Verbatim theatre makers are not obligated to follow guidelines relating to their interview practice; nor do such guidelines exist for this work in the way that they are outlined for oral historians. However, in this chapter and the following chapters in this *HOW TO* section of the book, I draw upon what I consider to be best oral history interviewing practice, if and when I deem it to be applicable to the creation of a play from interview content. In this way, I believe that the best possible outcome can be attained for verbatim theatre processes, both ethically and practically. At times, I will also highlight how and when the interviewing procedure for oral history purposes and for scripting a play might diverge.

If you already have a collection of interviews that you intend to make into a play, you may want to skip over the initial section on how to source narrators, but there will hopefully be much to interest you in other parts of this chapter. If you have settled upon the subject matter of your play, but have not yet conducted any interviews, your task is now to prepare for the interviewing process and to identify and contact the potential narrators.

This Chapter is Divided into Four Parts

- Preparing for the interview
- The interviewer/narrator relationship
- Conducting the interview
- Practical and ethical considerations when working with narrators

Preparing for the Interview

Who Will Conduct the Interviews?

There is a good chance that the person who came up with the idea of creating a verbatim play will want to follow it through from seed to fruition and be involved in all stages of its production. They have identified the themes or subject matter they wish to address through a piece of theatre and will often want to conduct the interviews themselves. Sometimes, though, playwrights want others to help in the interviewing process. This could be because there are a large number of people to interview, or it might be that other participants in the project (students or community group members or professional actors) want to be involved in meeting and hearing first-hand from those whose stories they will subsequently perform. Whoever the interviewers are, they should understand the basic premise of good oral history practice and be trained appropriately.

How the Interview Will Be Recorded

Audio recording is by far the most common format for verbatim theatre interviews, but video is also an option. Video recording is more complicated as a technology. Even the simplest shooting (with a single still camera) requires more expensive equipment, a videographer to handle the equipment and a much larger digital storage capacity. The extra equipment and the additional people in the room can potentially disrupt the intimate nature of an interview. An additional consideration is that an oral, rather than video, recording can produce a more relaxed atmosphere in the interview situation and can sometimes lead to fuller disclosure from the narrators. Ethical concerns are also heightened when narrators are recorded by video for the purpose of creating theatrical productions, particularly when the play tells the stories of people from marginalised communities or vulnerable narrators.

Audio recording is basically easier, less expensive and less intrusive, but in certain circumstances, video recording might be considered by theatre makers, for example, if they intend to employ a video element in the performance, showing narrators on a screen.

WILD GEESE

Wild Geese is the name of a series of plays and what are termed 'video ballads' about forced migration, produced by Birmingham-based Banner Theatre in the UK. In 2004 and 2006, the company toured *Wild Geese*, describing the piece as 'a song and video ballad of exile and migration that uses live music and video to combine the stories of Irish nurses, Asian textile workers, Iranian refugees and Chinese cockle-pickers'.[2] The theatre makers' thinking behind this theatrical choice was that, by employing video footage of the refugees speaking, they were avoiding ethical pitfalls by presenting a more immediate and less edited form than would have been the case if actors had spoken the words of the refugees. However, the theatre makers still had overall control of the framing narrative.

In my own work, I have always used audio recordings for interviews, and although companies such as Banner Theatre have explored other forms that carry with them exciting possibilities, in this book, I provide guidelines on creating verbatim theatre from audio-recorded interviews. On this matter, I agree with Alecky Blythe's assessment that 'Cameras may present something closer to actual reality, but audio allows for greater access to underground worlds'.[3]

Practice Makes Perfect

If you are new to interviewing or if you need a refresher, be sure to conduct and record a few practice interviews – maybe with friends – to ensure that you are perfectly comfortable with both the interview and the recording process. Your friends will probably not be experts on the subject at hand, but you can interview them about something else, just for the practice. You will learn how your recorder works, practice how to listen intently to the narrator and discover how, during an interview, you must always have a question prepared in your head relating to what the narrator is telling you, in case they suddenly dry up or lose their way when they are talking.

Basically, you must ensure that your recording session always works the first time around! When it then comes to interviewing the 'real' narrators for your project, you will have gained greater confidence and probably a sharper focus about which areas you want to ask them about and, as the interviews proceed, your methods and manner will improve exponentially. Experience really is the best teacher in this regard.

Preparation of Questions

The Oral History Association Principles and Best Practices advises, 'Interviewers should prepare an outline of interview topics and questions to use as a guide to the recorded dialogue'.[4] However, I do not operate in this way, for either my oral history work or my verbatim theatre projects. In approaching the interview, I have no way of knowing what any narrator will tell me but, as the playwright or oral historian, I do have a clear idea what kind of information I would like to find out from them, or at least which areas the subject matter might cover. When I interview people for a verbatim play, I am not in the position of gathering research data or evidence, as understood within oral history work. In addition to seeking information pertaining to the subject matter of the play, I am also looking for narratives that are interesting, colourful, moving, unusual and ones in which I can detect dramatic staging potential.

I believe that working from a list of questions can interrupt the natural flow of an interview and is therefore not helpful for verbatim theatre interviews. It can also create a kind of 'call and response' type of encounter, rather than an informal conversation, albeit a situation in which one person (the narrator) is speaking more than the other. The less formal an interview is, the more likely narrators will tell their stories in a relaxed way, which can, in turn, result in a more interesting narrative and provide richer material for your final script. If you know a certain amount about your subject matter beforehand, but not so much that you come across to the narrator as the expert, and you have a clear idea about what you would like to hear about from the narrators, then you will not need a prepared list of questions. If you are new to interviewing and have concerns that you might lose the thread of the questions you intended to ask, I advise that, beforehand, you jot down some general topics as a guide to the conversation, to which you can refer if necessary.

When the Subject Matter of the Interview Is of a Sensitive Nature

Verbatim theatre as an art form lends itself to the interpretation of social ills for a public audience, and sometimes the narrators upon which the play is based have suffered trauma through experiences such as forced displacement; genocide; war; emotional, physical or sexual abuse; or in other ways. Playwrights ask narrators to share their stories, not only with a single interviewer in a private setting, but for theatre makers who could possibly interpret them out of their life-context and for the stage, where they could be reinterpreted by audience members. *Interviewers need to understand the weight of the favour they ask, and the gift that is given by the narrator.* Playwrights who are interviewing people about topics that have involved trauma must tread carefully and seek proper guidance in terms of whether to, or how to, approach such narrators. This could involve extensive research about the topics addressed, meeting with group leaders of organisations who are engaged with members of the vulnerable population that you wish to approach and lining up counselling support for anyone who might appreciate such help after being interviewed.

The example below, about the play *From the Mouths of Mothers*, shows how one playwright worked with sensitive subject matter and vulnerable narrators involved in her production.

FROM THE MOUTHS OF MOTHERS

Amanda Stuart Fisher created a play called *From the Mouths of Mothers* which is based on interviews with mothers whose children had been sexually abused. It was performed at the Pleasance Theatre, London, in 2013. Within such a project, there was clearly a strong imperative from both the playwright and the narrators that the production could serve 'the common good,' in that a wider audience would be made aware of a matter which is seldomly discussed in the public arena. It was also felt to be important that the theatre makers attempted to safeguard the narrators from any adverse repercussions from their involvement.

Stuart Fisher's work was commissioned by the UK charity Mosac, which provides emotional and practical support for non-abusing parents and caregivers whose children have been sexually abused. Mosac's counselling coordinator invited narrators she thought might be interested and deemed to be emotionally able to contribute their stories. Mosac oversaw the theatre project and, after the performances, a Question and Answer session was held with the audience and an invited panel. During these post-show discussions, the work of Mosac was mentioned, and information about the charity was also provided in the programmes. In the production of this verbatim play, the writer, producer and other company members demonstrated an in-depth understanding of the ethical implications of their work with a vulnerable group of narrators.[5]

Identifying Narrators

One of the more obvious ways to begin finding narrators is to contact people you already know who may be able to tell you about their experiences relevant to the play. These may be members of one particular community (for example, Greek Cypriot families who live in North London, or older women who camped outside the Greenham Common Military Base as an anti-nuclear peace protest in the UK in the early 1980s, or Syrian refugees who fled to European countries after the civil war). Often, when you find the right person, they can recommend others. In fact, it may be that person's recommendation that opens the door for you into the community. When you have made a list of potential narrators, then you can expand your search to more formal channels as needed. These might include the following:

• Contacting leaders of community groups who work with members of the population you wish to approach. If you take this route, ask for contacts and introductions. Whenever possible, meet with people who are in close contact with members of the groups that you seek. Face-to-face meetings demonstrate a commitment from you and a respect for the leaders of the groups and their work.

- Posting flyers and announcements at libraries, museums and community centres.
- Targeting social media and online communities. Look for websites and Facebook groups, ask to join them, then request permission to post information about your project, explaining why you are seeking narrators.
- Making recruitment calls via local radio. Contact the radio station, explaining what you are working on and what your proposed call-out or interview would be about.

Just as there is no one way to invite narrators for your project, there are also no guarantees about the way they will respond. If your first efforts get no responses, revise and expand your communication channels.

In some circumstances, though, it may be better to not advertise too widely. If you get more responses than you are practically able to follow up, you will be faced with difficult choices in how to politely decline someone's generous offer to be interviewed. One word of caution – you may get volunteers who are simply 'eager beavers' wishing to participate in a project. I have noticed, over many years of seeking narrators to both verbatim theatre productions and oral history projects, that some people who have heard about a project I am working on contact me to tell me how much they have to say and how great their desire is to be interviewed. But these forthcoming and seemingly gregarious people do not always prove to be the best narrators and sometimes, surprisingly, they soon run out of things to say during the interview. By contrast, someone who has had experience relevant to your project but who seems a little shy or self-effacing, and might say to you: 'I really don't know if I've got anything to say that will help you', can turn out to be a most interesting and animated narrator. On numerous occasions I have found this to be the case.

The degree of difficulty in finding the 'right' people to interview is usually proportionate to the sensitivity of the subject matter and people's willingness to talk to a stranger about personal matters relating to it, especially on a recording. Depending on the nature of the project and your relationship to the community at the heart of it, you may need to build trust among its members. This can take a long time, especially if you do not come from that community yourself. One way to proceed is to find someone who is respected in the community. If you can cultivate such a relationship, he or she can be the conduit between you as an 'outsider' playwright and the community you wish to document. So, if you are seeking narrators who, by virtue of the subject your interviews address, may be reluctant to talk to a stranger about their experiences, then this will affect the way in which you look for them.

I have worked on a couple of oral history projects where I had to find transgender people as narrators. Owing to historical and contemporary prejudice against members of this population, I found it relatively difficult to find sufficient numbers of narrators and on neither occasion did I find that the fact that

I am a lesbian myself (and therefore a member of the LGBTQ community) necessarily helped me in these instances. The people who I finally found only agreed to be interviewed by me after a leading person from their community who knew me had spoken to them about the project and my previous LGBT-related work; in effect, giving the narrators a 'thumbs up'.

People from communities that have been historically silenced may be conflicted about sharing their stories with people they don't know. On the one hand, they may be distrustful and concerned that their experiences might not be accurately conveyed, but there is also the possibility that they could be delighted that you are interested in what they have to say and appreciate that you want to share their narratives with a wider audience.

How Many People Do You Need to Interview for Your Script?

This question has no one definitive answer! If you are creating a play about two or three people speaking about something that has happened to them, you might not need to interview anyone else for your piece and you could choose to interview them a few times each, in order to delve more deeply into their lives and experiences. But, generally, I would say that is it unusual to interview such a small number of people and I would advise you to secure a minimum of eight to ten interviews for any play. This number could extend to fifteen or even twenty.

As the playwright, you can potentially face problems when interviewing too many people for your script and then realising that some of the interview content you have acquired is not suitable for inclusion – or, more precisely, that excerpts from other interviews have provided you with sufficient dramatic content. The extra recorded conversations might give you a broader perspective on the topic and deepen your understanding of it, but you will then have to explain to some of the narrators that their interview content will not be employed. For one play I researched, one narrator (out of twenty-four) gave me an interview in which there really was nothing that I thought suitable or relevant to the play I was creating. But a feeling of guilt at completely omitting this woman's contribution got the better of me and, finally, I decided to include just a couple of her 'lines', so I could tell her that some of her interview had been employed in the script.

But interviewing narrators and then letting them know that nothing they said will be used is clearly problematic. Furthermore, if your narrators are from a sector of society whose voices are rarely heard, then by not including their story in the final production, they are at risk of being silenced once again. So be careful when you select your narrators, both in regard to the number of interviews you seek and in the narrators you choose. And when you do talk to them about your project, explain that you are collecting some personal stories as material for a play and that *some* of the excerpts will be used in the final piece. This will minimise disappointment and make your final scripting decisions a little easier.

Oral historians might examine the selection of narrators to assess if the sample was large enough to achieve the purposes of the research. But in verbatim theatre, since the aim of interviewing is to find interesting and relevant stories which can be dramatised – rather than as a means to gain research data and information – the numbers of narrators approached is determined by the playwrights who decide when they have attained sufficient interview material to create a script.

The Interviewer/Narrator Relationship

The previous section provided guidelines on how to identify the best narrators for your project and get them to agree to be interviewed. This section provides suggestions on how to cultivate the interviewer/narrator relationship throughout the project.

When you have found your narrators, you must give them some information to prepare them for their role and attempt to ensure that they feel reasonably comfortable with the process. This involves introducing yourself, telling them about the project and explaining why you think it is important (see **Appendix 1** for an example of a written approach), and contacting them in the way you believe they would be most receptive to your idea: phone, email or letter or a personal introduction from a mutual acquaintance; providing your own contact information.

Include the Following Information When You Initially Contact the Narrator

- Explain why you selected them to be interviewed.
- Describe the project to which you are inviting them to contribute.
- If your project is funded, mention the funding body supporting it. If it is conducted in association with an organisation or group, mention their name.
- Explain your own involvement with the project and your qualifications. Are you the playwright, or an actor in a theatre company, or an oral historian, or a teacher, or a student, or a community group member? Tell them why you think your project is interesting or important and in what way you see them as being of value to the project.
- Explain what will be expected of them and how much time the interview will take (usually between one and two hours). Be sure to mention whether it is audio or video.
- Assure them that they have full control throughout the process and can change their mind at any time about their involvement. Explain that they will be asked to sign an informed consent form. Invite them to ask questions at the time of the initial meeting and any time before or thereafter.

- Let the narrator know what will happen to the recorded interview – it will be transcribed and excerpts from the interview might be employed in a playscript.
- Thank them and tell them you would be honoured if they will participate.

When the narrator agrees to be interviewed, set up a time and date for an in-person meeting, preferably at a location of their choice. This could be at their home, at your home or some other place, such as a quiet room at the archive, library, school, college or theatre with whom you are working.

Creating a Permission Form

Oral historians agree that a signed permission/informed consent form is an essential part of the practice. The Oral History Association in the US has clear, time-tested guidelines for gaining consent from narrators, which propose that:

> Oral historians ensure that narrators voluntarily give their consent to be interviewed and understand that they can withdraw from the interview or refuse to answer a question at any time. Narrators may give this consent by signing a consent form or by recording an oral statement of consent prior to the interview.[6]

(See **Appendix 2** for an example of a consent form for a verbatim theatre play).

Following the guidelines of oral history practice, I also recommend that playwrights secure a signed consent form from narrators, but I suggest that this takes place after, rather than before the interview, when the narrator knows what they have said and a degree of trust has been built up between the interviewer and narrator. Although most verbatim theatre practitioners employ consent (or permission) forms, there are no prescriptive guidelines stating that they must do so. This is one of the main differences between oral history and verbatim theatre processes, but in your own work in creating a play from interviews, I strongly advise you to adopt this form of best practice.

Recording Devices

In oral history projects, recordings are frequently archived with the possibility of many people hearing them in years to come and, for this reason, the quality of recording in oral history work needs to be of the highest standard. But in verbatim theatre work, the original recording is rarely used after the interview has been transcribed and seldom archived in a public repository. Therefore, the recording standard generally needs to be sufficient only for transcription purposes. The main difference between a recording made for an oral history project and one made for a verbatim theatre script is that, usually, the playwright will be the only person who ever listens to it.

Many different brands of portable digital audio recorders are available, with which potential interviewers may already be familiar, and choosing the right one depends very much on your personal preference and budget. When recording verbatim theatre interviews, I have always chosen to use a small hand-held digital recorder, and would recommend this, but the ubiquitous mobile phone is another option for recording interviews. The mobile device itself is unobtrusive and non-threatening, easy to use and inexpensive, since most people have access to one.

Since the recording is generally only heard by the playwright and transcriber, it does not need to conform to the higher recording standards held in the oral history world, but exceptions can occur if the theatre director intends to let the actors listen to the recordings in order to help them develop the parts they are playing. Additionally, some playwrights choose to include excerpts of original recordings in the staged version of the play, a theatrical device which occurs in *The Line* by Gina Shmukler (one of the examples explored in **Chapter 14).**

In the form of verbatim theatre known as Recorded Delivery, which is employed in Alecky Blythe's productions, or what is referred to in Australia by playwrights such as Roslyn Oades and Stuart Young as 'headphone-verbatim', the actors are fed an edited audio script, which they repeat on stage.

LITTLE REVOLUTION

Little Revolution is a play by Alecky Blythe created in her company's Recorded Delivery style. Interviews were recorded by Blythe from narrators during and after the Hackney riots of 2011 in London. The edited recordings were played live to the actors through earphones during the rehearsals and the performances and they repeated what they heard, including every stutter, hesitation or cough. In this way, it could be argued that the representation of those who were interviewed in a mimetic fashion is as close as it can possibly be to an accurate one. But the difference between Blythe's working process and productions by other verbatim playwrights who do not work in this way is that there is no transcription process involved, only an editing of the recording. In much of Blythe's work a written script is therefore never required or produced, since the director and actors work entirely from recordings.

In the kind of productions created using Recorded Delivery or headphone verbatim, a high-quality original recording is important so that the actors are able to hear the voices of the original speakers as clearly as possible. As mentioned previously, this book does not provide guidelines on how to create this type of theatre, but it is always interesting to learn about the wide variety of plays produced using different verbatim forms and techniques.

Conducting the Interview

The purpose of an interview for verbatim theatre is different from that of oral history, in that the playwright/interviewer will be mainly seeking content that has dramatic potential, in addition to it being informative and contributing to the ideological aims of the piece. But many of the tried and tested interview techniques in oral history practice apply in equal measure when conducting an interview for a verbatim play.

Bring to the Interview

- A consent form for the narrator and the interviewer to sign.
- Recording equipment, consisting of at least one recorder (I always take a second, so that I have a back-up of the recording), batteries, external microphone (if a higher quality recording is required), extension cord, as needed.

When You Arrive

- Have a brief friendly chat with the narrator. Remind them about the purpose of the interview and the subject matter you would like them to speak about.
- Explain that you will be recording them as they speak about their experiences and that, at the end of the interview, you will ask them to sign an informed consent form. Before the recorded interview begins, ask them if they have any questions or concerns.
- Set up your recording device as near to the narrator as possible. I often perch my recording device on the arm of the chair on which they are sitting if possible, rather than on a table. Some oral history scholarship states that it is sometimes best for the microphone to not be visible to the narrator, but I totally disagree with this directive, since I think it is very important that the narrator is reminded that their words are being recorded throughout the interview. While not wanting your narrators to be 'on their guard' about what they say, you also need them to remember that what they are saying may be made public at some point.
- Before you begin the recording, listen for external noises (outside or inside the room) which may affect the recording. Ask the narrators if you can close a door or window if necessary, or move a loud ticking clock. Beware of rustling papers near the microphone or, if you are both sitting at a table, you might want to remind the narrator that emphatic hand gestures, such as thumping the table (an action which, incidentally, I have found many narrators frequently perform!) can distort the recording, and to try to avoid them. Turn off your own mobile phone and ask the narrator to turn off theirs', so that the interview will not be disturbed.
- Let your narrator know that they can stop the interview at any point, either if they need a short break or if they wish to terminate it.

During the Interview

- **Face your narrator**. Some oral history guidelines recommend sitting at a forty-five-degree angle with your narrator such as on an L-shaped sofa. However, I prefer sitting directly opposite the person I'm interviewing, across from them at a desk or if in their home, on a separate chair facing them, and not alongside them on a sofa. See what works best for you as you develop your own technique and gain more experience and confidence.

- **Engage with the narrator**. Make eye contact with your narrator. When I interview narrators, before I turn the recorder on, I say to them, 'I might occasionally look down at the recorder to check that it's still recording, but when I do that, just carry on talking'. I mention this because I have noticed that sometimes when I look at the recorder, it can interrupt the narrators' train of thought and they sometimes stop talking altogether. Give the narrator your full attention. If the interview seems to be losing steam, always have a follow-up question ready that either relates to the topic about which they were speaking or initiates a new area of discussion.

- **Establish a conversational flow**. As the interviewer, you should speak less, rather than more, during the interview. Remember that you are there to listen. Exceptions to this rule are if the narrator dries up and needs help moving forward or if they need you join in the 'conversation' to make them feel more comfortable. Once you begin transcribing, you may be surprised at the amount of times your voice appears on the recording, but in much verbatim theatre work, it is only the narrators' words that will be used in the script, not your own.

- **When the narrator speaks about familiar topics**. If the narrator speaks about something with which you are familiar, it is helpful to nod and show your recognition or personal understanding of the subject as an encouragement for them to continue. But, at other times, nodding or agreeing vocally with narrators has the potential to stop them from explaining something, since they will pick up on your gestures and assume that you already know what it is they are telling you. In this case, employing body language to express keen interest is usually enough to encourage narrators to continue.

- **The arc of the interview**. Although every interview is different, sixty to ninety minutes is a commonly accepted length. It allows time to go into depth on the important topics but it is not so long that it tires people out. If the narrator shows no signs of ending their narrative and the interview has lasted two hours, then I would jump in at that point and diplomatically suggest that it might now be time to wind up.

- **Ending the interview**. The interview is best wound up with a comment from the interviewer along the lines of 'Is there anything I missed that you would like to tell me before we finish?'

- **After the interview**. It is advisable to take cues from the narrator about how to negotiate time after the interview. I usually don't linger for too long, since my experience is that narrators often seem quite tired by the end. On the other hand, take care that you do not appear to rush out, as that may suggest an abrupt ending to a deeply personal conversation. There should be a clear boundary between the end of the recorded interview and the conversation that follows – marked by turning off the recorder and saying something to the effect that the formal interview is ended. Sometimes the narrator will become energised and might want to talk more, in which case you can ask them if it's OK for you to turn the recorder on again. Remember that if they tell you something after it's turned off, however fascinating it may be, in the form of 'word-for-word' verbatim theatre for which this book provides guidelines, those comments are not able to be used in the scripting process.
- **Follow-up interviews**
  You may wish to schedule follow-up interviews for any of the following reasons:
  * You sense that your narrator has more to tell you.
  * The narrator seems emotionally or physically tired from the current interview.
  * The subject matter discussed was traumatic for the narrator, and it seems best for the narrator to speak about the topic over time, rather than all at once.

Keeping the Interview on Track for Your Purposes

During an interview, a narrator sometimes veers off from the subject at hand. When this occurs, your job is to steer them gently back onto the topic you wish to hear about. It may be that you have to let them finish a long story before you can do this, so as not to interrupt or to seem rude, but the interview has been set up by you for a specific purpose – to gather interview material you will be able to employ in your script; so, it is important to get the narrator back on track. The more experienced you become, the easier it will be to guide them back to the topic.

Also, when narrators begin speaking about something which you see as having dramatic potential, you can delve a little deeper and ask them to elaborate or explain it in different words. Doing so can often prompt a narrator to give a fuller and sometimes more colourful version of the event, which, in turn, will ultimately provide you with material for a more interesting script. This requires close listening by the interviewer, since, while you are encouraging the narrator to share stories relevant to the subject matter of your play, at the same time, you will also be envisaging theatrical possibilities relating to the narratives being told.

Practical and Ethical Considerations

Narrators' Levels of Confidence

My experience of interviewing for oral history projects and verbatim theatre has shown me that people vary greatly in their degrees of confidence during an interview. Those who have never previously given an interview can be worried about the value of what they can contribute; therefore, you may need to provide them with a degree of safety and trust in you, as the interviewer, and in the project. One way this can be achieved is by taking more time to outline exactly what the project is for, and reiterate, before you turn the recorder on, what it is that you wish them to speak about.

If you interview people with high public profiles, such as politicians, lawyers or academics, you may notice that such narrators need less encouragement than others, since they are used to sharing their views publicly. However, I have noticed that politicians and 'political animals', when asked about a period in history that they have lived through, or memories of a particular event, can sometimes speak about their own experiences in quite a detached kind of way. Although they are relating information pertinent to the subject at hand, they sometimes do not reveal how they *felt* about the events they remember, believing that you will be after a more factual account of the matter. At times, this can result in a seeming lack of personal attachment to the material they are talking about, which can, in turn, produce a rather flat narrative.

Very occasionally, it might be the case that narrators tell you that information about their personal or family history can already be found in an existing publication, or might be published in the future, so there is no need to for them to share those same stories with you! This happened once when I was working on a community oral history project, gathering interviews from residents of Blackheath, an area in South East London that has a large working-class population, but where many well-to-do people also live. I interviewed a man who, judging by his house and his accent, appeared to me to be wealthy and upper-class, and almost every time he was about to answer a question, he stopped himself, explaining that the stories he could tell me would most likely be published in his autobiography, if he were to write one. He said that he would therefore not share those experiences with me. Whether or not he had any interesting narratives to relate, and whether or not he was ever going to write an autobiography, I never found out! But it seemed as if he regarded his memories as some kind of currency that he wanted to keep and 'spend' himself, rather than hand over to me for my own purpose.

Conversely, while researching this same community project, I found that the narratives I recorded from most of the working-class narrators in the same area were generously given, naturally flowing, vibrant, colourful and frequently very humorous. Within the working classes, at least in the UK, there has, historically, been a long tradition of passing stories down verbally, through the generations, rather than in printed form. I am aware that my observations are verging on generalisations but, at the same time, share them as an interesting observation and reminder that every story, every narrator and every interview situation is different. Remember to be flexible and to engage completely with the person sitting across from you, who is sharing their personal memories and perspectives.

Narrators Who Prepare Written Memories

Sometimes when you begin an interview, you will find that the narrator has written down their memories, either to share with you during the interview or because they think it will help you for the project. They may have had concerns about their ability to remember. Or, they may believe that the value of written recollections is of greater importance than the spoken form (since written versions of history have frequently been privileged over oral ones). Or they may have some other reason. In such circumstances, I would advise you, in as kind a way as possible, to urge them to look over what they have written and then put the piece of paper down and tell you about it in their own words.

In oral history projects, the relating of narrators' written accounts is generally discouraged because it is seen as lacking the spontaneity of a spoken 'conversation'. It is often the case that spontaneous words and phrases that come to a narrator's mind in the moment have a very different style of tone and delivery from the written word. In both oral history and verbatim theatre work, the spoken word, rather than the written account, can have a deeper emotional impact and, when scripted and performed, can provide greater dramatic potential.

In documentary theatre work, where documents other than interviews are employed in a script, then written journals or accounts can be used as source material. But if, as a verbatim theatre playwright, you choose to work in a way whereby your script only contains words spoken by 'real' people, then, in order to be true to this process, you will not employ written material in the final piece.

Pros and Cons of Group Interviewing

If you are researching a subject where a number of people have a shared experience – either of a period of time or of an event, one option is to interview them as a group. As the narrators begin to talk about their memories, additional recollections are stimulated by listening to other group members. Having witnessed this during an oral history project, I observed the narrators 'bouncing off' each other as they recalled events which they might not have otherwise remembered.

Conducting group interviews for either oral history or verbatim theatre projects, however, can sometimes make the transcription process extremely difficult, since the transcriber has to identify each voice during the interview.

In a group situation, especially if it involves reminiscing, people will often talk over each other, usually with rapidity and excitement about the matter being addressed. One way to mitigate the difficulty of sorting out voices is to video the exchange, but then there is always the concern that the presence of a film crew, however small, might restrict the level of the narrators' disclosure.

Potential for Triggering Trauma

I would suggest that the 'golden rule' of interviewing, in all situations, is to be polite and respectful to the narrator and aware of their physical or psychological needs. But the final section in this chapter relates to an extremely important matter in the interviewing process, which is that some interview topics are more likely than others to trigger traumatic memories – and you must be aware of this possibility and sensitive to such an occurrence.

Often, the interviewer is aware of the potential for evoking a traumatic memory, but at other times, it can happen out of the blue. Everyone has topics they find difficult to discuss, whether or not they are identified as a member of an 'at-risk' community. Rarely are oral historians or playwrights trained therapists, and if they are eliciting difficult and painful memories from the narrator, they cannot be expected to psychologically contain such a situation. One thing we can do, however, is to line up psychological support or referrals for narrators who might find their interview to be a traumatic experience, in any way. We should inform the person or organisation we have in mind for a referral and let the narrator know that support is available for them, should they need it. Another option is to tell any narrators you deem to be vulnerable that if, after the interview, they feel upset or disturbed by what they have spoken about, that you would be happy to give them a follow-up call the next day to talk about it, if they would like that. I have done this on several occasions and found that even if narrators have not needed to speak with me after the interview, they have seemed appreciative of the offer.

The likelihood of triggering a traumatic memory during an interview is the exception rather than the rule and should not scare playwrights away from tackling difficult material. That said, the playwright should consider the potential for triggering trauma when the project is being planned, seek appropriate extra training and gain an in-depth understanding of the subject matter that will be covered, in order to be fully prepared for a difficult interview.

I have found that by the time the interview has been arranged and the project explained, most narrators often know what they want to talk about, even if it might be a painful subject for them, and they are ready to share their stories. But this does not mean that it will not be a difficult experience for them. It may well be. And you must be ready to support them by being observant and caring and maybe asking them at certain points if they would like to have a break. If they say 'yes', then you can turn off the recorder and check with them after a little while to see if they would like to continue, stop completely or perhaps talk more at another time. With sufficient notification and information about the project beforehand, narrators will have a good idea of what they are letting themselves in for by agreeing to share their stories in this way, so it's not as if you are catching people unaware. But it is always advisable to be highly vigilant with narrators discussing subjects in which painful memories could be triggered unexpectedly, and it is your responsibility to prepare for such scenarios as best you can.

Notes

1 Oral History Association, "Principles and Best Practices: Principles for Oral History and Best Practices for Oral History," 2009, https://www.oralhistory.org/about/principles-and-practices-revised-2009/.
2 "*Wild Geese* (2004/2006)," Banner Theatre, March 4, 2020, https://bannertheatre.co.uk/portfolio/wild-geese-20042006/.
3 Alecky Blythe, "Alecky Blythe," in *Verbatim Verbatim: Contemporary Documentary Theatre*, ed. Will Hammond and Dan Steward (London: Oberon Books, 2008), 84.
4 Oral History Association, "Principles and Best Practices."
5 For the playwright's reflections on this project, see Amanda Stuart Fisher, "That's Who I'd Be If I Could Sing: Reflections on a Verbatim Project with Mothers of Sexually Abused Children," *Studies in Theatre and Performance* 31:2 (2011): 193–208.
6 Oral History Association, "Principles and Best Practices."

8

AFTER THE INTERVIEW

Transcribing and Preparing for the Scripting Process

After the interview has been conducted, oral historians and, usually, verbatim theatre playwrights transcribe it: a process outlined in this chapter which also discusses some of the ways in which the transcription process differs between the two disciplines. Oral historians regard the interview as a form of historical documentation of the spoken word. The whole recording and transcript, if one exists, will be preserved and, whenever possible, made accessible to researchers and also to members of the public. In verbatim theatre however, the playwright, in looking through a large amount of interview material, is faced with the task of rigorously pruning the content and selecting stories, phrases, descriptions, responses, and other comments for inclusion in the script. These excerpts are ones which best suit the writer's artistic, ideological, pedagogical or political aims for the piece and will appear in the final production, but the interview transcription is frequently never seen by anyone other than the playwright.

Record Keeping in Oral History and Verbatim Theatre Work

In oral history practice, information about the interview, which is termed metadata, is collected and entered into a record keeping system. Interviewers will record any information about the interview they deem important to their ultimate goal for the project, including personal details about the narrator (date of birth, parents' occupations, place of residence, education, career, family members and so on). Other information such as the circumstances of the interview, the narrator's relationship to the topic at hand and even technical data about the recording can be documented. Some oral historians create a summary of the interview content which can guide researchers to the interview. Additionally, if the oral history project is archived, the archivists might also require the documented background information about narrators, a transcript of the interviews, a copy of the consent form, information about funding sources for the projects and any other available documentation relevant to the project.

However, in verbatim theatre work, the transcript of the interview is all that is needed for the playwright to produce a script. After the play is written, it is rare for the interview recording or the transcript or any information about the narrators to be entered into a public record keeping system or preserved, either for general or limited access.

After a verbatim theatre interview, the next steps for the playwright are as follows:

1   To transfer the recording file of the interview onto a trusted computer as soon as possible, make copies and save in at least two places – perhaps on your personal computer, a computer associated with the project and the cloud (see OHA best practices for more detailed advice about this step).[1]

2   At the beginning of each transcription, name the person who was interviewed, the person who conducted the interview and what date it occurred. Playwrights can, of course, write up their own reflections and document any part of their own working process if they choose to, but such steps are not necessary for the purpose of creating a script from interview content.

3   To transcribe the recorded interview.

Transcribing the Interview

As in oral history practice, the transcription process of the interviews secured in verbatim theatre is an integral stage of the project. In most plays created from interviews (Recorded Delivery/headphone verbatim being one notable exception) a written form of documentation is essential, since the transcriptions will provide playwrights with the future content of their script. Transcription is a lengthy process, so allow adequate time for this in your project schedule. Even for experienced transcriptionists, a one-hour recording can take five hours or more to transcribe. I transcribe whole interviews but some playwrights choose to transcribe only the excerpts that they consider of relevance and potential use in the final script. If you are short on time and have a sufficient budget, you can outsource transcription to a professional, but I would only advise taking this step in exceptional circumstances. I believe that the time a playwright spends on transcribing is time well spent. Listening closely to the original recording while transcribing it brings me closer to the narrator and the essence of their thoughts. Since the narrator might eventually be a character in the play, this feeling of getting to know them and their voice and intonation a little more informs my ideas concerning theatrical possibilities. The transcription process also provides an opportunity to see which parts of the interview jump out at me as being excerpts that I might want to include in my script.

After I have transcribed an interview, I listen to it again while reading the transcript, and edit it accordingly. Every time I do this, I notice mistakes which I made the first time round but would not have spotted unless I had gone through the whole procedure again. I have also discovered that, rather than listening to an interview from the recorder, when I listen to the interview played back through an earpiece or headphones, I manage to pick up the slightly harder-to-hear passages more successfully. Once in a while though, you will still find it necessary to write '*inaudible*' in an interview transcript, however diligent you have been in your work.

There have been productive discussions in oral history scholarship and practice regarding exactly how faithful to the narrator's speech a transcript should be. For example, the question of whether words like 'um' and 'er' and 'you know' should be included has been addressed and many working in that field believe that it is useful to faithfully transcribe all such iterations since it can help the person who is reading the transcript (who may not have the recording to listen to) to better understand the narrators' meaning. It can also help the oral historian who uses the interview as a means of research.

In verbatim theatre work, however, it is usually only the playwright who works on the transcription process and later reads the written form of the original interview when they are at the point of scripting the play. The playwright will often have been the interviewer, and so I would say that it is up to the playwright to include as little or as much information as they think helpful in the transcript about the *way* that words were spoken; how many 'extra' words were spoken (i.e. the 'ums' and the 'ers'), when and where they appear and what might be regarded as significant pauses. For example, by writing '*long pause*' in the transcription, if the playwright conducted the interview, she may recall how the original narrator behaved at that moment and may also have an idea why there was a short break during their narrative.

Within my own verbatim theatre work, I have found that leaving in many natural expressions can provide me with more alternatives at the point of the scripting process, and even during rehearsals, when I will then have the choice to either include them or omit them. The more attentive the playwright is in trying to accurately reproduce the narrator's words, phrasing and dialect, the richer the quality of the interview material will be at the point of selecting excerpts for the script. But since transcripts of interviews for theatre projects are rarely ever part of the public record, the ultimate decision about exactly how to transcribe lies solely with the playwright.

Reproducing Speech

In whichever country we live or work, we all speak in different ways and with different accents and varying use of language. Sometimes you will transcribe an interview in which the narrator speaks with a very strong accent, which will consequently affect how the words they say are pronounced. In England, for example, it may be the words 'havin' or 'givin' where the final 'g' has not been emphasised. In such cases, you will have to decide whether you will transcribe exactly what you hear, phonetically, or what you think the word your narrator is saying would be, if they had not abbreviated it. Such decisions arise frequently in the transcription process and I would recommend that, where possible, you write what you *hear* the narrator say, rather than the word or the phrase that you might *understand* the narrator to be saying.

In my own plays where I have interviewed narrators for whom English is their second language, I have transcribed their words exactly as they were spoken. I have not edited or corrected them. An example of this is in my transcription of the interview with an Iranian contributor to *Rights of Passage*. The following extract is from the play, and I transcribed the words 'Hamed' (not his real name) spoke to me as I heard them.

HAMED: When I compare girlfriend, a friend who is a girl, and a boyfriend as a friend in childhood, the girl was, you know, for me simply like a sister. But the boy, when he was attractive and handsome, especially if he was older than me, sometimes I had a dream about him. I had a very beautiful bicycle, and in my dream, I lend him my bicycle, and it was one of my favourite hobby that he... I try to say in English, that we are both on one bicycle, and actually he drive the bicycle – not me, but I am at the front.

And it's like somebody support me who is bigger or stronger. He drive, but we're both together, and I could remember that it was very nice for me that sometimes I feel his hug and the heat of his body.[2]

This excerpt ended up as the opening monologue of the play. While certain parts of it are grammatically incorrect, I was keen to use the words exactly as the narrator spoke them, since I felt that their *sense* was perfectly clear and believed that it created a dramatically moving narrative.

There have been times, however, when I have sent excerpts I wished to use in scripts to the narrators, and they have been slightly taken aback at seeing their spoken words captured in document form in a way in which they know is not the most grammatically correct. For example, when a narrator is interviewed soon after they first arrive in a country (as occurred in my play about asylum seekers in the UK), and then, a few months' later, when I send them their excerpts to review, their ability to speak English will usually have vastly improved. In such cases, the narrator will be aware of how the transcribed version of their interview differs from how they now think English 'should' be spoken. In one case, a narrator mentioned this to me, saying that he felt that he was coming across as less well-spoken than how he would have preferred to have been represented. We had a long discussion about the matter, and I finally persuaded him that if the actor used the narrator's original accent during the final production, it would help in the dramatic portrayal of that narrator by making it sound more authentic – something that I believe ultimately occurred in the play. The narrator seemed happy with my argument and, when he attended the show, with how he was portrayed on stage. But for me, this discussion raised an interesting issue concerning representational choices within a script of the original narrators for the play.

Factual Inaccuracies

Within any form of personal narrative, possibilities of factual inaccuracies exist. If you notice inaccuracies during the interview, I would advise you to let them go and allow the narrator to keep talking. The only exception to this is if the narrator is asking you to confirm a particular incident, fact or date which you know to be inaccurate, in which case you may want to offer your own opinion. At the transcription stage, though, if you spot an error that you remember noting during the interview, or if you discover an inaccurate comment that you had not picked up beforehand, you may add a footnote to remind yourself to rectify the error should it be included in the final script.

All memory is fallible and subjective and oral historians have discussed at great length how, when a narrator describes something that may be factually incorrect, their narrative may provide clues about additional meanings of historical experience as well as relationships between individual and collective memory. Such meanings can be explored in depth and may enable a greater understanding of testimony. But, for the purposes of writing a play based on interviews, you will not want any historical facts to be mis-conveyed during the production – whether or not they were stated by the narrator, since this could lessen the potential impact of the piece and might cause confusion to audience members.

Preparing for the Scripting Process

Choosing Which Verbatim Form to Employ in Your Script

As the playwright, you must decide whether your scripted play falls into the category of 'strict'/'pure'/'exact' verbatim (all these terms involve similar processes) or 'massaged' verbatim, or something else entirely. The first category – strict/pure/exact – suggests that the play's text will consist *only* of words spoken in an interview by a narrator. Massaged verbatim describes a form of writing where the script is *based* on interviews with real people but, rather than their exact words being spoken on stage, the 'essence' of their narrative is conveyed by actors.

My own opinion is that the way a playwright chooses to script the interview content impacts the power dynamics within a project. When playwrights paraphrase the narrators' words or dramatically present their own interpretation of something that has been told to them in a way that is not completely faithful to the original version, they are, of course, exerting their editorial and artistic rights, but possibly at the expense of the narrator. My own reason for adhering as strictly as possible to the spoken words of the narrators in my scripts is based on two premises: Firstly, I believe there is something that 'rings true' about hearing the voice patterns, comments, descriptions and experiences, as delivered by the original narrator – the 'real' person – as opposed to either a more fictional narrative or an actor or playwright recreating what they recall a narrator having said to them. And the other argument I make for exact verbatim is that narrators are frequently invited to come to see the play which has been scripted from their interviews. When this occurs, if the content of the script is exact verbatim, they immediately recognise that what they said in the interview is being spoken word-for-word on stage by the actor. I have seen narrators light up when they hear their own words repeated in a performance piece, and I believe it gives them a sense of agency within the production process.

These two points form the premise of my decision to work with what I consider to be 'pure' or 'exact' verbatim theatre, whereby I can tell an audience (in the foreword to a script or in programme notes or in publicity material) that the words spoken during the play were spoken directly to me during the preparatory interviews. In the following chapter, I lay out guidelines for scripting your own play from interviews using the narrators' exact words.

Confirming the 'Heart of the Project'

This is now the time to settle upon the 'heart of the project'. When you first conducted the interviews, you probably had some idea about the theme of the play or at least the subject focus. Now you must craft some of that interview content into a script. Be prepared though to change course if some interesting new material interview content piques your interest. You might also want to re-visit some of the initial notes you made at the beginning of the project, so it may be helpful to now ask yourself:

1   What subject did you want the play to address?
2   What is your own angle or opinion?
3   What do you want the audience to come away with?

The answers to these questions may have altered during the interviewing process, and they may change yet again as the writing process develops.

Your agenda as the playwright, which will have been an important factor and a driving force from the project's inception, will continue to exert its influence upon this stage of scripting. Even when the play is created in a style that is exact or pure verbatim – in that every word in the script was spoken by a narrator – you as the playwright are still the overall editor of the piece and your creative work now consists of identifying interview excerpts which you deem to be useful and relevant to the play and the direction in which you now intend to take the piece.

Notes

1 Oral History Association, "Principles and Best Practices: Principles for Oral History and Best Practices for Oral History," 2009, https://www.oralhistory.org/about/principles-and-practices-revised-2009/.
2 Clare Summerskill, *Rights of Passage* (London: Tollington Press, 2016), 7.

9

SCULPTING YOUR PLAY

From Transcript to Playscript

The next task in creating your play is to select content from the transcribed interviews which you might include in your script. This step may seem a little daunting, but just remember that – unlike a playwright who writes fiction, inventing the content from their own imagination – you already have in your possession all the 'lines' that will finally appear in your play. It is just a matter of working out how the material can be arranged in a way that best advances the creative and ideological aims of your project; deciding who, out of your narrators, will become the principal characters in the piece, and what the overarching storyline of the piece will look like. The three main components of your play that you need to begin to identify, and then develop relate to its:

problematic ?

a   THEMES
b   CHARACTERS
c   PLOT

These areas are addressed in detail below but, before you work through those subjects, it might be helpful to think carefully about where you are now in your process. The brief questionnaire below (in Box 9:1) will remind you of your original goals, sharpen the focus of your aims and ensure that you are fully prepared to begin scripting your play.

THEMES, CHARACTERS, and PLOT

Identifying THEMES

At the point when you conducted the interviews for your play, you probably had some strong opinions about the main subjects or themes that you wanted your piece to address. As the interview period progressed, you will undoubtedly have

BOX 9.1

Q: What are your goals in writing this play? Tick those that apply.

A: To work with a community group or students on a play that addresses a subject which is of interest to them and to other community members or students. ☐

A: To create a professional piece of theatre performed by professional theatre makers, researched and scripted by an oral historian or a playwright who has interviewed a number of people about a particular subject or theme. ☐

A: To create awareness about a matter which you deem to be of political or social importance and to educate audience members about that topic. ☐

A: To motivate audience members to become actively engaged with work relating to issues addressed in the play. ☐

A: Some other reason: (note down your own answer to this question.) ☐

Q: What practical resources do you already have in your possession or need for this next stage?	**Have**	**Need**
A: Recordings of interviews conducted with narrators which are now transcribed.	☐	☐
A: Signed consent forms from the narrators and their contact details.	☐	☐
A: An office or appropriate space to work in as you lay out the interview material at your disposal and settle upon themes, plot and the main characters who will appear in your play.	☐	☐
A: Resources – in the form of other publications to which you can refer for further advice. (See Suggested Reading in **Appendix 6**.)	☐	☐

honed your ideas about how you want to approach these themes dramatically. The task you have before you now, of 'sculpting the play', begins with looking for content within your interview transcriptions that relates to the theme of the play.

If many people spoke about one single subject which you are keen to include in the script, you can highlight all those references, then choose which of the narrators' stories were the most powerful or relevant to the play's theme and what you want the production to say. You can also select several versions of the same event, allowing some of the 'characters' to share differing opinions based on their own personal experiences. If you look for differing views about a subject or event within the transcribed material at your disposal, you can explore how you might like to employ them dramatically.

Many verbatim playwrights find it useful to physically spread out printed versions of the transcribed interviews in front of them. In this way, you can see what the potential source material is and mark up excerpts that seem relevant, which you may later decide to employ in the script. You may want to cut out excerpts from the transcripts as a way of organising your interview content in preparation for scripting.

Identifying themes and related excerpts from narrators can help you clarify the main areas that you want your script to cover, provided, of course, that they align with your own objectives for the piece. In the face of numerous themes addressed by narrators, you will need to decide which are the most important ones and, however interesting or entertaining others might be, you will soon realise that you can't include everything. Your work at this stage is to greatly reduce the amount of interview material, looking for only the most relevant and dramatically powerful excerpts.

As a verbatim theatre playwright, you cannot simply 'make up' the content of your script. By creating a play from interviews – and advertising it as such – you can only employ what has been said by your narrators. While this could, in some ways, be seen as artistically restrictive, it will eventually contribute to the overall power of the piece, especially when audience members fully comprehend that everything in the script was said by a 'real' person. The key point for you as the playwright to understand is that everything you need in your final script is already in the interview material you possess. I have never worked on a verbatim play that has ultimately felt incomplete, either because it lacks certain information or because there were not enough moments of dramatic tension or plot development. It is simply a question of *looking* for this kind of content within the original interviews and using it as productively and creatively as you can.

Finding the Play's Main CHARACTERS

The 'Characters' in the Play Will Be Narrators You have Interviewed

Just as the dramatic content cannot be invented for a verbatim play but must evolve from what has been said in interviews, the characters in your play cannot be invented either, since they will have originally been people you interviewed. Determining who the principal characters are in a verbatim play usually occurs after all the interviews have been completed and, at the scripting stage, you must decide who you want them to be. They will probably include the narrators who related the most relevant or interesting stories and the ones who shared their narratives in the most engaging, moving or even humorous way. This is an area in which fictional drama and verbatim theatre differ substantively in that, as playwrights working with interviews, we actually meet the 'real-life' people who are going to feature in our productions.

RIGHTS OF PASSAGE
When I was researching *Rights of Passage*, based on interviews with lesbian and gay asylum seekers in the UK, I found it quite difficult to line up

potential narrators owing to the relatively niche subject matter the play addressed and the sensitive nature of the stories that I sought. When I did manage to find people to interview, although I did not know the details of their personal experiences, I hoped that they would be narrators whose stories fitted in with my own aims and agenda in creating the play. My intention in writing the piece was to highlight the specific hardships that LGBT asylum seekers face, both in their countries of origin and during their encounters with the UK Border Agency and the Home Office. I was also particularly interested in the matter of lesbian, gay and bisexual asylum seekers having to somehow *prove* their sexual orientation to a judge or Home Office official.

The first person I interviewed was a Malaysian gay man and, as I listened to his story, I knew immediately that he could be a main character in my play. The tale he told me was one that involved knowing that he was gay from a very early age, gaining a scholarship to attend a college in Scotland, supported by a Muslim educational board in Malaysia, and then coming out to some of his fellow students. His sexual orientation was vindictively reported by a fellow Muslim Malaysian student to his funding board and he had his grant withdrawn and was told to return to Malaysia. He decided that he could not do that since he would risk persecution there and, instead, he stayed in Edinburgh, earning money when he could as a waiter and also as a prostitute. Several years later, he learnt that he could claim asylum in the UK based on his sexual orientation. He was eventually successful in doing that and nowadays, he actually works for the UK Home Office because, as he told me in his interview, 'The Home Office gave me my life back'.

I mention this example of Izzuddin, as he was called in the play, to demonstrate how one person's interview can provide a playwright with a 'ready-made' story which already contains a distinctive dramatic or narrative arc. A dramatic arc is when a character or a situation moves from one state to another and change is thereby effected. The dramatic arc of Izzuddin's life story was clear but it was up to me, as the playwright, to decide which excerpts of his interview should be used in the script. For *Rights of Passage*, I finally decided to have three main characters in the play, Izzuddin being one of them, and I interwove their stories throughout the piece.

During the process of conducting interviews, sometimes you will find yourself making decisions about who you arrange to meet based on semi-formed ideas of what you would like your final script to look like. For example, in researching *Rights of Passage*, Izzuddin was the first asylum seeker I interviewed and, after deciding that he was going to be a main character in the script, I then sought out other narrators who came from different parts of the world. To complement and contrast the part of Izzuddin, I decided to look for a lesbian or gay man from an African or Afro-Caribbean country, and a lesbian or gay man possibly from the

Middle East. So, my idea of how the final casting would look was in my mind during the interviewing period, and in that regard, it partly determined the direction of my research. The play's dramatic content therefore came about as a result of a back and forth process of development between my concept of the play and the real stories that I was discovering during the interview process.

The decision about how many main characters will be in your script is often informed by how many actors you have at your disposal in the final production. If you are creating the production with professional actors, financial considerations may limit cast numbers, but an extremely common practice in verbatim theatre is to have a set number of actors each playing multiple parts. In this way, contributions from many narrators can be heard and dramatised in the play. The tour of *Rights of Passage* was funded by Arts Council England, from whom we secured a sufficient, but not a huge budget which allowed us to pay the wages of four actors who ended up performing more than forty characters in the play, albeit some who only spoke a line or two. However, a year later, a student group at Cambridge University working with the charity Oxfam (a charitable organisation focussed on the alleviation of global poverty) staged the play with a cast of ten performers, which meant that the actors did not have to each play so many different parts. Both productions created interesting staging options but, whatever your play, its subject matter, or where you intend to perform it, deciding upon your final cast size is a necessary step at the writing stage of the production process.

When you have settled on the main characters around whose stories the script will revolve, you then have to work out how many minor characters appear in each scene. Again, this will be related to cast numbers, but remember that, although actors can play multiple roles, if, for example, there are only two men in a cast, but four in your intended scene, this may be problematic, unless the female actors take on the male roles. Be alert to such possibilities during the scripting process.

Also, look for ways in which you can demonstrate the dramatic *journeys* of your main characters during the play. *Rights of Passage* followed a chronological path whereby we first met the main characters in their countries of origin; we saw examples of the prejudice they suffered there on account of their sexual orientation; we then followed them as they travelled to the UK and witnessed their encounters within the asylum system. Towards the end of the piece, we learned that two of the three main characters had attained asylum, but that one was still awaiting a decision – thereby creating a dramatic 'cliff-hanger'. In this way, verbatim theatre work can resemble fictional forms of theatre, whereby an audience is able to meet the characters at the beginning of their story, follow them as they go through certain experiences and see what their situation is at the end of the play. But remember that not all questions posed in the script need to be fully resolved by the final scene, if you feel that this choice would aid the play's dramatic structure.

Option of Composite Characters

One option to the playwright having to settle upon just a few main characters in the piece based on which narrators told the most interesting or relevant stories during their interviews is to create 'composite' characters. This means that characters in your play could be called by any names, but the 'lines' they deliver are made up from sections of different narrators' stories. When working in this way, the play can still be called verbatim, in that the exact words of the narrators are still being employed, but dramatic license allows for the creation of a character who delivers lines originally spoken by another person or several other people.

ONCE UPON A LIFETIME

I wrote a play for the UK reminiscence theatre company, Age Exchange entitled *Once Upon a Lifetime;* which was based entirely on interviews with older working-class women living in South East London. Several of the women told me stories which were in many ways similar to each other. The narrators had generally left school when they were fourteen and had gone to work in the service industry as maids for rich families. They later married and had children. Another experience some of them shared was that their husbands had left home to fight in the Second World War and, during that period, the women had raised their children alone, continuing to work, while also helping the war effort in various ways. The husbands who eventually returned, were often met by young children who did not always recognise them as being their fathers, because they had been away so long.

After hearing so many stories with narratives reflecting similar life experiences, the artistic director of Age Exchange, Pam Schweitzer and I decided that, rather than creating a play which would have several different women narrating parts of their own life stories, the piece would feature one single women, Elsie, who was, in fact, a 'real' person, still working as a cleaner at the age of eighty-two. We interviewed her several times and included many of her life experiences in the piece, but we also employed stories in the script that had been told by the other narrators and these were given to the main character to perform. In this way, we created a composite character, based on a real person.

After this play was performed in residential homes, sheltered housing, and day centres, mainly to other older women who had lived through the same time period as Elsie – the central character – after the show, many audience members told us that they felt as if they were watching their own stories being enacted and hearing about experiences that they had also gone through. This was the first time that I have worked with the idea of a composite character in a play and it turned out to be a very effective theatrical device, resulting in a particularly memorable production.

Seeking the PLOT

Once you have identified the themes of your play and have a good idea about the principal characters, you need to work on developing the plot of your script. The plot consists of all the main events that are addressed in the piece which are presented as an interrelated sequence. Working out the play's plot therefore basically entails deciding where you will start the piece, what happens to the characters the audience will meet and how you want the play to end.

Where to Start and How to End Your Script

In real life, a person's story or even the story of a community is a continuous one. It will have begun long before you met the narrator who talks to you about their experiences and continue for them long after you have conducted the interview. But for a play, there must be a starting point where you (and the audience) jump in and the subject matter and/or the main characters are introduced. Figuring out where to start is one of the most difficult decisions to make. It can sometimes be a little easier if the plot or the direction of the play is a clearly chronological one, where you could begin at, or just a little while before, the time that the events that the play addresses occurred, and provide some background about the community or the individuals involved. In a play that follows a chronological timeline, the content can then build up to the main event (if the interviews have addressed one particular occurrence) and the play can conclude when the whole story has ended.

Many verbatim plays, however, rather than focussing on one particular event, have as their subject matter an experience that was shared by several separate narrators who maybe do not know each other. In such cases, you can also look for a timeframe for each individual's story which may be described in the form of:

1   A beginning or introduction – providing information about the character and his or her background or circumstances at the point where we meet them.
2   The middle part of the play – which might involve one or several of the narrators speaking 'out' to the audience or sharing stories with each other about critical areas of their experiences. These narratives can be scripted in dialogue form between cast members whenever possible, rather than just delivered as monologues.
3   The end – winding the play up but letting the audience know, through the words of the characters, what finally happened to them as a consequence of the events or experiences they had been through and also how they felt about them at the time, and in hindsight.

At this stage in your scripting process, you might find it helpful to write a couple of pages about how you think the play could finally look – especially working on ideas about the dramatic arc of the piece. This draft outline might involve making decisions about the main stories that you would like to include and working out which characters will narrate them. You could think about creating either a beginning, a middle and end version of events, or some other kind of order to the stories you are presenting. Then you may want to experiment with how you could divide the piece into scenes. Once you have laid out some possibilities, be prepared to shift the scenes around in a different order and, as you work, you will find that your ideas become clearer. Then look once again through all of the interview content, searching for any other excerpts that tie in with your chosen themes and the play's current direction.

TENSION, CONFLICT and HUMOUR in Your Play

Whatever the playwright's agenda for a piece of verbatim theatre – political, social or ideological, and, of course, artistic – your job is to create a script that will engage an audience on a dramatic level. You must therefore look for dramatic possibilities in the transcriptions and be prepared to work with these sections when structuring the script, rather than simply deciding what story you want to tell and then looking for narrators' excerpts that fit in with that story.

Some of the content you obtain from the interviews, especially when it relates to a matter of social or political concern, when placed in a script, may risk coming across simply as a kind of academic debate, stating people's different views and understandings of the subject or theme addressed by the play. But the form in which you have chosen to present this information is a theatrical one and so you must be constantly vigilant that you do not create a piece which is too dry and merely relates political or social facts. A good piece of verbatim theatre is one where the personal voice is situated at the very forefront of the drama. In order to achieve this, you need to look for incidents in your interviews which convey **Tension, Conflict**, and **Humour**.

Tension is the feeling that is produced in a situation when people are anxious and do not trust each other, and when there is a possibility of sudden violence or conflict. Dramatic tension therefore is literally the suspense of the narrative. But tension is also closely linked with timing so, ideally, tension should be seen to build in the drama. However, if it builds too slowly, it might die in the middle of a scene, and the audience might lose interest at that point, but if it builds too quickly, it may appear ineffective or artificial.

Conflict is the basis of all good theatre and a component of any great story, and it is closely related to tension. In a story, the central conflict is defined as the main opposition, obstacle or complication that characters need to navigate in order for the story to reach a conclusion. So, conflict is the challenge the main characters need to solve to achieve their goals. As a verbatim theatre playwright, you need to look in the interview material for any stories or parts of stories where there is tension or conflict and, when they relate to your subject matter, try to include them in your script.

In interviews provided for a play about asylum seekers, for example, there will often be stories which contain a great deal of both tension and conflict. A narrator's life may have been under threat in their country of origin. The journey to seek safety in a land that is not their country of origin will undoubtedly have been one which was fearful at times, if not dangerous. Narrators might also share experiences of undergoing official interviews with border control agencies who have the power to grant or decline asylum – safety – to the applicant. And audience members will want to know what the final outcome was for the characters who have shared their stories on stage. In plays addressing other subjects which may be less traumatic, the playwright will have to search for moments of dramatic tension or conflict in order to keep the attention of the audience members and make them care about what happens to the characters. Remember, also, that tension can appear in several forms including reflections of anger, shame or confusion. The more experience you gain creating plays from interviews, the quicker you will become at identifying such content.

One of the curiosities of a verbatim theatre script is that it will generally contain narratives which are spoken in the present (since the words in the play were ones which were told to the interviewer) about things that have happened in the past. Because of this, you may have to look extra carefully for possibilities of dramatic tension since, even if you do identify moments of action or crisis, they will be described in the past tense. Narrators will have composed (and recomposed) their memories about a particular event or period as the years have gone by and so the relating of these incidents might not contain the same sense of urgency that fictional events dramatically performed in the present tense can convey. One of the tasks for verbatim scriptwriters and directors is to find ways to heighten the dramatic tension of narrated stories that occurred in the past.

Another type of dramatic content to look out for is when narrators tell humorous stories. With scripts that address matters of a serious or even a traumatic nature, it may initially not seem appropriate to include narratives of a humorous nature, but in my own plays, I have always deliberately sought light-hearted stories that I can employ, precisely *because* much of the subject matter is serious. It is a part of the human condition to look at the funnier side of difficult situations or experiences, and I have found that including excerpts of this kind can provide much-needed light relief during an otherwise hard-hitting piece of theatre.

GATEWAY TO HEAVEN

One of my favourite stories in my interviews for *Gateway to Heaven* came from the narrator, Carol, who explained how, in the 1960s, because she was a lesbian and wore 'drag' (dressed in men's clothing), she was unable to find work. She told me that, because of this, she became a cat burglar! She then described a wonderful incident when she and her gay male friend had climbed up the side of a building and in through a window to an apartment only to find themselves in a sitting room while the owners were watching television. She and her friend decided to simply walk as quickly as they could past them towards the front door, and Carol explained how the couple who were sitting on the sofa just looked up briefly in surprise at them before turning again to what was on the television. As she spoke, I immediately saw staging possibilities in my head for this scene that would reflect conflict, tension and humour all together, and I resolved to include it in the final script and performance.

A Note on Scripting 'Real' People's Narratives

As a playwright, one of the most exciting things about working with other people's words, rather than inventing the script content yourself, is that you will come across ways of speaking that you would never have thought of on your own. Generally, these turns of phrase or expressions will pop out from the transcripts and, when employed in the play, they will be the ones which remind the audience that your piece is a verbatim piece and that the stories the characters are telling were all originally spoken by a 'real' person.

One example of an almost throw away memory that I decided to include in the script of *Vis à Visibility*, a play about experiences of disabled LGBT people, came from Jenny who told me about a time when was admitted to a psychiatric hospital. The words she spoke in my interview with her, which were then included in the script where she acted herself and delivered her own 'lines', were as follows:

> Unfortunately I became really quite mad and ended up back in hospital. I was engrossed in my own madness and at that point I thought I was a moth. It wasn't bad. The difficulty was the inability to fly. I was earthbound, which was a bit of a problem!

Although this was about a time where she had clearly been suffering mentally, I always thought that anecdote to be a particularly delightful and humorous one, knowing that I could never have thought up such 'lines' for a fictional script.

Settling Upon the Final Content and Direction of Your Play

To think carefully about the content and direction of the script, you may want to approach this stage of the process as if you were investigating one or several questions:

1   What happened to the people who were interviewed, or what did they make happen?
2   Why did it occur?
3   How were those who lived through it affected?
4   What happened to them afterwards?
5   What can be done in the future?
6   And finally... What is the story I wish to tell?

The following section is about the play *Minefields and Miniskirts*, written by Terence O'Connell from interviews gathered by the oral historian, Siobhan McHugh. After a brief description of the piece, I have answered the numbered questions above, in relation to this production.

MINEFIELDS AND MINISKIRTS

This playscript was adapted by Terence O'Connell from Siobhán McHugh's book of the same name which had been published in 1993, ten years before the theatre production. In July 2004, the play premiered in Melbourne and then toured Australia. McHugh interviewed one hundred women about their role and experience in the Vietnam War, an area of study which had been largely ignored by historians. The narrators included nurses, secretarial staff, journalists, entertainers, and the wives, mothers, and sisters of servicemen. Half of McHugh's interviews were about the war zone and half were based on memories of women on the home front, both during and after the war.

As well as presenting personal testimony, the content of the play addressed the matter of National Service in Australia, since the Vietnam War was the first time that conscripts had been sent overseas to a war zone. The piece also reflects the country's internal discussions about whether the war was justified.

Questions and Answers about the Script's Content and Direction, in Relation to *Minefields and Miniskirts*

1 *What happened to the people who were interviewed, or what did they make happen?*

The narrators were all women who had been impacted by the Vietnam War; so the play was based on their experiences of the war.

2 *Why did it occur?*

Some background information was provided in the play about how the war started, the level of Australian involvement during the war and how the country was divided in its support for the conflict.

3 *How were those who lived through it affected?*

Some of the women interviewed were wives and girlfriends of men who had fought in the war and returned to Australia suffering from post-traumatic stress, a condition which had a knock-on impact on the women who cared for them. Some of the women who had been in Vietnam also suffered from this condition. Some of the women who were interviewed had lost loved ones who had fought in the war and all of the women were changed by their involvement in the war.

4 *How do they feel about the situation now?*

Some women became involved in the anti-war movement which, in turn, led them to re-evaluate women's role in society.

5 *What can be done in the future?*

A play about war will almost always result in an audience assessing for themselves what they believe the benefits or risks of engaging in conflict to be, particularly when troops from their own country are sent to fight in another one.

6 *And finally... What is the story I wish to tell?*

The story that McHugh and then O'Connell wished to tell was one of unofficial and under-documented versions of history. In this way, previously unheard stories in the form of oral histories allowed the playwright to create a theatre piece which increased the amount of coverage of the issues addressed.

Before you begin scripting your piece, apply the questions presented above to your own play in order to help you to firm up its content and direction.

Now we move on to the writing part of the process which, in verbatim theatre, might also be seen as an editing process, since we are adapting passages from the transcribed interviews, rather than writing a fictional play from scratch.

10

SCRIPTING OPTIONS AND TECHNIQUES

The scripting process of a verbatim play is similar to fictional theatre writing, to the extent that the content has to engage the hearts and minds of an audience. Most plays, of any kind, will address one or more main themes, and will have one, or a few, principal characters whose journeys the audience follows closely throughout the piece. As discussed in the previous chapter, there will also be moments of tension, conflict and humour. But it helps to note the ways in which fictional and verbatim theatre writing diverge. This chapter outlines those differences and addresses some of the challenges of writing a play from interview transcripts. It also provides advice on how to structure your script and identifies decisions you must take during the writing process that impact the final production in the form of performance logistics and also artistic and ethical representation.

Decisions about Representation

As a verbatim playwright, you have to make important choices about faithfully representing the words of the narrators while also trying to attain your artistic goals. You will need to select interview excerpts which inform the content of the piece and advance the dramatic narrative, and you have to decide which characters will speak which words – a step that involves knowing who in your cast is available and able to take on certain parts in the play. These decisions are ones that are both creative and practical.

For example, if you want the play to be a two-hander (a piece with a cast of two actors), then you must decide whether the two actors are to be male or female. If both are to be female, then you will probably find times when male characters appear, or are mentioned in the script, such as someone's father or brother, or another male role that is integral to the story. In such cases, you will have to ask yourself questions such as "Will the female actor then play the male role?" If you don't want this to occur, then your whole play will either have to not have any men in it who say anything, or you could come up with some theatrical device whereby they are still able to be heard, perhaps in the form of a pre-recorded voiceover.

Similarly, if your play has characters who are all of the same ethnicity, or are differing ethnicities, then choices around which actor plays which character will again arise. For example, your cast may consist of four actors and the text of the play may include stories provided by narrators who are white European and Afro-Caribbean. At the point when the actor playing the Afro-Caribbean narrator describes an event which occurred in his childhood and other characters are needed to help act this out, do the white actors play the part of the Afro-Caribbean roles? And if so, what are the implications, both dramatic and political, of this choice of representation? These are decisions which you must make at the writing, rather than at the casting, stage of your production.

(For an example of a play where cross-race and cross-gender casting is employed, see *The Line,* by Gina Shmukler in **Chapter 14**.)

Creating Scenes

Dividing your script into scenes is helpful for a number of reasons. First, short breaks between scenes provide breathing space in the action for both cast and audience. Scene divisions are also useful to the director and actors simply as points of reference. No hard and fast rules govern the best length for a scene; rather, the divisions are mostly determined by the dramatic flow. The ends of scenes do not necessarily need blackouts, where all the stage lights go off and then come on again to mark a new scene. They can be indicated simply by a pause in the action or the stage lights dimming slightly, during which the actors could move a chair or table into another position on the stage in preparation for the next scene; or music can be played as a sound cue (see below for further discussion about this option).

Intervals, Endings and Titles

Intervals

You must decide upon the approximate length of your play and whether or not it will have an interval. Any play under about seventy-five minutes would probably not need an interval but, if your play is longer, then I strongly advise that you include one. If you do have an interval, then look for ways in which you might be able to build up to a theatrical climax just before it comes. A typical dramatic device at this point could be the introduction of a new but vital piece of information being disclosed about one of the characters. Alternatively, the script could contain an event or development which might deeply impact one or several of the characters. The audience will then be keen to return after the interval to see how the story continues during the next act. Most plays nowadays are no longer than two acts, so at the beginning of the second act, you could choose to resolve the question or tension that you set up just before the interval; or you could move on to new territory entirely.

Endings

Endings of plays, verbatim or otherwise, are also important, and you will have to decide how your play finishes. At this stage in your writing process, ask yourself:

1   What questions have been answered during the course of the play, and which questions have been left unanswered?
2   How do you want audience members to feel as they leave the theatre?
3   If you have seen your play as a way to highlight an issue, do you think you have covered that issue sufficiently and, crucially, in a way that is dramatically engaging?
4   Do you think that your audience now has a deeper understanding of the issue raised in the play?
5   Do you intend your play to create a call for action from audience members about the issue it addressed? Or do you simply want to leave them with the bare facts of the matter (or as near as you have been able to represent them) and let them think about the subject in their own time?
6   If you have used your play as a way to pose a question, have you successfully achieved that?

Title

Your play will need a good title. You may not have started the interviewing project with a particular title in mind, or not even have thought of one by the time you begin the scripting process, but at some point, you need to settle upon a strong title for the piece. When you have some possible ideas, ask friends or colleagues for their reactions to your suggested titles in order to pick the one that will be the most popular, descriptive, appealing, catchy or intriguing.

Possibilities around Juxtaposition

The dramatic juxtaposition of different thoughts, events or memories (placing them close together or side by side, especially for comparison or contrast) is an effective technique in verbatim theatre scripts. It opens the door to a theatrical portrayal of different understandings of an event, and it can present opposing arguments relating to a matter being addressed in the play. In essence, this scripting technique is a way of presenting interview excerpts in dialogue with each other.

The excerpt below provides an example of dramatic juxtaposition from *Gateway to Heaven*, based on interviews with older lesbians and gay men, that conveys varying opinions from several narrators about their views on sport, in relation to their sexual orientation.

CAROL: If you were a little bit different, if you read – especially me going and getting Freud from the library – and if you took an interest in the arts, which I did, whereas most girls were just shagging their boyfriends and dancing. I liked boys to play games with, football, that sort of thing, but not to go out with.

COLIN: At my school we had to play rugger whether you liked it or not! I hated rugger. It was a vile revolting idiot sport.

ROSIE: I was very good at sport.

GERARD: God, how I hated it! Rather be doing reading or whatever.

ROSIE: I think I was probably in love with my P.E. teacher.

COLIN: I couldn't hit a tennis ball or play cricket to save my life.

ROSIE: And then I went to a girl's P.E. college and I thought I was bound to find someone there that I could talk to.

GERARD: Football's such a brutish game. I was absolutely useless at it, and I just knew I was different from the other boys.[1]

When this scene was staged, the characters threw a ball between them as they spoke their lines, some (the women) throwing and catching it enthusiastically and competently and others (the men) finding the whole exercise somewhat repugnant! Although the narrators' comments do, in fact, verge on the stereotypical, they were the exact words that were narrated in interviews and setting them in juxtaposition with each other made this part of the script and the information imparted (combined with the ball throwing) somewhat humorous and more interesting, dramatically, than it might otherwise have been.

Timelines and Chronology

A play does not always need to follow a chronological timeline. As the playwright, you have the creative freedom to present excerpts of the interviews you have secured in whatever way you choose, as long as you remain faithful to the content of narrators' words. Feel free to experiment with any form or idea that occurs to you and see if you can make it work dramatically in a way that presents the interesting and exciting stories in the transcribed interview content and secures the audience's attention.

There is one area of verbatim theatre writing unique to the form, to which you must pay attention at this stage of your scripting process. The narratives in your interviews will have been spoken in the present, even though all incidents related by the narrators happened in the past and, in this way, we already encounter a break in the logic of the timescale of the drama. One way of working with this is for the actor/character to speak 'out' to audience members as if they are, in fact, the interviewer receiving the story that is being related.

When a past event is mentioned, that incident can be narrated by the actor, turning alternately to the audience and other members of the cast, with some of the story being acted out on stage. Another way that narrators' stories can be presented is through 'flashbacks' of events that happened in the past being dramatised on stage. In this way, we can time-travel through the narrators' lives but still be with the characters now, in the present, as they reflect on past experiences. Many of the decisions around staging and delivery of lines will take place during the rehearsal room as the director and the actors explore dramatic possibilities but, during the scripting period, the playwright will also have to consider theatrical options relating to this matter.

One of the finest dramatic possibilities available in verbatim theatre is for a character to basically tell the audience a good story. This can often begin with an actor explaining exactly where the drama is set and then developing the narrative from that point onwards. For example, an actor may say: 'During my childhood, that would have been in the Seventies, every summer, me and my mum and dad would stay in a caravan by the coast for a week'. The actor could deliver this line 'out' to the audience (rather than to a fellow actor) and then turn to the other actors on stage who play the parts of the parents, sitting perhaps 'by the sea' with a thermos flask and wearing coats and scarves (if the play is set in England!).

Another option involves taking your chosen stories from the transcripts and laying them along the same timeframe as each other, even though the events might have happened to the different narrators at completely different times.

RIGHTS OF PASSAGE

In *Rights of Passage*, we hear accounts from three main characters who all sought asylum in the UK. In reality, one of their stories (Izzuddin's) is historic, in that he gained asylum and refugee status over twenty years before I interviewed him. Another of the stories, about Hamed – the Iranian gay man who sought asylum – occurred a couple of years before my interview with him. And the third 'character', a lesbian Ugandan (Miremba) was still in the asylum process at the time that I was writing the play. I made the decision to theatrically present these stories alongside each other and did not state that one happened much longer ago than the others.

Working with Monologues

When you lay an oral history interview transcript next to a theatre script, you will notice they are structured in a very similar way. In the case of an interview transcript, you see the names of the interviewer and narrator followed by the words they spoke. In the case of a theatre script, you see the name of each character followed by their lines. Hopefully, in the interview transcript, the narrators' responses will be far lengthier than the questions or comments made by the interviewer but, when searching for material to include in your play, your focus will be on what was said by the narrator rather than by the interviewer. If you find that the narrator spoke about a matter which you want to include in your script, one obvious way to employ their narrative is to omit any questions or comments made by the interviewer. This will leave you what appears to be a monologue. If you follow this procedure with all the interview material, you will then have a series of monologues from which your play can be created. However, these will now consist of one or several narrators speaking, seemingly without interruption and often at some length, about the subject the play addresses or about a particular personal experience. The challenge for you is to work with such content in a way that creates an interesting script and an engaging final production.

Direct Address

A common theatrical device used by verbatim playwrights when working with monologues is for the character in the play to speak 'out' to the audience, rather than to a fellow actor/character as is usual in more fiction-based theatre. Speaking out to the audience breaks the 'fourth wall' of more traditional forms of theatre, where the audience understands they are watching an action that takes place without their presence being acknowledged. This style of direct address was frequently employed as a dramatic device throughout the twentieth century in forms of propagandist, documentary and verbatim theatre. Consequently, its use in theatre created from interviews which address political or social matters, voiced by actors who represent those who historically may not have been given a platform from which to speak, makes sense, both ideologically and artistically. One outcome of the device of direct address is that the audience is invited to share the role of the interviewer.

STILL LIFE

Still Life is a testimonial play written by Emily Mann, first performed in 1981, about how the Vietnam War affected three lives: a Marine veteran, his estranged wife, and his mistress. In her playwright's notes, Mann informs us that: 'The characters speak directly to the audience so the audience can hear what I heard, experience what I experienced'.[2] The narrator-now-actor is telling her story directly to the audience, which has an added impact of engaging audience members in a deeper and more immediate way than if they were simply watching characters in a fictional piece of theatre speak to each other. This form of direct address, as employed in Mann's testimonial theatre, can also be used by verbatim playwrights whose intention is to raise awareness about a particular subject or concern. The narrative delivered out to the audience enhances the sense of urgency about the subject matter and creates a bond between audience members and the character who is speaking to them.

William Shakespeare's plays contain some of the greatest soliloquies even written, delivered 'out' to the audience rather than to other characters, but these are almost always interspersed with longer scenes of action and dialogue which drive the plot forward, and they are also fictional narratives. One of the main challenges for verbatim theatre writers creating a script which mainly consists of actors delivering monologues is to find ways where this does not become repetitive as a dramatic device or regarded as a theatrical limitation. It is therefore of critical importance to explore additional ways, other than direct address, of employing interview excerpts in your script. One device used by verbatim playwrights during the scripting process or developed by the director during the rehearsal period is for the characters to share their stories with each other on stage. In this way, the narrators' telling of their experiences, as spoken in their interviews, is witnessed by another character or characters on stage, rather than being told directly out to the audience. An example of this might be a scene where the characters share stories with each other about their drug or alcohol addiction in a support group setting. The set and scenery could depict a community or church hall, and the characters in the play might be sitting in a semi-circle, speaking their lines to each other, but in a way that the audience has a clear view of them.

Creating Dialogue from Monologues: Secondary Dialogue

Another means of avoiding the creation of a script which only contains monologues is to look for 'secondary dialogue' which involves generating dialogue from one monologue. For example, in some interviews, narrators might tell you a story in which they refer to different characters in that story. They may say something along the lines: 'He said ... then I said ... then he said to me ... so I said to him...', and so on. Look out for any natural 'conversations' of this sort in your interview transcripts since this would be a very good place to start creating a scene involving secondary dialogue which still uses the exact words spoken by the narrator but allows other characters to enter into the story.

Example 1: Scripting *Gateway to Heaven*

My play, *Gateway to Heaven*, was produced in 2005 and toured twice nationally in the UK. Below are some excerpts from Carol's transcribed interview, followed by an example of how I scripted dialogue from her monologue and introduced other characters in the dramatisation of her narrative. Carol was the ideal contributor to a verbatim theatre play in that she is a natural storyteller. In her full interview I found countless examples of interesting, entertaining excerpts relevant to the play's theme that lent themselves perfectly towards being dramatised (as seen in the previous example about her cat-burglar episode). Many of the narratives she provided were also easy to adapt to a form of secondary dialogue. As she spoke, she would quite naturally set up several extra characters in her stories, who, when I scripted the story, could easily be acted by other cast members. The actress who played Carol could tell parts of the story 'out' to the audience in the form of direct address and then turn to other actors on stage, speaking to them and reacting to lines they spoke as extra characters in her story.

Excerpt from Carol's original transcribed interview[3]

Once, we'd come out of The Boltons [*a pub*]; I'd had a little drink, I'd started to drink by then. Everyone drank, it's the gay scene isn't it? Drink, drink, drink. We'd come out The Boltons, we walked down Earls Court Road. Now, the only loo open was the men's, so me and Rusty – she was in drag as well – go into the male toilet. We'd gone straight into the cubicle of course, wouldn't even look at what they were doing... Some straight guys saw us going in, called the cops, they were always outside the station, and they arrested us. Took us in a bloody white Maria, took us in. Everyone was in uproar, screaming and shouting, because Earls Court was full of mostly queens. They locked us up for the night. We had nothing. We just had what we was wearing. So even if we'd wanted to change and go into court we couldn't. So, we go into court the next morning and the judge was there and the whole gay population has turned up. It was just amazing. It was like something out of a film set. It had got round that everyone had been arrested and everyone took days off work and the court was full of queens and a few gay women. Not many gay women because there weren't that many around then. So, he said to Rusty (her drag name was Rusty, mine was Caz, see), he said 'Miss Rusty Martindale, I see you come from Manchester'. So she said 'Yes your honour'. He said 'Why didn't you go home to go to the toilet?' And I think she said something like 'Well, Manchester is a terrible long way to go for a pee'. And the court was in uproar. It was fantastic! And I think they fined us a pound each. A pound was a lot of money in them days. And I said to him 'There was no women's toilets open, it was the only toilet available and we had to go in there' And he fined us a pound. But when you gotta go, you gotta go, haven't you?

Scene Created from the Interview Content Above[4]

CAROL: And there was this one time, we'd come out The Boltons, and I'd had a little drink, 'cos everyone drank, it's the gay scene isn't it? Drink drink drink. And we walked down Earls Court Road. Now the only loo open was the men's, so me and Rusty...

RUSTY: And I'm in drag and all

CAROL: We go into the male toilet, straight into the cubicle of course.

RUSTY: But some straight guys saw us going in, called the cops and they arrested us.

POLICEMAN ENTERS arresting RUSTY and CAROL

RUSTY: Took us to the station in a white Maria.

CAROL: Everyone was in uproar. There was all this screaming and shouting because Earls Court was full of mostly queens.

RUSTY: They locked us up for the night, we had nothing. We just had what we was wearing so even if we'd wanted to change to go into court we couldn't.

CAROL: The next morning the judge was there and the whole gay population has turned up. It was just amazing, like something out of a film set.

PAUL: It had got 'round that they had been arrested and everyone took days off work and the whole court was full of queens and a few gay women and all. And this judge he says to Rusty:

JUDGE: Your name is Miss Rusty Martindale?

RUSTY: Yes, your honour.

JUDGE: And I see that you come from Manchester.

RUSTY: Yes, your honour.

JUDGE: Now, I have to ask you why did you use a gentleman's public convenience and not go home to use your own toilet?

RUSTY: Well, your honour, Manchester is a terrible long way to go just for a pee.

CAROL: And the whole court was in uproar. It was fantastic!

JUDGE: Silence! Silence in this court! So, ladies, it would appear that there are no mitigating circumstances at all?

CAROL: There was no women's toilets open, it was the only toilet available. And when you gotta go, you gotta go.

RUSTY: And they fined us a pound each.

CAROL: And a pound was a lot of money in them days.

Bending My Own Rules!

In this scene, I took a little dramatic license in creating a few extra words for the Judge when he says 'Silence, silence in this court'. I also added very short lines for Rusty which were not actually spoken by her in her interview, where twice she says: 'Yes, your honour'. This decision was not taken lightly, since I pride my scripts on being as near to 'exact' verbatim as possible, where there is nothing said in the text that was not spoken by a narrator. But I justify my choices by my belief that there always needs to be a little room for rule-breaking in creative work and, in this case, my desire for this scene to work theatrically overrode my original intention that no extra lines be created, and I made the decision to add a few extra ones. So, even though I occasionally make similar minor additions to my plays based on interviews, I can still tell myself and others that the narrators' words are always used 'verbatim – word for word' in the final script. When the scene described above was staged, it was one that was particularly vibrant, fast-moving, highly entertaining and easily dramatised – all thanks to Carol's storytelling expertise.

*Note: There is a short scripting exercise for you to experiment with in **Appendix 3**.*

Notes

1 Clare Summerskill, *Gateway to Heaven* (Machynlleth, Wales: Tollington Press, 2019), 10.
2 Emily Mann, *Testimonies: Four Plays* (New York: Theater Communications Group, 1997), 34.
3 From an interview with Carol in 2005 for my play *Gateway to Heaven*. Excerpts from the interview are published in Clare Summerskill, *Gateway to Heaven: Fifty Years of Lesbian and Gay Oral History* (London: Tollington Press, 2012).
4 Summerskill, *Gateway to Heaven*. (Machynlleth, Wales: Tollington Press. 2019), 18.

11

BEYOND THE SCRIPT

This chapter deals with matters that the playwright must address towards the end of the scripting process but before actors are cast and the rehearsal process begins. In order to inform and complete the writing process, the playwright must be aware of set design and staging possibilities for their piece. As outlined in **Chapter 1**, theatrical options range from a playreading without costumes, set or props, presented to an audience by actors either sitting on chairs or acting script-in-hand, through to a full-scale theatrical production. Having a clear idea, at this stage, of how you envisage the final performance will impact certain aspects of your work on the script.

Some considerations when planning the staging possibilities are as follows:

1   **Budget** – If you know that you will be working with a sufficient amount of funding for your production, then your staging possibilities will inevitably be greater than if you are working with limited finances.
2   **Intended audience** – Do you want the play to reach as wide an audience as possible, maybe in theatres around the country? Or is the piece tailored for a smaller audience who might come from the same geographical locality as those whose stories are being told through the piece?
3   **Performance space** – Again, choices around this matter often depend on the available budget, but you may already know that your play is intended for a particular audience which, in turn, will determine where it will be performed, such as residential homes, community centres or schools.

Set Design and Staging Possibilities

Set design is an important part of the creation of a professional theatre production, whether it be for small-scale touring (when the theatre set has to be relatively small and often fit into the back of a van) or for larger theatre venues, where the set can stay in place for the duration of the theatre run and does not need to be assembled every time the show is performed. It is usual for a set and a costume designer to be brought into the production process sometime before the rehearsal period begins. They will work on design ideas with the director and sometimes with the writer, with the understanding that, during the rehearsal period, further developments relating to scripting and staging might arise which will impact their designs.

Even though you might employ a set designer, if your play is going to be a staged performance (rather than actors simply presenting a reading of the script) as the writer, you still need to think about how the play could work design-wise and about whether your writing choices can realistically be achieved in the final production. For example, do not be too ambitious about setting your scenes in different locations with little time provided in between the changes, if they have no hope of being realised at the design stage.

Stage Directions

A playwright must include stage directions in their scripts that show the director and the actors how the writer intends a whole scene – or one particular moment during a scene – to work theatrically. A simple stage direction might be *'Jean sits on her bed, staring into space'*. Or, a more detailed example might be *'Jean throws a lighted match into a wastepaper bin and watches as the flame catches and smoke begins to fill the room'*. It will be up to the set designer and the director, and the safety regulations in the theatre, to determine if and how such a stage direction can be realised. The director might, of course, decide that the scene would work better if the actor mimed the whole event, or if it was staged stylistically in some other way that represented what was occurring, rather than acted it out explicitly.

THE LINE

At the beginning of her script of *The Line,* first performed in 2012 in Johannesburg, South Africa, the playwright Gina Shmukler provides some information about the origins and purpose of the play as well as laying out some of her ideas about how the production should be designed and staged. Under the heading 'About the Text' she includes the following statement:

> The text is quoted verbatim. The language is punctuated in the script so as best to indicate the rhythm and speech patterns. Where punctuation is missing, the phrase is continuous.[1]

And under the heading 'About the Staging', among other directives, she writes:

> The metaphor of 'crossing the line' is reflected in the design and staging of the play. The wooden chair with steel structure is the *witness* and *researcher* position placed upstage at the tip of a triangle. The wooden bench is the *victim's* position

stage right. The Morris chair is the *perpetrators'* while the arms of the Morris chair is the *politicians'*.[2]

We can see from Shmukler's notes about her text that she had thought carefully about staging possibilities for the play while she was writing it and wanted her ideas to be implemented when the piece was performed. She is also keen that the title of her play, *The Line*, be represented symbolically in the set design and that the title and the concept behind the title be understood as relevant to the dramatic action.

Technical Options for Your Play

In numerous theatre productions, it is quite common nowadays to see images projected onto a backdrop, either at the back or sides of the stage, which enhance the dramatic action or atmosphere. For the Artemis Theatre tour of *Rights of Passage*, when the three main characters were relating incidents that had occurred in their countries of origin (Malaysia, Uganda and Iran), video clips showing street scenes from those places were projected onto a square column which formed part of the set.

In verbatim theatre pieces, sometimes excerpts of the original recordings taken from interviews with the narrators are played at points during the live performances. If you chose to employ this device, make sure to inform the narrators, whose voices will be heard, about this before they attend the show, as it may cause them to be surprised or even uncomfortable. They might, of course, like the idea that their voices are being used in this way, but checking that they feel all right about you making a theatrical choice which involves them beyond having their interview content scripted, which is what they will have originally agreed to, reflects good ethical practice.

Employing Sound Cues in the Play

Since a verbatim play, by its very name, can have a natural tendency to be quite wordy, with interview excerpts continually being delivered by the actors, you may want to look for theatrical devices, other than simply the actors' delivery of narratives, that can enhance the dramatic action in the play. One way for this to occur is by inserting music cues at certain moments in the performance. In every verbatim piece I have produced, I employed several sound cues because I find that the right piece of music, even if it is only a very short snippet, can complement the drama that is occurring on stage. I might choose an upbeat music cue for a dance scene, or a slow love song for an intimate moment, or a culturally specific music cue to take the audience to a country or region where the spoken narrative is situated. In *Rights of Passage*, for a scene set in Tehran, I discussed with the Iranian narrator what kind of music might suit the mood, and together we settled upon an appropriate song.

Live Music during the Piece

You may decide to have actors singing or playing music during the performance. In the UK over the last few decades, there have been many examples of verbatim theatre company members acting, singing and playing instruments during the shows. All of Pam Schweitzer's productions at Age Exchange were performed in this way, as were many of Ivan Cutting's verbatim productions at Eastern Angles (the Ipswich-based small-scale touring company, which frequently draws upon memories of narrators living in the county of Suffolk in the UK). If the songs performed in the show relate geographically, or are age-specific to audience members, or are generally well-known, then the audience members will often join in with the actors. This shared experience can heighten the level of enjoyment and meaning for both the cast and the audience.

HOME

Home by Nadia Fall, is a verbatim piece created from interviews conducted in an East London hostel for homeless youngsters. The residents have been on the streets as a result of a number of contemporary social issues including family breakdowns, gang violence, and unplanned pregnancy. The play was first performed at The Shed, a temporary studio venue at the National Theatre, London, in 2013. The content of the script is partially verbatim (word-for-word interview content) and also includes some fictional content.

One of the most effective aspects of the show is the large extent to which music is employed. Some songs are simply accompanied by acoustic guitar, but the show is also interspersed with Rihanna megamixes and rap numbers. The most striking and mesmerising of all the musical contributions is from a character who does not speak but who, instead, delivers her story through body language and beatboxing. This is clearly a bold, and highly exceptional theatrical choice in a play which aligns itself with verbatim theatre, but the engaging character of Jade is brought to life by twice UK Beatbox champion, Grace Savage and demonstrates to the audience that Jade's story is one that doesn't easily fit into words. It also serves to remind audiences, playwrights and scholars alike that verbatim theatre is continually developing and evolving as a dramatic form.

Songs and sound cues, musical or otherwise, can provide well-needed breaks or changes of atmosphere within the action. In plays which address especially hard-hitting or sensitive subject matters, the audience will be more able to digest the performance if their experience is not merely a white-knuckle ride where they are holding on to the edge of their seats in shock or horror or distress until the final curtain falls. Since verbatim plays often tackle matters of social or political urgency or injustice, considering how to convey the content in a way that is informative but never *too* harrowing or upsetting for the audience is important. Music or other sound cues can fill these moments of stress and tension as well as indicate mood changes, the introduction of a new character, or a transition from one topic to another. Effective use of the right music at the right time can contribute greatly towards audience members still being able to honestly say afterwards that they *enjoyed* watching the production.

Working with Narrators after the Interview Stage

Sending Narrators 'Their' Excerpts

A common practice in oral history is for the interviewer to return the interview transcript to the narrator for review and approval, ensuring that the narrator's intention and voice have been accurately conveyed. In verbatim theatre, this is not a standard practice and, although some theatre makers operate in this way, it is not automatically assumed that the narrator will be consulted again by the playwright after the interview.

When I have completed a script, I always send the narrators the excerpts of their interviews that I would like to use in the play. At this stage, I do not require them to fill in another consent form, since they have already agreed to have parts of their interviews included in the script, but I do ask them if they are happy for me to include the excerpts I have selected. There has only ever been one incident where a narrator told me that she did not want me to employ the excerpts I sent her. This occurred because I had employed the real name of her ex-husband (which she had used during the interview) and, on seeing the excerpts, the narrator asked for her ex-husband's real name to be removed, a request which I immediately agreed to and we settled upon another name for him.

I believe that contacting narrators about which excerpts of their interview you wish to employ in the play is both respectful and also an action which affords them a degree of agency in the production process of the play. It allows them to reflect upon what they initially said and to consent, once again, to the use of their interview excerpts, now understanding in a far clearer way how their words will be used in the creation of script.

I have noticed that sometimes people who work, either in what might be regarded as high profile professions (politicians, barristers, head teachers, local or national policy makers, for example), or narrators who are particularly aware of legal implications often pay close attention to the fact that the words from their interview will be spoken in a public arena. They also realise that they, as narrators, may be identified as the original speakers. Other narrators might not show so much concern about exactly what the playwright intends to do with their interview content. Ethical vigilance must be applied in equal measure with narrators from all backgrounds and professions, but if a narrator asks you detailed questions about the final script or performance, and wishes to know more about exactly how their contribution might be employed, then you must try to see their interest not in any way as a disruption to your work, but very much a part of it. As playwrights, we have full control over interview content which will represent the narratives of real people, and we must work respectfully and empathetically with narrators who have concerns about how we portray them. Within my own working practice, the basic rule around these matters that I follow has always been: 'Do as you would be done by'.

Notes

1 Gina Shmukler, "The Line" (2012) written and directed by Gina Shmukler (unpublished).
2 Shmukler, "The Line."

12

REHEARSAL AND PERFORMANCE

You are now at the stage where you need to think about some practical requirements in producing your play. These include finding:

- a rehearsal space
- a performance space
- actors for your show

The Rehearsal Space

Your actors will need a rehearsal space. You might be able to find a suitable room at no cost, but often you will have to pay for one and must factor this expense into your budget. The rehearsal space needs to be large enough for the director and/or writer to work with the actors, and it can sometimes be used to store costumes and props that the actors require both during the rehearsal period and, later, for the final show. If you are very fortunate, you and your company members might be able to rehearse on the stage of the theatre where your show will be performed.

The Performance Space

If you are working with professional actors and have a sufficient budget to pay for a set and the wages of your company members, one option is for the show to be 'programmed' by a theatre in your local area or even by several theatres in different locations. Programmed, in this sense means that the theatre agrees to having your play performed there, helps you to advertise it and arranges a financial 'split' with you, whereby you (or your company or group) and the venue divide the box office income on an agreed percentage. Financial arrangements with theatres often take quite a while to put into place, and some theatre companies begin working on their tour bookings up to eighteen months or two years in advance of the first rehearsals for the show.

An option to being programmed by a theatre is to hire a theatre space on a daily, or even an hourly basis (if you are only going to be using the theatre for one performance). Hiring a theatre can sometimes work out a little more expensive than the production being programmed, but this is not always the case, for example, if your shows are very well-attended and you make enough money back from ticket sales to cover your costs and make a profit. Such an arrangement does, however, usually mean that your theatre company, rather than the venue, has the main responsibility of publicising the show and securing audiences. Booking arrangements with theatres inevitably vary from venue to venue and country to country.

Performing your production in a non-conventional theatre space is another alternative. This option continues the tradition adopted by the earlier verbatim theatre companies in the UK, who, depending on the subject matter addressed in the piece and the target audience, would present their shows in venues such as community centres, village halls, residential homes, sheltered housing, hospitals, schools or Trade Union headquarters. Many small-scale theatre companies still work this way, and verbatim theatre pieces which are based on specific events or issues and targeted to particular audience members often work well in smaller spaces. These venues are also conducive to creating an intimate atmosphere whereby actors dramatically share stories or memories with the audience, who may then, in turn, be encouraged to participate at the end of the piece in a facilitated discussion. Another advantage to performing plays in such venues is that you, or whoever produces and markets your production, can liaise well in advance with those who run these venues to ensure that groups are targeted who will have a particular interest in the subject matter addressed by the play.

Finally, if you are working with students in a school or college, you may already have access to a performance space which would be suitable for your purposes. It could be a hall or even a theatre venue, and your cast and projected audience numbers will usually determine the size of the performance space required.

Actors for Your Show

You will probably have decided at the beginning of your project whether you intend your play to be performed by professional actors or by members of a community group or students with whom you may already be working in some capacity.

STAYING OUT LATE

Staying Out Late is a play that I created from workshops with older lesbians, bisexuals and gay men addressing their fears and concerns about how they might be treated on account of their sexual orientation when receiving care in later life, either at home or in residential care. After six workshops held over six weeks, during which we addressed the subject matter through group discussions and themed improvisation, the final show was enacted by the workshop participants, joined by two professional actors. For a few of the scenes, I interviewed some of the participants who agreed to act excerpts from their own interviews. I subsequently transcribed parts of their interviews and, during the rehearsal period, they were given back those excerpts to learn and then perform.

In hindsight, my thoughts on working this way are that, although it was certainly a powerful and engaging experience to hear an actor speaking their own 'lines', telling their own story, this theatrical device was also accompanied by certain challenges. It was difficult for the participants, who were not professional actors, to learn and relate the exact words that I had scripted for them. During the performances, I noticed that they seemed happier to tell their stories in a different, more improvised version than the one they had tried to learn. This may have been partly to do with memory issues, but my feeling was that, on some level, it didn't make much sense to them to learn lines when it was their own story they were telling! Improvisation is a powerful dramatic form, but it is, by its very nature, unstructured and therefore, some of the content the writer may want to convey can easily be lost during performances. Furthermore, improvisational theatre is not verbatim theatre as defined in this publication.

Choosing actors to interpret and perform the interview content in the script is one of the first tasks faced by the director. Working with either amateur or professional actors, the director (or you, if you are the playwright and director) must hold auditions to find strong actors, able to perform verbatim theatre and suited to play characters in the script. Some directors look for actors who physically resemble the original narrators; others look for actors who resemble what they see as the character who the playwright has 'written' in the script; others simply select actors on their artistic merit. Verbatim theatre is frequently presented as an ensemble acting type of performance, where all of the cast members are active in many of the scenes, playing many different roles. This means that they are often required to attend all of the rehearsals, rather than be called in only for 'their' scenes, as is more common with fictional pieces of drama. The kind of actors you seek must therefore be willing and able to work in this collective way.

As mentioned previously, when a script has been created from interviews, more often than not it will contain monologues which the actor will, at times, be required to deliver 'out' to the audience. Many professional actors might not have worked in this style before; so, to make best use of the audition time, they could be asked to read from the script, performing passages in this way. I have found that actors who have had previous experience working in smaller, non-traditional theatre venues are often comfortable in breaking the 'fourth wall' and speaking directly to the audience. Similarly, I have noticed that auditionees who have worked as stand-up comedians or cabaret performers adapt relatively easily to this breaking of the fourth wall.

The Rehearsal Period

During the rehearsal period, actors learn their lines and work with the director on their character development and on staging options. The length of the rehearsal period can depend on a variety of factors which include how much funding is available and whether the actors are full-time professionals or have other jobs as well. If the actors are balancing their participation in the project with other jobs or studies, whoever produces the play will have to work with a degree of flexibility to secure the amount of rehearsal time required for the production.

Professional actors expect to work five or six full days a week but need to be paid professional rates. The rehearsal period for a full-length show in professional theatre can last anywhere between three and six weeks working full-time. In my opinion, four weeks is generally a sufficient length, but this period will probably have to be longer if actors can only rehearse part-time.

Some of the actors may have experience with verbatim theatre work; for others, this will be their first time. These actors may face certain challenges in playing a 'real' person, as opposed to performing a fictional character created from a playwright's imagination. In verbatim theatre, a point will come during the rehearsal period when either the director or the actor, or both, will make a choice about whether they wish to work in a mimetic style when portraying a narrator or whether they will search more for the 'essence' of the character. A mimetic version would entail the actor trying to impersonate or act exactly like the 'real' person they are playing, talking like them (as heard on the interview recording) and – if they have the chance to meet them – possibly taking on their physical attributes. Seeking the essence of a character, however, might involve never encountering that person in real life or even listening to their voice on the interview, but rather 'finding' the character through the lines of the script.

Some actors will be intensely curious about the person whose lines they are speaking and may ask the writer and interviewer questions about what their characters are like in real life. The actors might want to listen to the narrators' full interviews to get a better feel for them or to have the opportunity of hearing their natural speaking inflections, dialect or accent, which will not always be apparent on the printed page. It is usually up to directors to decide whether or not to make the original tapes available for the actors, but sometimes actors make this decision themselves.

During the rehearsal period of *Rights of Passage*, one actor and the 'real' person he was playing made contact with each other through social media and they discovered that their life stories, as gay Malaysian immigrants to the UK, had been very similar (I'm still not sure who approached who initially!). The actor asked the narrator about a particular section of his story in the play because he believed some additional information about the original narrator and what he had been going through would help him in his acting process. Their meeting went very well and, after speaking about the specific incident, the actor felt that it had greatly informed his understanding of the role. After the production finished, the narrator told me that he had appreciated meeting the actor during the rehearsal period and valued being involved in the production process in this way.

But not all actors want to meet the 'real life' characters they are playing and not all narrators will wish or need to meet theatre company members. Some actors and narrators may want to meet each other only *after* the show has been performed. One of the actresses in *Rights of Passage* who played the part of the Ugandan lesbian, Miremba, met the narrator she was portraying after the first night of the show, an encounter which proved to be deeply meaningful for both of them. Decisions about when and whether the theatre company members meet the characters they play are taken variously by the director, the playwright and the actors themselves, and, of course, by the narrators who must always feel comfortable with such an arrangement.

'Am I Me Now, or Them, Then?'

In addition to the need for actors to be able to work with the 'direct address' technique, the nature of many verbatim theatre scripts means that actors will also be faced with theatrical transformations of time and place during their performances, which generally do not occur as frequently within fictional forms of theatre. The most common example of this is when an actor is required to deliver a speech during which they are talking in the present about an event that occurred in the past. An actor new to verbatim theatre might ask the director, "So, if I'm speaking in the present, but about the past, am I playing the character who is me now, or me then?" This question relates not only to the actor's understanding of the conceptual premise of the play, but it can raise an additional question about whether the actor telling stories in the present (or the 'now') is an older version of themselves when they are acting past events. I have found that, rather than over-thinking this process, actors often resolve these matters on their own during the rehearsal period as they work with the script. Guided by the director, the appropriate interpretation and delivery of their lines then becomes clear to them.

A director will usually look for ways for actors to tell some of the stories being enacted as if they are happening in the past and some of them in the present. At other times, the actor is clearly reflecting upon an event and might be required to act whatever emotion the original event brought up for them. But this is exactly what the rehearsal period is for: searching for, and then settling upon theatrical methods of expression and forms of staging that work for the actors and enable the play to engage an audience and create the greatest dramatic impact possible.

Workshopping issues to do with memory can sometimes be beneficial during a rehearsal period. In pieces that I direct, one of the exercises I conduct with actors is to ask them to pair up and tell each other stories about a significant childhood memory and then have the person who was the 'listener' tell the story they heard back to all the other company members. Through this exercise, both the listener and the actor-narrator realise just how important correct repetition and interpretation is for someone who shares experiences that are dear to them. Sometimes the listener is more concerned about relating an exact version of the actor-narrator's story back to the others than the actor-narrator is! I recommend this exercise to all verbatim theatre practitioners, since it contributes towards a greater understanding of the narrators' experience and role in the production.

Feedback and Involvement of Narrators

The value of narrators who contribute their stories to a verbatim playwright is immeasurable. Without the narrators, there would be no script and no final production. But their involvement and role within verbatim productions has not, to date, been widely examined within theatre scholarship. Historically, it has often been a common practice in small-scale verbatim theatre processes for narrators to be invited to rehearsed playreadings, where their feedback is sought, valued and occasionally used by the playwright to help rework parts of the script. Then, at the point when the final production is staged, narrators are invited once again to attend the performance and, if post-show discussions are held with the cast, the playwright, the director and sometimes professionals who work in the area addressed by the play, narrators can also be asked to participate.

13

OVER TO YOU, NOW!

The focus of this book on the connections between oral history projects and verbatim theatre has demonstrated that the bridge between these two disciplines is a relatively easy one to cross. Understanding the fundamental differences between the two practices is also important. As an oral historian, you may have worked for quite a while in ways which have become second nature to you – keeping meticulous records, striving for a degree of impartiality in the interview situation and making sure that every single word spoken by both the interviewer and the narrator is preserved fully intact for the historical record. As you now move towards taking up your role as a theatre practitioner – becoming, in effect, a playwright – you will understand that some of the working processes you have followed as an oral historian do not necessarily apply when creating a play from interviews. This is not to say that there is a 'relaxing of the rules' in verbatim theatre processes but, it simply highlights the different outputs in each area of work. Now you are ready to call yourself a theatre maker and are equipped with the basic knowledge of how to create a verbatim script and present it on stage.

Theatre practitioners who have read this book will, hopefully, have been both intrigued and informed by the connections explored between plays based on interviews and the practice and theory of oral history. As a theatre professional, you already understood about working with scripts, theatre venues, actors, directors, designers and other company members and, as a playwright, you might have already produced a verbatim play. Now, you are aware of discussions in oral history scholarship that are relevant to your theatre work.

The close connections between the two disciplines are mainly discussed in the earlier chapters of this book but are also mentioned, intermittently, throughout the remaining ones. My intention has not been to explore these

connections merely as an academic exercise but, rather, to deepen the understanding of the work of verbatim theatre and oral history practitioners and to
inform and enhance both practices. More specifically, and quite intentionally,
I call upon verbatim theatre practitioners who always strive to create works of
dramatic merit and often seek to use their artistic talent to inform and educate
audiences to turn to existing debates within oral history in an attempt to hone
their own working methods, particularly in relation to matters of an ethical
nature.

In theatre productions which stage the testimonies of 'real' people, ethical
concerns are inevitably foregrounded and I have proposed some ethical guidelines that I strongly encourage verbatim theatre makers to follow. In **Chapters
4** and **5,** addressing ethical considerations, several of the steps I suggest for
your own verbatim theatre work extend significantly further than most playwrights' concern that they 'do no harm' to narrators whom they interview and
portray as characters in their plays. The steps I outline require that verbatim
theatre practitioners purposefully identify ethical concerns that arise within
their work. This process includes examining power dynamics in the interview
situation, exploring theatre makers' own agendas in creating the play, reflecting upon possibilities of appropriation or exploitation and recognising both the
risks and the benefits that narrators can experience during their involvement in
verbatim theatre productions.

Armed with an understanding of some of the ethical implications of theatre
work created from the stories of 'real' people, and a basic outline of the practi-
calities of creating a piece of theatre, it is now time to embark upon your own
verbatim play.

Two weeks before I submitted this manuscript for publication, I had the
great fortune to see a new play in London, created from interviews with homeless people in the UK. Not only was it a piece based on interviews – which initially drew my attention – but it also addressed a subject matter that piqued my
interest, homelessness, which is such a topical concern in our society. Through
personal narratives, the play provided much information about the issue and, in
that way, satisfied my own desire to leave the theatre knowing more about this
important matter than I did when I arrived. But it was an additional delight to
experience a truly excellent dramatic production. I can honestly say that the
play was one of the finest pieces of theatre that I have ever attended, verbatim
or otherwise.

In a relatively small venue, the set design and the theatrical choices taken
by the theatre company members worked perfectly in the space. All three actors were superb – tackling some of the staging challenges of verbatim theatre
(mentioned previously in this book) with professional expertise, such as alter-
nating between delivering some lines 'out' to the audience and then speaking
others to their fellow performers. At times, monologues that I assumed came
from original interview content were cleverly divided into dialogic exchanges,

and at other points, dialogue material (such as a scene between one of the characters and a staff member of a homeless organisation) was conveyed by one actor playing both characters: a dramatic device that worked extremely well. To me, this demonstrated how a factor sometimes regarded as a theatrical limitation in verbatim theatre – the dramatic presentation of monologues – can be successfully addressed in artistically innovative ways.

After the show ended, it was announced that there would be a short break before the audience was invited to reconvene for a discussion in the theatre space. The Question and Answer session that followed was initiated by the playwright/director who was joined on stage by one of the actors, two women who work for homeless charities and a man who describes himself as a 'homeless artist and activist'. Most audience members returned for the discussion which consisted of questions mainly relating to homelessness, rather than to any choices about the development of the script or the staging of the piece. The playwright said that she was very keen for the production to be seen by a wider audience, particularly by those in positions of power or influence, and she asked if anyone personally knew a Member of Parliament who they could invite to the show! There was a general agreement from the playwright and the other speakers who joined her on stage, as well as from the audience that far more must be done to address homelessness and that politicians and citizens alike must work harder to understand the causes, possible solutions and the lived experience of those impacted by homelessness.

As far as I could tell, none of the narrators were present in the audience, and I had no knowledge of how the playwright had worked with her interview material or addressed ethical considerations involved in her research and practice. But the piece reflected several of the steps in creating a verbatim play that have been discussed in this book: How a playwright or oral historian comes to an idea for a piece of theatre, finds people to interview with experience of the subject matter addressed, approaches a sensitive subject matter in a seemingly careful and respectful manner and then creates a powerful and informative script which is presented flawlessly by the performers. And at the point where some audience members might assume that their theatrical experience had ended, they were then invited to participate in a discussion about the subject matter and left the venue even more knowledgeable about the issue than they had been when the play finished. From comments made in the post-show discussion, it was apparent that many of us were as determined as the theatre makers to go out of the theatre and into the world with the intention of raising further consciousness about homelessness or even endeavouring to affect some form of change in regard to this matter.[1]

This production reassured me that, although various forms of verbatim theatre have been around for several decades, there is absolutely no doubt that theatre makers and audiences alike have a deep and continuing appetite for dramatic representations of personal narratives. The piece showed how the expertise of theatre professionals, when focussed on a subject matter of political and social concern, can, through an alchemistic process, produce a form of entertainment in which personal narratives reach deeply into the hearts and minds of those who are fortunate enough to be in the audience. Sharing this experience with you about recently seeing such a powerful play will, I hope, encourage you to passionately, thoughtfully, ethically and artistically put into practice all you have learnt in this book. I wish you all the joy and fulfilment that your project will invariably bring to you and all those involved – oral historians, theatre makers, future audiences and, of course, those without whom your production would never be possible – the narrators.

Note

1 "No Sweat" was written and directed by Vicky Moran (created alongside members of the LGBTQIA+ ex/homeless community). First performed at The Pleasance, London 2020.

PART IV

Examples of Work by Verbatim Theatre Playwrights and Companies

14

EXAMPLES OF PLAYS CREATED FROM INTERVIEWS

Contents

Introduction

I have selected these examples of verbatim theatre, documentary theatre and oral history performance projects from around the world to illustrate a variety of ways in which theatre created from interviews can be employed as a call to social awareness. This chapter shows how practitioners have used different research, scripting and production methods to achieve their goals.

Like a Family and *The Laramie Project* are dramatic productions based on interviews with hundreds of community members about an event or period of time. They both demonstrate connections between the ways in which playwrights created those pieces and oral history methodology. *Like a Family* provides an example of oral history performance which was an improvised piece of theatre, not scripted in the form of 'exact' verbatim. But the emphasis Pollock and her 'student-actors' placed upon the experiences and the expertise of the narrators in this work is of relevance to verbatim theatre practitioners. I had the pleasure of interviewing Della Pollock about this production and have included some of her reflections. *The Laramie Project*, a play which has previously been mentioned in this book, shows how a community can tell a single story through many voices, a subject which has also been addressed in oral history scholarship.

In examining *Gateway to Heaven*, I illustrate how the insider positioning of a playwright can impact narrators' disclosure in their interviews for a verbatim script (a matter previously discussed in **Chapter 3**). When creating this play, I perceived that the level of trust in me, as the writer, and in the project, increased because I share the same sexual orientation and some of the same experiences as the narrators. *The Line* by Gina Shmukler is a play based on subject matter of a sensitive nature, which partially draws upon narratives provided by vulnerable narrators. In this production, the playwright makes several interesting staging choices concerning the dramatic presentation of violent episodes and flashbacks, which are addressed in this section.

The next two examples examine the work of the UK theatre company, Ice and Fire, and the work of an individual playwright and performer, the renowned American theatre practitioner, Anna Deavere Smith.

In the research period of *Rights of Passage*, another of my plays, I was faced with challenges of working ethnographically with members of LGBT asylum seeker groups and, in discussing this play, I address some of the challenges that entailed. And finally, I turn to *Parramatta Girls*, a piece by the Australian playwright, Alana Valentine, who, while still working closely with narrators she had interviewed, chose to present a semi-fictional version of events in the final dramatisation of the piece.

These examples illustrate a variety of working methods used to create theatre from interviews, and you can select elements from each to adapt to your own project. They will provide you with a deeper understanding of some of the scripting methods and dramatic choices employed by playwrights working in this field.

Example 1: *Like a Family* – Della Pollock

Oral History Performance Which Reflects Michael Frisch's Concept of 'Shared Authority' and Informs the Working Practices of Verbatim Theatre Playwrights

The Project

Like A Family was devised in 1988 in the US by Della Pollock and her students, who then performed in the piece. The production was created from a series of published interviews combined with further interviews conducted by Pollock's student-actors. Pollock refers to *Like a Family* as an 'oral history performance', rather than a verbatim play.

In the 1970s and early 1980s, six interviewers from the Southern Oral History Program at the University of North Carolina (UNC), Chapel Hill, conducted more than 300 interviews with working-class Southerners in the Piedmont Industrialisation Project. The period covered by these interviews ranged from the late nineteenth century, when economic pressures pushed farm families in that region away from the land and toward factory work, to the General Textile Strike of 1934. The interviews were combined with materials drawn from the trade press and letters written by workers to President Franklin D. Roosevelt. They provided a detailed account of cotton mill life, work and protest, and were published in *Like a Family: The Making of a Southern Cotton Mill World* (1987).[1] At the time of the book's publication, Della Pollock, then a young lecturer at UNC Chapel Hill and now a renowned scholar on oral history performance, attended the book signing of *Like A Family* and met the primary author, Jacquelyn Dowd Hall. Hall mentioned that she was eager for the material in the book to somehow be dispersed amongst the community from which it came. Pollock also felt strongly that the content deserved a wider audience and decided to create a theatre piece based on the interviews.

Devising and Rehearsing the Play

Rather than employing professional actors, Pollock invited a group of eleven of her students at Chapel Hill to participate in the project as actors and researchers. These student-actors listened to the audio recordings of the original mill workers and conducted additional research and interviews. They talked to contemporary mill workers and family members of the original narrators. This process of sending actors out into the community to seek local knowledge and history, and for that to then be presented dramatically back to audience members who came from the same population as those who have given their stories, is notably similar to the methods employed by Peter Cheeseman in his Stoke Documentaries.

Pollock had originally intended to write a script version of *Like A Family* for her student-actors but, instead, opted for an improvised performance. Instead of narrating verbatim excerpts of the interview material, Pollock encouraged the student-actors to: 'Stay with the gist, with the heart of what has been conveyed'.[2] During the rehearsal process, she asked them questions such as 'What is the ethical and moral thread that is being used to stitch up all the pieces and what are the key images that consequently get emphasised and re-emphasised? Is there a refrain, a point of reception?' She explains: 'I wasn't working with the mimetic style, so the actors were not trying to act the characters or be the characters'. Through this dramatic choice, Pollock felt that she was representing the narrators in a more truthful way than if actors had conveyed their spoken words in an exact verbatim style of production.

The Tour and Audience Response

The students toured the production of *Like a Family* to six mill communities in the Piedmont area of North Carolina. The performance venues ranged from church basements to an American Legion hut to a Union Lodge. Audience numbers varied between 11 and 200, and they consisted of members of the community: former and current mill workers, their relatives, friends of mill workers, community members, children and students. In the performances of *Like A Family,* Pollock placed the audience members who had personal experience of the subject matter as the 'experts' – the teachers – during this theatrical exchange. In the lengthy post-show discussions, the audience was invited by the cast to share memories of the subjects addressed in the piece. This demonstrated that the students were eager to gain a deeper understanding of the history of the mill workers. Pollock explains:

> There were so many ways we built the performance as involving demonstrations of not knowing, of not understanding, of not having previously known, of starting to learn because of the privilege of listening, and of constantly provoking questions that only the people in the audience could answer.

Pollock suggests that the reaction of community members from which the interviews came was: 'That student is hearing my story'. Her understanding was: 'They heard themselves being heard'. In this way, although audience members may have, to some extent, foregone the promise of 'the real' if one understands that term as being an exact repetition of interview excerpts, Pollock's belief is that they were gaining something more in the form of their stories having been fully heard and received by the listener.

Like a Family shows how the stories that theatre practitioners gather in the form of interviews can be redistributed back to the members of a community, whose numbers make up an audience. Narrators in *Like a Family* were seen by Pollock as providing expert witnesses, adding their testimony and experience to the wider canon of historical knowledge and understanding, with the interviewer as the recipient of this generously shared expertise. Through Pollock placing the narrators and their fellow community members as the experts, and the student-actors as those who were eager to learn from them, the project reflected certain tenets of oral history, as later described by Frisch's notion of 'shared authority', whereby oral history is understood as being a joint process of learning and exchange.

Example 2: *The Laramie Project* – Moisés Kaufman and Members of the Tectonic Theater Project

Dramatically Presenting Voices from a Community and Creating Performed Historiography

The Laramie Project is probably the best-known interview-based play in the world. It was the second most produced play in the US 2000–2001 theatrical season and has been performed internationally. Although, in the US, *The Laramie Project* is referred to as a documentary play, in its form it closely resembles the verbatim theatre methods of production that many theatre companies in the UK have employed since the late 1960s, as the script content is largely based on interview material combined with occasional journal entries from the members of Tectonic Theater Project.

Interviewing for the Script

The Laramie Project was created from interviews which examined the reactions of residents of Laramie, Wyoming, to the brutal torture and murder of a gay university student, Matthew Shepard.[3] On 14 November 1998, a month after Shepard was killed, Kaufman and members of his theatre company travelled from Denver to Laramie and began the first of six visits to the town, conducting more than 200 interviews there. The interviews were later edited down by a small group of writers from Kaufman's Tectonic Theater Project, led by Leigh Fondakowski.

The interview excerpts employed in the script cover a wide range of views, not only about the version of events that people recalled after Shepard's death, but also personal opinions on what might have happened between the victim and his attackers leading up to the murder. Some thought that the incident was a homophobic attack, some that it was drug-fuelled, others that it was a robbery gone wrong, and some thought it was a combination of all three of these factors.

Performed Historiography

Because of the social and political significance of this murder, recorded versions of the crime would have been logged in records at police and governmental departments and accounts of the incident would have been found in the transcripts from the trial of the accused. Numerous references to the event would also have been made in newspapers and on TV both on a local and a national level. But the creation of a play which covered Shepard's death in even more detail by interviewing residents about what they thought had happened and asking how they felt about it opened up an even broader discussion, leading to far wider coverage of that event than would otherwise have occurred. This example shows us how a piece of theatre based on interviews can not only produce a dramatic interpretation of events and a springboard for local, national and even international discussion, but can, arguably, provide a version of performed historiography. *The Laramie Project* tells a many-sided tale, compiled from a collection of interviews with a diverse range of people whose opinions about Shepard's murder might never, otherwise, have been sought or recorded.

In this work, we can observe a close connection with oral history projects where narrators talk about the impact of a particular event on themselves and their community. Alessandro Portelli tells us:

> At the core of oral history [...] lies one deep thematic focus, which distinguishes it from other approaches and disciplines also based on interviewing and fieldwork, such as anthropology, sociology, and folklore: the combination of the prevalence of the narrative form on the one hand, and the search for a connection between biography and history, between individual experience and the transformations of society, on the other.[4]

Here, Portelli explains how oral history differs from other disciplines which also employ interviewing as a method of gaining knowledge for research purposes, singling out oral history as a practice in which deeper historical meaning can be created because of its attention to individual testimony. This process is reflected in *The Laramie Project*.

Theatre Company Members Listening to a Community

There is a longstanding tradition within oral history of gathering stories from several members of one community. The Oral History Association's 2010 pamphlet 'Using Oral History in Community History Projects' defines community as 'any group of individuals bound together by a sense of shared identity',[5] and community oral history projects are described in Sommer et al.'s *Planning a Community History Project* as 'an interrelated set of interviews about an event or way of life in a community'.[6] The term 'community' can refer to a geographical area or locality, and it can be used to describe people who share aspects of a social identity, such as members of the LGBTQ population, or BAME (Black, Asian and Minority Ethnic) narrators, and sometimes oral history projects combine the two meanings of the term.

The oral historian Linda Shopes offers advice to those working on oral history community projects that are geographically bound:

> First, conceptualise a community history project around a historical problem or issue rather than a series of life-history interviews. A community is formed around the intersections of individual lives: what are

the points of connection, tension, or alienation? What historical problem defines the community, and how can this problem be explored through questions to individual narrators?[7]

Shope's suggested approach bears a notable resemblance to Kaufman's aims in his work when he states: 'I am interested in history (both recent and past) and how we look at it in a communal setting. How do we learn stories, tell stories and use pre-existing narratives to construct and re-construct our own identities?'[8] Kaufman informs us, 'From a formalist perspective, I was also excited about creating a piece with the company as the listeners of the town'.[9] Again, similarities can be observed between this play and community oral history projects where interviewers record a number of narrators speaking about a shared experience. In such work, Shopes advises, 'Scholars can learn that local people often have thoughtful if haltingly articulated understandings of how change happens; lay people can learn how what is local has links to national and international developments'.[10] Kaufman is a theatre maker and not an oral historian, but this play shows oral historians how interview material gathered from members of a community can reach far beyond an archive and be dispersed internationally in the form of a dramatic production.

Example 3: *Gateway to Heaven* by Clare Summerskill

The Advantages of Being an 'Insider' Playwright When Conducting Interviews with Members of a Marginalised Community

The Production

Gateway to Heaven is based on interviews with twenty-four older lesbians and gay men in the UK and portrays their experiences of living in a society where the majority of people's sexual orientation differed from their own. The play draws its title from the Gateways Club, a famous lesbian bar in Chelsea, London, which opened in 1931 and featured in the 1968 film, *The Killing of Sister George*, and Heaven, a popular dance club for gay men in London's Soho district, which closed in 1980. The play was written by myself, directed by Kate Crutchley and performed by members of my theatre company, Artemis. I had known some of the narrators beforehand, and others were suggested to me by friends and colleagues. A few of them had a public profile of which I and other people within the British LGBT community were already aware and other narrators were less well known.

After I had created the script from interviews, we invited narrators and members from LGBT groups and organisations to a rehearsed playreading at Oval House, London, followed by a Question and Answer session with the cast, writer, director and some of the narrators. The following year, there was a three-week run of the play, also at Oval House, followed by two national tours.

The script follows a chronological timeframe, from the 1940s to the 1980s, beginning with several of the actors delivering accounts, mainly in monologue form, which had been shared by the narrators, about their childhoods. They explain how, and when, they first knew that they were lesbian or gay or had felt themselves to be in some way 'different'. The play then dramatises the narrators' memories of personal, social and political events, which include the 1967 Sexual Offences Act and the Greenham Common Peace camp.[11] Throughout the piece, music cues from the periods shown were employed during and between the dramatic action and the last scene of the play was set in the mid-1980s, when it was generally agreed by the narrators that lesbian and gay legal rights had made substantial gains in the UK and public support had advanced significantly.

Interviewing Members of a Previously Criminalised and Shamed Community

For a majority of the lifetimes of older lesbian and gay men, homosexuality had been regarded by society not only as criminal but also as a sickness, and there has always been a moral and social stigma around women loving women. The American Psychiatric Association officially declassified homosexuality as a mental illness in 1973, but it was not until 1992 that the World Health Organisation finally followed suit. Furthermore, being lesbian or gay has generally been perceived by Western Christian societies as religiously reprehensible. Some, if not all of these factors will contribute to how an older gay man or lesbian speaks about their experiences when being interviewed.

Oral history, in its pursuit of unearthing the history of marginalised and under-documented communities, is ideally suited to seeking testimonies from older lesbians and gay men, and verbatim theatre is a means whereby their narratives can be widely shared through dramatisation. However, when members of a community are interviewed who have previously been criminalised, silenced or shamed, ethical concerns abound.

In common with members of other oppressed sectors of society, lesbians and gay men may welcome the opportunity to be interviewed about their lives, most especially when their stories might benefit others from the same population or educate other audiences. As people whose lifestyles have been historically criminalised or judged to be morally and religiously reprehensible and whose experiences have been under-documented, by agreeing to be interviewed about their past experiences, older lesbians and gay men are engaging in a political act. Their narratives will contribute towards a previously barely visible, but ever-growing body of historical documentation, and by sharing personal testimonies in this way, their own sexual orientation and life experiences can be validated.

A Shared Identity

In interviewing situations where narrators come from marginalised or vulnerable communities, as discussed previously, there is always a danger of exploitation of narrators or appropriation of the interview material by those initiating the projects. But older lesbians and gay men who share their stories, either with oral historians or with verbatim theatre playwrights, are taking additional risks when they agree to be interviewed in regard to coming out to the interviewer (and later to audience members, if their stories are identifiable), and hoping that they can do so safely and without adverse repercussions. The level of trust a narrator from this population holds in both the interviewer and the project itself is therefore of particular significance. Substantial legal gains and advances in societal understanding have made it much easier for people to identify as lesbian, gay or bisexual nowadays, but in the stories that older lesbians and gay men narrate about their past, there will not only have been memories of being shamed by others, but some narrators will also have battled, over their lifetimes, with a sense of internalised homophobia.

From my own oral history work with LGBTQ people, and also when interviewing LGBTQ narrators for verbatim theatre projects, I have always felt that when I am open about my own sexual orientation as a lesbian, they usually see themselves as speaking to 'family'. Moreover, they understand that, together, we are creating a form of historical record, reflecting the term 'shared authority', whereby both parties are bringing expertise in the form of knowledge and lived experience. I therefore suggest that when a playwright holds an 'insider' position when working with older lesbians and gay narrators, that a deeper level of disclosure can occur in the interview; which, in turn, provides more options for the playwright at the scripting stage.

Example 4: *The Line* by Gina Shmukler

Dramatising Trauma

The Line, by Gina Shmukler, is created from interviews she conducted in Soweto, Johannesburg, with victims and perpetrators of the xenophobic attacks that swept across South Africa in May 2008. It was first presented at The Wits Arts and Literature Experience in May 2012, and, shortly thereafter, the production was invited to the Market Theatre, Johannesburg.

The playwright interviewed those who were affected by, or who witnessed, the attacks and some of the perpetrators. Narrators' names have all been anonymised except for that of Nadine Hutton, a photojournalist who covered the attacks. Eliza, another narrator, is a Mozambican national who speaks Zulu, which is translated for the audience by one of the actresses in the play. During the violence, Eliza's shop was looted and her family brutally tortured. Her niece was raped, and her husband and brother killed. One other narrator, given the pseudonym David, was a perpetrator of the attacks and admits to assaulting migrants during the riots.

The Writer's Intentions in Creating the Play

Shmukler wished to theatrically present first-hand testimony from those involved in the shockingly violent acts which had been carried out against foreign nationals in 2008 in South Africa: attacks which were to reoccur again in 2015 and which have been viewed as some of the most harrowing episodes of post-Apartheid South Africa history. Shmukler's concern about this subject was also informed by her own Jewish identity and her interest in the Holocaust and other incidents of human atrocity. She explains: 'The Line explores the process of perpetration, from neighbour to violent foe, and attempts to re-humanise both perpetrator and victim whilst investigating what makes good people do bad things and how one crosses "the line"'.[12]

The playwright's interest also lies in questioning how trauma can be represented theatrically. She asks: 'How do we create theatre out of trauma, and how do we put trauma on stage and do justice to the magnitude of the event?'[13] The Line demonstrates how traumatic narratives can be performed in a way that is dramatically engaging and politically educational for the audience. In her production, Shmukler takes a number of decisions which enhance the impact of the narratives she includes in the script, intensifying the theatrical experience of the audience.

Scripting Choices

- **Inserting the voice of the researcher in the script**
  Shmukler writes herself into the play as the researcher character. The narrators are introduced by the researcher in the form of a voiceover and the audience are told their age, gender and occupation, where the interview took place, and the playwright's initial impression of those interviewed. As in The Laramie Project, the interviewer inserting themselves into the narrative reminds audience members that the monologues they hear were originally part of a two-way conversation. Some writers believe that this form of dramatic device highlights the fact that the testimonies the audience is hearing are from 'real' people and not a purely fictional account, thereby increasing the authenticity of the piece.

- **Casting**
  The play was written for two actresses, one black woman and one white, with one actress playing all the white characters and the other, all the black characters. There are six different characters in the piece, and the performers are cast across gender. Shmukler explains this choice in the following

way: 'The absence of the stereotypical black violent male on the stage not only enabled the play to go beyond representation, but also was a powerful device in the context of a play that could possibly re-traumatise its audience'.[14]

- **'Flashback' and 'Attack' scenes**
Throughout the script, at various points, Shmukler introduces what she terms 'Flashback' and 'Attack' scenes. The 'Attack' points are where the narrated monologue becomes more of an 'in real time' account, rather than one describing an incident that occurred in the past. The flashback scenes are, again, narrated verbatim from interview excerpts but they occur at specific moments in the action, so that the audience understands that horrific past events can still traumatise a person in the present. Shmukler is interested in 'the language of trauma', and the flashbacks relate to this concept.

There is a vibrant soundscape in the final production, where, during the flashback and attack scenes, the music designer, Charl Johan Lingenfelder, combines ambient music with sound and voices from the original interview material. This is a powerful device which heightens the dramatic tension and also serves to provide short breaks from the monologues. Shmukler explains: 'While the silence that followed offered the audience a pause in the action of the play, the *flashback* offered me both a structural tool in the writing and a dramatic tool in performance'.[15]

Example 5: Ice and Fire

Performing Political Theatre as Playreadings

Ice and Fire is a UK theatre company known for exploring human rights stories through performance. It was founded by Sonja Linden and Sara Masters, and Christine Bacon has been the artistic director there since 2009. Ice and Fire create full scale dramatically fictional productions, and they also present playreadings of scripts written from interview material. In this section, I will focus upon their playreadings. These include *On a Clear Day You Can See Dover* (2012), that weaves together factual information and testimonies gathered from interviews with migrants at the French port of Calais seeking to enter the UK, and *The Afghan Monologues* (2011), created from the real words of men and women from across Afghan society, as well as Western commentators from the front line. Another piece the company present is *The Asylum Monologues*, a first-hand account of the UK's asylum system in the words of people who have experienced it. Written by Sonja Linden and Christine Bacon, it premiered at Amnesty International in June 2006 and has been touring the UK ever since. On their website, Ice and Fire state, 'The script is regularly updated and because we have a large number of different testimonies, it can be adapted for bespoke events which may have a particular focus (e.g. children in the asylum system, access to health care, etc.)'.[16]

Christine Bacon founded Actors for Human Rights, which is a network of more than 700 professional actors across the UK who are dedicated to drawing public attention to human rights concerns. The actors are called upon to perform the playreadings, which are usually presented with the performers seated in chairs, reading the script out to the audience. This kind of presentation means that the plays can be performed at short notice in non-theatrical environments, with only a very brief rehearsal period required. Bacon described this process to me in the following way: 'We rehearse for two hours and then we're on – directly addressing the audience at all times… Are you listening? Are you listening?'[17]

Overtly Political

The Ice and Fire website states: 'We want to empower people and communities to express their rights through the power of sharing stories and transporting performance'.[18] Speaking about *The Asylum Monologues*, Bacon explains, 'The objective of the script is sort of nakedly campaigning'.[19] She is aware that in packaging the pieces as entertainment, rather than as a political debate or event, the company can draw an audience that will consist not only of those already interested in the issues that the piece addresses, but also a far wider public.

Valuing the Narrators

Much of Ice and Fire's work involves working with vulnerable narrators who are frequently suffering from traumatic experiences, but the theatre company members are particularly sensitive to this fact and work in ways which demonstrate their respect for and appreciation of those who share their stories in interviews.

When asked how she views the narrators' involvement, Bacon states:

> The idea is that we're borrowing their testimony for as long as they are happy for us to do that. And we make it very clear that 'This is your story. Anything you don't want to answer, just say. We will send you a transcript when it's finished and you can change anything you like and it will be honoured. You can withdraw your permission at any time'.[20]

About her narrators, Bacon explains, 'I keep in touch with a lot of them so I can update the audience on what's going on. We update the stories, the testimonies, if significant things change as well in their lives, and add those details to the story'.[21] This demonstrates one of the advantages in working with verbatim theatre that is presented in the form of a playreading, rather than scripts learnt by actors in a rehearsal period and performed in a theatre for a run or a tour.

Reciprocity

Although accusations of appropriation by verbatim theatre practitioners can arise because of the nature of the work, it is also the case that certain benefits can be identified for those who share their stories. Bacon points out that several of the asylum seekers and refugees who she has interviewed are activists themselves. Many of them have left their country of origin because they stood up to the authorities there and because they believed in speaking out. She explains that because of this, rather than seeing themselves as being in any way exploited by the theatre company, the narrators 'have an implicit understanding of what activism means and why it's useful, and why is it useful to speak out and get stories heard. In every case, it was always "Ah, finally somebody's actually wanting to listen to us! I don't have to just be in the shadows anymore"'.[22]

Example 6: Anna Deavere Smith

A Solo Performer Creating Multivocality

Body of Work

Since the late 1970s, the American actress and playwright Anna Deavere Smith has researched, written and performed her own one-woman plays, which are based on interviews but not always presented in pure (or exact) verbatim form.

Her work often focusses on social and racial disharmony in the US and two of her best-known productions are *Fires in the Mirror: Crown Heights and Other Identities* (1994) and *Twilight: Los Angeles* (1992). *Fires in the Mirror* addresses the Crown Heights conflicts in the early 1990s between African Americans and Jewish people, and features interviews with a number of narrators, ranging from black gang members to Jewish housewives. *Twilight: Los Angeles* is a piece about the urban uprising and racially motivated violence in Los Angeles following the Rodney King murder.

Working Process

Much of Deavere Smith's work involves her embodying the speech, intonations and physical gestures of real people whom she has interviewed. In this way, she searches for the *essence* of a narrator, rather than always relaying word for word excerpts from the interview, and she rehearses by listening to the interviews on headphones and repeating phrases that she hears. About her play *Notes from the Field*, Deavere Smith states: 'the words are verbatim. The words are exactly what the people said. When I was a girl, my grandfather said, "If you say a word often enough, it becomes you", and that's really my technique'.[23]

Multivocality

One of the most original and theatrically impressive qualities of Deavere Smith is her ability to portray a variety of individuals of different class, ethnicity, age and gender. As an African American woman, she is aware that she meets both her narrators and the subject matter as someone holding that ethnicity. However, in playing so many roles on stage, she seeks to provide a space for multivocality within her productions.

> I don't believe that when I play someone in my work, that I "am" the character. I want the audience to experience the gap, because I know if they experience the gap, they will appreciate my reach for the other. This reach is what moves them, not a mush of me and the other [...] more a desire to reach for something that is very clearly not me....[24]

In her plays, while acting a variety of characters, she will juxtapose monologues which present different points of view. As the writer, she has carefully selected the content of the piece and yet she does not offer any overarching personal narrative or intervening statements during her work. Rather, she wishes to rely upon the words of the characters to speak for themselves. She says: 'These performances are polyphonic, both in the sense of representing multiple voices and in their refusal to synthesise differences in any intervening personal statement, any *authorial* commentary'.[25]

An audience might assume that, as an African American, Deavere Smith may wish to convey a particular interpretation of her subject matter, particularly since so many of her plays address matters of social discord based on racial tensions. But she strives to create a critical distance between herself and her characters. Speaking about the production *Twilight: Los Angeles*, she states: 'I was afraid that my own ethnicity would tell this story about L.A. in a way that reduced it to black and white – that's what I knew about race in America, black and white'.[26] She explains how she thought that she had: 'better not rely on my own judgement to watch out for the black voice'.[27] To allay this concern, she decided to employ three dramaturgs of varying backgrounds and ethnicities to help her with the piece: Elizabeth Alexander, an African American poet from the University of Chicago; Dorinne Kondo, a Japanese American anthropologist and feminist; and Hector Tobar, a reporter of Guatemalan descent.

Speaking for Others

Playwrights who create productions based on interviews will often have to make political as well as artistic choices. These include determining the subject matter which the piece will address and deciding whether it will be about a community or group of people who are from a similar background to the theatre company members, or whether they intend to gather stories from people about whom they may have previously had little personal knowledge or shared experience. When narrators do not share the same experience or identity as the playwright, then the writer must decide how she will represent those narrators. As addressed in **Chapter 5**, if theatre practitioners (or, indeed, oral historians) wish to 'give voice' to stories that have not previously been widely heard, then ethical considerations arise when someone who comes from another community chooses to present them dramatically. Deavere Smith recognises the importance of these concerns and after she had worked with the dramaturgs she brought in to help her with *Twilight: Los Angeles*, she admitted: 'There I learned a lot about '"who can speak for whom"'.[28]

Example 7: *Rights of Passage* by Clare Summerskill

Working Ethnographically with Members of a Vulnerable Community

As discussed in **Chapter 5**, over the last decade, there has been a noticeable increase in the production of verbatim plays based on stories provided by asylum seekers and refugees. The focus for my own play, *Rights of Passage,* was on the experiences of lesbian and gay asylum seekers, both in their country of origin and in the way that they are treated in the UK asylum system. There are seventy-three countries – mostly in the Middle East, Africa and Asia – where homosexual activity between consenting adults is illegal and twelve countries in which homosexuality is punishable by death.[29] Furthermore, when lesbian, bisexual and gay people come to the UK to seek asylum on account of their sexual orientation, they are asked to provide 'proof' – something which is often extremely difficult for them to do, since frequently they will have no witnesses to support their case. Consequently, many are refused asylum, locked up in detention centres (where they can suffer homophobic attacks) and sometimes forcibly sent back to their country of origin, where their lives will be in greater danger than when they left if their communities and the authorities know that they have been refused asylum on account of their sexual orientation.

The more I heard about the treatment of LGBT asylum seekers, and personally came to know people who were suffering as a result of UK Border Agency and Home Office procedures, the more shocked I became. As a verbatim theatre playwright, I wanted to produce a piece based on the testimonies of people who had undergone these harrowing experiences. I was aware that such stories held powerful dramatic and staging possibilities, but my main motivation in the creation of a script based on these matters was to inform a wider public by means of a theatre production and national tour about what I considered to be a seriously underreported matter that showed the UK's immigration system, as well as its commitment to the terms of the 1951 Refugee Convention, in an extremely bad light.

The Play

I scripted *Rights of Passage* from interviews with lesbian and gay asylum seekers and refugees in the UK. The play also includes interview excerpts from people who work in a legal capacity with LGBT asylum and human rights, and people who work for organisations which support LGBT asylum seekers. It was first performed in 2016 by members of my theatre company, Artemis. The script describes the journeys of the three main protagonists: Miremba, a lesbian from Uganda; Izzuddin, a gay man from Malaysia, and Hamed, a gay Iranian man. The first act is staged primarily in their varying countries of origin, showing incidences of persecution that had led them to seek a safer and freer way of life in another country. The second act focusses mainly on their experiences within the asylum system in the UK. By the end of the play, the audience has learnt that two out of three of the main characters have attained refugee status, but one of them is still awaiting the outcome of her application.

Employing Ethnography in Verbatim Theatre Practice

The stories that I sought from narrators for this play were of a deeply personal nature, involving traumatic events that they had endured on account of prejudice against their sexual orientation. I wanted to work in a way that reflected respect for them and their experiences, while also creating a piece of theatre that raised political and social awareness about their situations, and bearing in mind the playwright Julie Salverson's warning that: 'Thoughtlessly soliciting autobiography may reproduce a form of cultural colonialism that is at the very least voyeuristic'.[30]

Over the five-year period in which I researched this play, I became personally acquainted with members of some LGBTQ asylum groups and organisations in England. This occurred mainly through attending protests and demonstrations which highlighted LGBTI human rights abuses and supported individual asylum seekers who faced imminent deportation.[31] Most of these actions were organised by the London-based LGBTQ asylum group, Out & Proud Africa. I also liaised with the Croydon LGBT asylum seekers group, Rainbows Across Borders. I gave a talk about my theatre and activism work to their members, and I offered free writing workshops for LGBTQ asylum seekers and refugees (entitled *Writing the Journey*) to members of the LGBTQ asylum seekers support organisation, Micro Rainbow.[32]

The play was initially presented in 2014 as a rehearsed playreading at Oxford House, London, funded by the Arts Council England as part of a research and development project. Members of London-based LGBTQ asylum groups were invited to attend the event for free, and their travel expenses were reimbursed. There was a post-show discussion with panellists who included people working for LGBTQ asylum groups in London, the Iranian contributor to the play, the actors and myself. In 2016, the full production opened with a week-long run at Chelsea Theatre in London and then toured for a six-week period to twelve other theatres around England.

I made contact with certain LGBTQ asylum seeker and refugee groups in London, Coventry, Liverpool and Manchester which provide their members with legal, practical and emotional support and work towards raising awareness of the often life-threatening levels of homophobia that exist globally, particularly in Commonwealth countries. My theatre company arranged free tickets for members of these groups to several of the performances on tour, and we asked them to participate in the post-show discussions that we held. On the opening night at Chelsea Theatre, a group of twenty LGBTQ asylum seekers came to the show and we provided a separate room where they could go to afterwards to discuss with their group organiser and myself how the play had impacted them. A couple of the group members were slightly upset after having seen, in effect, stories of their own lives reflected back to them; but all of them assured me that the piece provided an accurate dramatic presentation of what they had experienced. They said that they were pleased that the issue of LGBT asylum was being addressed in a theatrical form and that a wider audience was being educated about the subject matter.

Example 8: *Parramatta Girls* by Alana Valentine

Employing Composite Characters in 'Massaged' Verbatim Productions

Alana Valentine is a critically acclaimed Australian playwright who has written some of her scripts using verbatim theatre methods. Her play, *Run Rabbit Run* (2004), about a football team's battle to stay in National Rugby League, was created entirely from interview content and her production of *Parramatta Girls* (2007), based on the testimonies of former inmates of the Parramatta Girls Home, is written in the style Valentine refers to as 'massaged verbatim'.[33] Rather than being created from exact interview content, the final piece was *based* on interviews and it was dramatically presented in the form of the women meeting up at a reunion.

Subject Matter

The Parramatta Girls Home, also known as the Industrial School for Girls and Girls Training School, was a state-controlled child-welfare institution located in Parramatta, New South Wales, Australia, which operated from 1887 until 1974. Its inmates were girls who had been committed to the institution as 'delinquent', 'neglected' or as juvenile offenders, and a large proportion of them were state wards. Some girls were sent there because they were orphaned, others because their parents had divorced and many of them were indigenous and had been taken from their families. In 2009, the Prime Minister, Kevin Rudd, made an apology on behalf of the nation to more than 500,000 indigenous Australians, many of whom suffered abuse and neglect while in out-of-home care during the previous century.

Playreadings

Valentine spent four years researching the play, and during that time, she interviewed thirty-five former residents of the home who had suffered physical abuse, excessive workloads, intrusive examinations and appalling conditions while being institutionalised. There were two public readings of the script as work-in-progress prior to the play's first season with Company B at Belvoir Street. The first reading employed only the spoken testimony of the narrators in a form of direct address out to the audience, and at the second reading, actors presented the stories in Valentine's 'massaged' verbatim form.

Narrators were invited to each public showing and were asked for their feedback on the developing scripts. Valentine believed that if the women initially saw the playreadings in a pure verbatim form, their trust in her and her working process would increase, and that they would feel, in the final production, that their stories had still been faithfully told, even though not word-for-word.

Final Version

The third draft presentation included fictional scenes, and the final version of the piece was what Valentine calls, 'A fully fledged drama with some story-telling aspects'.[34] The interviews she had gathered from all the narrators were reduced to being delivered by eight characters in the play. She explains her distinction between pure and massaged verbatim theatre:

> Pure verbatim focusses on exact transcripts of the interview material, where the contract between you and the audience is that the actors repeat *exactly* what the interviewee said, and as a playwright the focus is on their precise words. In massaged verbatim I am still interested in how they speak, but I don't reproduce the dialogue word for word; rather I use my skills to polish or boil down the interview material and create for audiences the *essence* of their speech. This can include characteristics not discernible from pure transcripts but apparent in the moment when interviewing a number of community members.[35]

Reasons Behind Valentine's Choices

It is interesting to examine Valentine's thinking behind various choices she made at different stages of this play's development. She says one main reason why she employed 'pure' verbatim in the first playreading was that her narrators had often mentioned to her that since the time they had been incarcerated at the Parramatta Girls Home, they had rarely spoken about what had occurred there and had feared that if they did, they would not have been believed. Hearing their own words spoken on stage in public was therefore hugely significant for them in this regard. The audience also included inmates of other institutions. The sharing and witnessing of the narrators' testimonies provides an example of how verbatim theatre created with, and for, members of one community can go far beyond simply performing dramatic representations and can validate those whose voices have been previously silenced.

A challenge that arises for all verbatim theatre writers who work with difficult and painful memories is to find ways in which that material can be dramatically presented that are not too harrowing for an audience to watch – however much the audience members may wish to be educated about the subject matter. Listening to stories that involved physical and emotional abuse, Valentine had the idea of staging the play as a reunion of some of the women. In this setting, she could portray some of the tragic events they had suffered, and at the same time, highlight the narrators' resilient spirits as survivors. She states, 'This is eight powerful, stroppy, funny women on stage triumphing over the horror that is thrown at them and laughing, crying and celebrating as they do'.[36]

Creating characters from interview excerpts that come from different narrators may or may not have been confusing for those who gave their stories and who then attended the play, but one of the strongest justifications for this dramatic device is related to the question of anonymity. Narrators from certain communities, particularly those who have suffered trauma and shaming, will often feel relieved when they see that a production does not specifically identify them. Instead, they perceive their experiences as woven into a much larger narrative, but still having the same impact as if they had been dramatically presented from one personal viewpoint. In *Parramatta Girls*, although the interviews were 'collapsed' in this way, the real names of the core narrators still appear as character names as a way of honouring them and their participation.

Another reason for Valentine's decision to employ massaged verbatim is related to the matter of institutional care in Australia and those who were historically abused within that system. This speaks to a wider issue of social injustice in that country. The stories that she heard in interviews and which are represented on stage were extremely personal and, at the same time, part of a collective narrative. She explains: 'Because the importance of individual experiences was their part in this bigger whole, I collapsed multiple stories into eight characters whose journeys transcended being victims to a punitive system'.[37]

Notes

1 Jacquelyn Dowd Hall, James Leloudis, Robert Korstad, Mary Murphy, Lu Ann Jones, and Christopher B. Daly, *Like a Family: The Making of a Southern Cotton Mill World* (Chapel Hill: University of North Caroline Press, 1987).

2 Quotations from Della Pollock (unless otherwise stated) from: Della Pollock, interview with Clare Summerskill, Chapel Hill, North Carolina, US, June 5, 2014.

3 Laramie is a city in, and the county seat of, Albany County, Wyoming, in the United States, approximately 130 miles north of Denver, Colorado, and is home to the University of Wyoming.

4 Alessandro Portelli, *The Battle of Valle Giulia: Oral History and the Art of Dialogue* (Madison, WI: University of Wisconsin Press, 1997), 6.

5 Cited in Barbara W. Sommer, with Nancy MacKay and Mary Kay Quinlan, *Planning a Community History Project*, Community Oral History Toolkit, vol. 2 (Abingdon: Routledge, 2016), 10.

6 Sommer, *Planning a Community History Project*, 23.

7 Linda Shopes, "Oral History and the Study of Communities: Problems, Paradoxes, and Possibilities," in *The Oral History Reader*, Second Edition, ed. Robert Perks and Alistair Thomson (Abingdon: Routledge, 2006), 268.

8 Caridad Svich, "Moisés Kaufman: 'Reconstructing History Through Theatre' – An Interview," *Contemporary Theatre Review* 13:3 (2003), 70.

9 Svich, "Moisés Kaufman," 70.

10 Shopes, "Oral History and the Study of Communities," 269.

11 The 1967 Sexual Offences Act decriminalised homosexual acts in private between two men over twenty-one in England and Wales but did not cover the Merchant Navy or the Armed Forces. The Greenham Common Women's Peace Camp was a series of protest camps which began in 1981 and protested nuclear weapons being placed at RAF Greenham Common in Berkshire, England.

12 Georgina Shmukler, "Trauma on Stage: Making Theatre about Xenophobia in South Africa using the "Structures" of Trauma" (MA research report, University of Cape Town, 2013), 4.

13 Shmukler, "Trauma on Stage," 4.

14 Shmukler, "Trauma on Stage," 50.

15 Shmukler, "Trauma on Stage," 34.

16 "Asylum Monologues (Launched June 2006), Scripted by Sonja Linden and Christine Bacon, "Ice and Fire," March 4, 2020, https://iceandfire.co.uk/project/asylum-monologues/.

17 Christine Bacon, interview with Clare Summerskill (via Skype), August 24, 2016.

18 "Asylum Monologues."

19 Bacon, interview.

20 Bacon, interview.

21 Bacon, interview.

22 Bacon, interview.

23 John Bucher, "The Power of Words: A Conversation with Anna Deavere Smith," *LA Screenwriter*, June 6, 2018, https://www.la-screenwriter.com/2018/06/06/the-power-of-words-a-conversation-with-anna-deavere-smith/.

24 Anna Deavere Smith, quoted in Dorinne Kondo, "(Re)Visions of Race: Contemporary Race Theory and the Cultural Politics of Racial Crossover in Documentary Theatre," *Theatre Journal* 52:1 (2000), 96.

25 Charles R. Lyons and James, C. Lyons, "Anna Deavere Smith: Perspectives on her Performance within the Context of Critical Theory," *Journal of Dramatic Theory and Criticism* 9:1 (1994), 45.

26 Anna Deavere Smith, "Not so Special Vehicles," *Performing Arts Journal* 17:2/3 (1995), 86.

27 Deavere Smith, "Not so Special Vehicles," 87.

28 Deavere Smith, "Not so Special Vehicles," 87.

29 Human Dignity Trust. "Map of Countries that Criminalise LGBT People," *Human Dignity Trust*, March 5, 2020, https://www.humandignitytrust.org/lgbt-the-law/map-of-criminalisation/.

30 Julie Salverson, "Performing Emergency: Witnessing Popular Theatre and the Lie of the Literal," *Theatre Topics* 6:2 (1996), 182.

31 There are discrepancies in this thesis (and more widely) in the acronym employed for members of the LGBT(QI+) population. Throughout this book I employ the letters of the acronym that are relevant to the play or subject under discussion or the letters of the acronym that are employed by the group or organisation to which I refer.

32 Out & Proud African LGBTI is a UK Charity that supports LGBTI asylum seekers and refugees: https://africanlgbti.org/. Rainbows Across Borders is a voluntary self-help group for lesbian, gay, bisexual and transgender (LGBT) asylum seekers who are fleeing persecution of oppressive homophobic/transphobic regimes: http://www.rainbowsacrossborders.org.uk/. Micro Rainbow International supports LGBTI asylum seekers and refugees by providing safe housing and facilitating access to employment, volunteering, training and education for LGBTI asylum seekers and refugees: https://mrifoundation.global/.

33 Alana Valentine uses the term 'ex-inmates' to refer to the Parramatta Girls, since the Industrial schools, as they were known, were like prisons in that children were committed by a court for a prescribed length of time and confined to the institution. Alana Valentine, *Bowerbird: The Art of Making Theatre Drawn from Life* (Strawberry Hills, NSW: Currency Press, 2018), 70.

34 This quotation is from a briefing from Alana Valentine, prepared for the original production of *Parramatta Girls*. Saskia Smith, "Teachers' Notes: Parramatta Girls by Alana Valentine," *Education at Riverside*, 2014, March 4, 2020, https://riversideparramatta.com.au/wp-content/uploads/Parramatta-Girls-Teachers-Notes-2014.pdf.

35 Valentine, *Bowerbird*, 105.

36 Valentine, quoted in Smith, "Teachers' Notes," 19.

37 Valentine, *Bowerbird*, 10.

CHECKLIST FOR PRODUCING YOUR VERBATIM PLAY

- Decide what subject, event or social issue you want to address.
- Decide whether you will be working alone as the playwright and interviewer – and possibly director, too – or with others.
- Apply for funding, if required for the project.
- If you intend to perform your final production in theatres, approach venues about possible dates.
- Select a recording device for the interviews and become proficient in using it.
- Find narrators to interview and contact them.
- Explain the nature of the project to narrators, and let them know why you want to hear about their experiences.
- Prepare consent forms and gain informed consent from narrators at the end of interviews.
- Transcribe the interviews.
- Create a script from the interview content.
- Send narrators the excerpts from their interviews that you wish to employ in the script.
- Approach and/or employ company members you will need for the production of your play.
- Find a rehearsal space and a performance space or venue.
- Begin advertising the performance dates to target audiences and to the general public, as required.
- Rehearse the piece with actors and a director (if this role is not undertaken by you as the playwright).

- Optional
  - Produce a rehearsed playreading of the script, performed by actors (script in hand) to an invited audience consisting of the narrators and other people knowledgeable about the subject matter the play addresses.
  - Hold a post-performance discussion with the audience members and narrators after the rehearsed playreading, asking them for feedback.
  - Incorporate the feedback into a revised version of the script.
- Rehearse with actors for a minimum of three weeks full-time or the equivalent amount of time if your actors are only available on a part-time basis.
- If required, publish the script so that it can be sold at performances.
- Perform the play.

APPENDICES

APPENDIX 1

APPROACHING YOUR NARRATOR EXAMPLES

Initial Email Approaching Narrator

Dear Ray

I was given your contact details by Geoffrey who said that it would be OK to write to you about a project that I'm working on. I am a playwright, working mainly with verbatim theatre (where scripts are created from interview content) and I am currently seeking people to interview for a play based on the stories of older LGBTQ people in London. I have secured a research and development grant from Arts Council England for this work and, after I have completed the interviews and the script, the play will be presented in the form of a rehearsed playreading to which you will, of course, be invited. At a later stage, I will apply to the Arts Council for an additional grant that would allow a full production of the play to be performed at theatre venues around the country, acted by members of my own theatre company, Artemis.

I would be very keen to interview you for this play and wondered if that might be possible. If you were interested, I could come to where you live for an interview or, you could come to my house if you preferred (I live in South London). Alternatively, we could both meet at London Archives where I could book a room.

If you have any questions at this stage, please do feel free to contact me, either by phone or email. I look forward to hearing from you.

Meanwhile best wishes from
Clare
Tel: (*provide phone number*)
Provide a website address if you, or your theatre company have one.

Follow-Up Email

Dear Ray

Thank you so much for getting back to me. I'm delighted that you willing to be interviewed for this project! Meeting you at your flat would be fine.

You asked about the remit of the interview, and the answer is that I am just interested in your memories of being a gay man in London. So, no, you don't have to prepare anything. Just maybe think a little before we meet about times in your life when you were involved in anything LGBTQ-related in London. It could be social, political, relating to work, clubs, pubs – anything at all, provided it happened in London (although you don't need to have been born in London).

As far as arranging a date for us to talk, I will call you on the number you gave me, and we can take it from there. Many thanks again for your interest in this project and I'm greatly looking forward to meeting you.

Best wishes from Clare
Tel: (*provide phone number*)

APPENDIX 2

SAMPLE CONSENT FORM FOR AN AUDIO-RECORDED INTERVIEW

The Project

The creation of a verbatim play based on interviews with older lesbians, gay men, bisexuals, transgender and queer people in London, scripted by Clare Summerskill.

The project is funded by the Arts Council England. If you have any questions, please contact me on *(provide email address)*........ or call me on *(provide phone number)*.

The Agreement

Interviewer: Clare Summerskill
Narrator: Ray Butler

☐   I am aware that my participation in this interview is voluntary.
☐   I understand the intent and purpose of this research is to create a play based on interviews which will be performed publicly.
☐   I would like to remain anonymous. I do not want my name or anything that might identify me to appear anywhere in the research or performance of this theatre piece, however, artist-researchers may use any personal information or stories I share in this interview for their theatre project under an anonymous or fictional name.
☐   I agree that the copyright of my interview content will be owned jointly by myself and the playwright and that such copyright is licensed for the purpose listed above.

Signature of Narrator _ _ _ _ _ _ _ _ _ _ _ _ _ _ _   Date: _ _ _ _ _
Signature of Interviewer _ _ _ _ _ _ _ _ _ _ _ _ _   Date: _ _ _ _ _

APPENDIX 3

SCRIPTING EXERCISE

Below is a transcribed excerpt of one of my interviews with a narrator for *Rights of Passage* who was called 'Miremba' in the play. Miremba is originally from Uganda, and the interview content describes conversations that took place between her and her mother. Your task is to read through it and adapt it in some way into a dialogue that could be used as a short scene (or scenes) in a script.

Tips

- Look for any possibilities of dialogue.
- Work out who the different characters will be in your scene.
- Write your version out in a scripted form. Showing clearly which lines are spoken by which characters.
- Include stage instructions if and where necessary.

Extract from Miremba's Interview

So here I go back home and I remember when I first went back home my mum, you know, came to me and we were sitting down and she said 'You know what? Miremba, I've never seen...' She goes 'Have you got a boyfriend?' And I say 'Erm, no, no I don't have a boyfriend' you know, 'I don't. I wanted to finish my studies first, you know, you always tell us – don't interrupt with boys until you finish school so, no no, I don't have a boyfriend'. 'OK, 'cos I've never never seen anybody and erm...'

She say, 'Ok, Ok, so you don't have anybody?' I say 'No, no, Mummy, I don't have any. I'm not even ready now to have a boyfriend, you know, I want to, I want to go back to Uni, do my Masters there and then maybe I'll settle down but not now'.

So that was the end of the topic. I don't know why she did ask, eventually I knew why she was asking 'cos after like, it was a month, it was a few weeks, she comes up and she say 'Oh, you know, you remember when I told you, when I did ask if you got a boyfriend you say, you know, you have a right age of marriage...' 'Cos now I was twenty... Yes, I was in my twenties. It's like, 'Oh, you are the right age of marriage, you know, you need to settle down. I don't want you to get apart from me, I don't want you to get pregnant. So, er, I think it's high time you get married'.

I was like: What? I'm not ready, you know? Why should I get married right now?' 'So, you know, you need to get married'. She say 'You need to get married 'cos I don't want you to...' She say 'I don't want you to get pregnant here'. Because in my family if you get pregnant at your parents, it's shameful to the family. So you have to preserve that cultural way, like. I got a chance to study but the other people don't, don't study. So, you know, it's a culture, like you study and then you get married and then you get kids and then you settle down – and you have to get a man. You don't have to get a man, 'cos I knew my sister, my own sister they got her a man.

APPENDIX 4

PROJECTED PRODUCTION EXPENDITURE

This is a list of some basic items of expenditure that you might need for your theatre production. Depending on the size of your budget and the kind of play you will be creating, some of these identified expenses will be more necessary than others.

Administrative Costs during Recording and Scripting Process

Access to printer and phone and computer
Recorders and batteries
Travel expenses for interviewers
Paper and print cartridges

Working Space Needed

Office space (for transcription and scripting process)
Room required for auditioning actors
Space needed for rehearsal process
Performance space – traditional theatre venue or community hall, or some
    other kind of space

Wages for Company Members

Actors
Director
Playwright
Stage manager(s)

Photographer
Graphic designer (to design flyers and posters)
Set designer
Lighting designer
Costume designer
Transcribers (if this work is outsourced)

Production Costs

Printing of flyers and posters
Props and costumes
Set building materials
Space to be hired for set builders, if required
Copyright payments on any sound cues employed in the show
Gels for lighting design

Touring Costs

Van driver (who could be one of the stage managers)
Van hire
Accommodation for company members if touring
'Per diems' – payments to actors in addition to basic wages to cover costs of
    eating on tour

APPENDIX 5

GLOSSARY

Acting/speaking 'out' to the audience – Delivering lines directly to audience members rather than to fellow actors, thereby breaking the fourth wall.

Appropriation – The act of taking something that belongs to someone else, usually without having the right to do so.

Asylum seeker – A person who has fled her/his own country and applies to the government of another country for protection as a refugee.

Audition – A short performance that an actor gives in order to show they are suitable for a particular play.

Blocking – The theatre term for the actors' movements on the stage during the performance

BAME – Black, Asian and Minority Ethnic is the terminology currently used in the UK to describe people of non-white descent.

Composite character – A character created from the narratives of two or more individuals.

Dramatic (or narrative) arc – The dramatic arc refers to three main sections: exposition, climax and dénouement, which are connected by rising action at the beginning and falling action towards the end. It is not unusual to find more than one dramatic arc in a complex story.

Dramatic juxtaposition – A technique in theatre writing in which two or more ideas, places, characters and their actions are placed side by side, for the purpose of developing comparisons and contrasts.

Ensemble acting – An approach to acting that aims for a unified effect achieved by all members of a cast working together on behalf of the play, rather than emphasising individual performances.

Ethnography – The study and systematic recording of human cultures. Also, a descriptive work produced from such research.

Fourth wall – A performance convention in which an invisible, imagined wall separates actors from the audience.

Improvisation – A performance that is not practised but is invented by the performers.

In the round – A form of theatrical staging in which the acting area, which may be raised or at floor level, is completely surrounded by the audience.

Insider/Outsider – The way in which these terms are employed in the context of verbatim theatre work as outlined in this publication refers to whether the theatre makers come from the same community or a different one as the narrators, and whether or not they have shared experiences. Employing the tools of intersectionality there are, of course, many variants and overlaps within these binary terms.

LGBT(QI) – LGBT stands for Lesbian, Gay, Bisexual, Transgender; and the Q and I, when used in the acronym, stand for Queer or Questioning, and Intersex.

Narrator – In oral history practice and scholarship, the word 'narrator' is usually employed to refer to the person being interviewed.[1] Some oral historians and scholars employ the term 'interviewee'.

Refugee – According to the UN Refugee Convention, a refugee is a person who is outside their own country and is unable or unwilling to return due to a well-founded fear of being persecuted because of their race, religion, nationality, political opinion or membership of a particular social group (including women and LGBT people).

Script – Abbreviated term for 'play script', which is a piece of writing produced for the stage, that includes a list of characters and can be divided into acts which are then divided into scenes.

Transcript – A written or printed version of material originally presented in another medium.

Note

1 Robert Perks and Alistair Thomson, "Introduction," in *The Oral History Reader*, Third Edition, eds. Robert Perks and Alistair Thomson (Abingdon: Routledge, 2016), xiii.

APPENDIX 6

SUGGESTED SOURCES FOR FURTHER INFORMATION ON VERBATIM THEATRE, DOCUMENTARY THEATRE AND ORAL HISTORY

Suggested Reading on Verbatim and Documentary Theatre

Anderson, Michael and Linden Wilkinson. "A Resurgence of Verbatim Theatre: Authenticity, Empathy and Transformation." *Australasian Drama Studies* 50 (2007): 153–169.

Belfield, Robin. *Telling the Told: How to Make Verbatim Theatre*. London: Nick Hern Books, 2018.

Brown, Paul, ed. *Verbatim: Staging Memory and Community*. Strawberry Hills, NSW: Currency Press, 2010.

Cantrell, Tom. *Acting in Documentary Theatre*. Basingstoke: Palgrave Macmillan, 2013.

Claycomb, Ryan M. "Ch(oral) History: Documentary Theatre, the Communal Subject and Progressive Politics." *Journal of Dramatic Theory and Criticism* XV111:2 (2003): 95–121.

Cox, Emma, ed. *Staging Asylum: Contemporary Australian Plays about Refugees*. Strawberry Hills, NSW: Currency Press, 2013.

Favorini, Attilio. "Representation and Reality: The Case of Documentary Theatre." *Theatre Survey* 35:2 (1994): 31–42.

Forsyth, Alison and Chris Megson, eds. *Get Real: Documentary Theatre Past and Present*. Basingstoke: Palgrave Macmillan, 2009.

Frisch, Michael. *A Shared Authority: Essays on the Craft and Meaning of Oral and Public History*. Albany: State University of New York Press, 1990.

Hammond, Will, and Dan Steward, eds. *Verbatim, Verbatim: Contemporary Documentary Theatre*. London: Oberon Books, 2008.

Jeffers, Alison. *Refugees, Theatre and Crisis: Performing Global Identities*. Basingstoke: Palgrave Macmillan, 2012.

Maedza, Pedzisai. *Performing Asylum: Theatre of Testimony in South Africa*. African Studies Collection, 66. Leiden: African Studies Centre, 2017.

Martin, Carol. *Theatre of the Real*. Basingstoke: Palgrave Macmillan, 2013.

Paget, Derek. "'Verbatim Theatre': Oral History and Documentary Techniques." *New Theatre Quarterly* 3:12 (1987): 317–36.

Pollock, Della. *Remembering: Oral History Performance.* Basingstoke: Palgrave Macmillan, 2005.

Salverson, Julie. "Change on Whose Terms? Testimony and an Erotics of Injury." *Theater* 31:3 (2001): 119–25.

Schweitzer, Pam. *Reminiscence Theatre: Making Theatre from Memories.* London: Jessica Kingsley, 2007.

Stuart Fisher, Amanda. "'That's Who I'd be if I Could Sing': Reflections on a Verbatim Project with Mothers of Sexually Abused Children." *Studies in Theatre and Performance* 31:2 (2011): 193–208.

Summerskill, Clare. "The Importance of Being Gay: The Perils and Possibilities of LGBTI Asylum Seekers' Involvement in *Rights of Passage.*" *Research in Drama Education* 23:2 (2018): 282–88.

Weiss, Peter. "The Material and the Models: Notes towards a Definition of Documentary Theatre." *Theatre Quarterly* 1:1 (1971): 41–43.

Suggested Reading on Verbatim Theatre and Ethics

Alcoff, Linda. "The Problem of Speaking for Others." *Cultural Critique* 20 (1991–92): 5–32.

Duggan, Patrick. "Others, Spectatorship, and the Ethics of Verbatim Performance." *New Theatre Quarterly* 29:2 (2013): 146–58.

Gibson, Janet. "Saying It Right: Creating Ethical Verbatim Theatre." *NEO: Journal for Higher Degree Research Studies in the Social Sciences and Humanities* 4 (2001): 1–18.

Luckhurst, Mary. "Verbatim Theatre, Media Relations and Ethics." In *A Concise Companion to: Contemporary British and Irish Drama*, edited by Nadine Holdsworth and Mary Luckhurst, 200–23. Oxford: Blackwell Publishing, 2008.

McDonnell, Bill. "The Politics of Historiography: Towards an Ethics of Representation." *Research in Drama Education* 10:2 (2005): 127–38.

Preston, Sheila. "Introduction to Ethics of Representation." In *The Applied Theatre Reader*, edited by Tim Prentki and Sheila Preston, 65–69. New York: Routledge, 2010.

A Selection of Published Verbatim and Documentary Plays Mentioned in This Book

Beck, Jessica and Helena Enright. *The Exeter Blitz Project.* Exeter: Short Run Press, 2013.

Blythe, Alecky. *Little Revolution.* London: Nick Hern Books, 2014.

Deavere Smith, Anna. *Fires in the Mirror.* New York: Anchor, 1993.

Fall, Nadia. *Home.* London: Nick Hern Books, 2013.

Hare, David. *Stuff Happens.* London: Faber and Faber, 2004.

Kaufman, Moisés. *The Laramie Project.* New York: Vintage Books, 2001.

Littlewood, Joan. *Oh What a Lovely War.* London: Methuen Drama, 1967.

Mann, Emily. "Still Life." In *Testimonies: Four Plays*. New York: Theatre Communications Group, 1997.

Norton-Taylor, Richard, ed. *The Colour of Justice: The Stephen Lawrence Inquiry*. London: Oberon Books, 1999.

Stuart Fisher, Amanda. *From the Mouths of Mothers*. Twickenham: Aurora Metro Publications Ltd, 2013.

Summerskill, Clare. *Gateway to Heaven: The Play*. Machynlleth: Tollington Press, 2019.

———— *Hearing Voices*. London: Tollington Press, 2010.

———— *Rights of Passage*. London: Tollington Press, 2016.

Suggested Reading on Oral History

Bergen, Teresa. *Transcribing Oral History*. Abingdon: Routledge, 2019.

Frisch, Michael. *A Shared Authority: Essays on the Craft and Meaning of Oral and Public History*. Albany: State University of New York Press, 1990.

McKirdy, Carol. *Practicing Oral History with Immigrant Narrators*. Abingdon: Routledge, 2015.

Perks, Robert and Alistair Thomson, eds. *The Oral History Reader*. Fourth edition. Abingdon: Routledge, 2016. *(This is the most recent edition, but previous editions have different content, which is why they have also been included in this reading list)*

———— *The Oral History Reader*. London: Routledge, 1998.

———— *The Oral History Reader*. Second Edition. Abingdon: Routledge, 2006.

Portelli, Alessandro. 1998. "What Makes Oral History Different?" In *The Oral History Reader*, Third Edition, edited by Robert Perks and Alistair Thomson, 63–74. London: Routledge, 1998. Originally published in: Portelli, Alessandro. *The Death of Luigi Trastulli and Other Stories: Form and Meaning in Oral History*. Albany: State University of New York Press, 1991: 45–58.

Ritchie, Donald A. *Doing Oral History. A Practical Guide*. New Edition. Oxford: Oxford University Press, 2003.

Ritchie, Donald A., ed. *The Oxford Handbook of Oral History*. Oxford: Oxford University Press, 2010.

Thompson, Paul with Joanna Bornat. *The Voice of the Past: Oral History*. Fourth Edition. New York: Oxford University Press, 2017.

Sommer, Barbara. W., with Nancy MacKay and Mary Kay Quinlan. *Community Oral History Toolkit*. V.1. *Planning a Community History Project*. Abingdon: Routledge, 2016.

Summerskill, Clare. *Gateway to Heaven: Fifty Years of Lesbian and Gay Oral History*. London: Tollington Press, 2012.

Yow, Valerie Raleigh. "Ethics and Interpersonal Relationships in Oral History Research." *Oral History Review* 22:1 (1995): 51–66.

———— *Recording Oral History: A Guide for the Humanities and Social Sciences*. Third Edition. London: Rowman and Littlefield, 2015.

Websites

Anna Deavere Smith: www.annadeaveresmith.org – Anna Deavere Smith's work with verbatim theatre is unique. This site provides some information about her acting, her productions and her working methods.

Artemis: www.artemistheatre.co.uk – My own theatre company, Artemis, produces plays reflecting the lives of those from marginalised sectors of society and most of our plays are created using verbatim theatre methods.

Currency Press/Alana Valentine: www.currency.com.au/verbatim-theatre-alana-valentine – Alana Valentine is one of a growing number of playwrights in Australia whose work includes verbatim theatre pieces.

Drama Online/Verbatim Theatre: www.dramaonlinelibrary.com/genres/verbatim-theatre-iid-2551– An informative summary of verbatim theatre written by Tom Cantrell, Lecturer in Drama, University of York, 2012.

Gateway to Heaven: www.gatewaytoheaven.co.uk – This site describes the production of my play *Gateway to Heaven* and also provides information about some of the contributors who were interviewed for the play.

Hearing Voices: www.hearingvoicesplay.co.uk – This site contains information on another of my verbatim plays, *Hearing Voices*, about the experiences of those suffering from severe mental health problems.

Ice and Fire: iceandfire.co.uk – Ice and Fire have produced many verbatim plays about members of vulnerable populations, including asylum seekers, refuges and migrants.

The Laramie Project: www.yidio.com/movie/the-laramie-project/19689 – Since *The Laramie Project* is such a seminal work, and has been discussed at length in this publication, it is helpful to watch the film version.

Oral History Association: www.oralhistory.org – This site offers guidance to best practice in oral history work.

Oral History Society: www.ohs.org.uk – Another site which outlines best practice in oral history work.

INDEX

Note: Page numbers followed by "n" denote endnotes.

Printed in Great Britain
by Amazon

58630364R00129